The Edinburgh History

The Edinburgh History of the Greeks
Series Editor: Thomas W. Gallant

Titles available
The Edinburgh History of the Greeks, c. 500 to 1050: The Early Middle Ages
Florin Curta

The Edinburgh History of the Greeks, 1768 to 1913: The Long Nineteenth Century
Thomas W. Gallant

The Edinburgh History of the Greeks, 1453 to 1768: The Ottoman Empire
Molly Greene

Forthcoming titles
The Edinburgh History of the Greeks, 1909 to 2012: A Transitional History
Antonis Liakos and Nicholas Doumanis

The Edinburgh History of the Greeks, 323 to 30 BC: The Hellenistic World
Joseph G. Manning

The Edinburgh History of the Greeks, 1453 to 1768
The Ottoman Empire

Molly Greene

EDINBURGH
University Press

© Molly Greene, 2015

Edinburgh University Press Ltd
The Tun – Holyrood Road
12(2f) Jackson's Entry
Edinburgh EH8 8PJ

www.euppublishing.com

Typeset in 11/13pt Adobe Sabon by
Servis Filmsetting Ltd, Stockport, Cheshire,
and printed and bound in Great Britain by
CPI Group (UK) Ltd, Croydon CR0 4YY

A CIP record for this book is available from the British Library

ISBN 978 0 7486 3927 4 (hardback)
ISBN 978 0 7486 9400 6 (webready PDF)
ISBN 978 0 7486 9399 3 (paperback)
ISBN 978 0 7486 9401 3 (epub)

The right of Molly Greene to be identified as the author of this work has been asserted in accordance with the Copyright, Designs and Patents Act 1988, and the Copyright and Related Rights Regulations 2003 (SI No. 2498).

Contents

List of Illustrations and Maps	vi
Series Editor's Preface	vii
Note on Orthography	viii
1. Thessaly	1
2. From Constantinople to Istanbul	22
3. Christians in an Islamic empire	57
4. The larger Greek world	87
5. The Greeks and the seventeenth-century crisis	112
6. Living with others	139
7. The patriarch's victory	163
8. The Ottoman court and the Greek Enlightenment	192
Timeline	216
Guide to Further Reading	217
Bibliography	218
Index	233

Illustrations and Maps

Illustrations

1. The palace of the *hospodar* of the Danubian Principalities in Bucharest — 108
2. Saints (Basil, Athanasius, and Cyril of Alexandria) with decorated vestments drawing on Ottoman motifs — 108
3. Decorative pattern drawn from Ottoman motifs. 1641, Catholicon (main church), Monastery of the Dormition of the Virgin, Spelaio, Macedonia, Greece — 109
4. Vase with carnations. 1671, Stegopole Monastery, southern Albania — 109
5. A prelate's pectoral, obverse side. Istanbul, late seventeenth century — 110
6. Myrrh flask. 1670, from Trabzon — 111

Maps

1. The Ottoman heartland in the Balkans — 17
2. Metropolitan sees that disappeared between 1483 and 1525 — 30

Series Editor's Preface

The Edinburgh History of the Greeks is a multi-volume, chronological series covering the history of the Greek people from antiquity to the present. Each volume combines political history with social and cultural history in order to tell the story of the Greek people over the course of recorded history in an exciting, novel and innovatory way. Drawing on the rich resources from anthropology, archaeology and history, as well as political science, philology, art, literature and law, the books will be diverse, abundant and vibrant.

The Greeks suffer from too much history, some have said. Indeed, library bookshelves sag under the weight of the massive number of tomes devoted to the history of Greece during the ancient, medieval and modern periods. This series differs from them by focusing on the history of a people, the Greeks, and not a place, Greece. The story will reflect the fluctuating dynamics of change while primary sources and accounts of the lives of individuals and communities will invigorate the text.

The history of the Greeks over the long durée must be told on a vast and at times even global scale, and so the Greek world is taken to include not just the area traditionally associated with ancient Greece or the territory of the modern Greek state, but to encompass all areas where Greeks have settled, including the diaspora of modern times.

Thomas W. Gallant

Note on Orthography

Throughout the book I have preferred modern Turkish orthography ("Bayezit" rather than "Bayezid") and the avoidance of diacritics except when necessary; thus, for example, *reaya* rather than *re'aya*. When using words of Arabic origin I use the Turkish rather than the Arabic spelling, so *medrese*, not *madrasa*. Greek words have been transliterated according to the ELOT system. The only exception to that is the names of Greek authors who have published in English and have not followed ELOT. Their names appear as published. For simplicity's sake I have used modern place names, so "Plovdiv" rather than "Philippoupolis." The only exception is the vexed question of Constantinople/Istanbul. When referring to the Byzantine period I have used "Constantinople," otherwise it is "Istanbul."

CHAPTER 1

Thessaly

Thessaly is not a destination in today's Greece. A hot and humid plain for much of the year, with undistinguished provincial towns, it lacks the attractions that other parts of the country possess in abundance. But it is in Thessaly that will be begin our story, for two reasons. First, it was there that, at least for the Greek lands, Ottoman rule took its most characteristic and creative shape. The word "creative" may startle a little; it is admittedly an unusual word choice when writing about the Ottomans, particularly if one is writing from the perspective of the various Balkan peoples. But it is indeed the apposite term because in the heartland of the Balkans the conquerors created a new society, for Muslims and Christians, rulers and ruled, alike.

Second, to start in Thessaly is to not start in Istanbul, and there is a reason for this choice. The history of the Greek people under Ottoman rule (as well as that devoted to the Serbs, the Bulgarians, and non-Muslim groups) has, until recently, been treated as synonymous with something called "the Greek Orthodox community." In this enduring view of the empire, the Greek Orthodox community, buttressed by the legal autonomy granted to it by the sultan, was "a self-enclosed entity with distinct boundaries and assumed to have a homogenous character." Moreover, the Ottoman context was external to this boundary (Ozil 2009: 12). New scholarship, a scholarship that this book embraces, is taking apart this venerable paradigm. Rather than starting from the assumption of the Greek community, it is asking what kinds of communities Greek Orthodox individuals belonged to, how these were constructed, and how they were sustained.

The Orthodox patriarch in Istanbul looms over the community in the older historiography. With the fall of the city to the Ottomans and the death of the emperor, he takes up his new position as head of the Greek Orthodox flock. To begin the history of the Greeks in the Ottoman Empire with the fall of Istanbul, in my view, is to reinforce this perspective. Our mind's eye is drawn inevitably to the Bosphorus and we imagine the patriarch's rule radiating outward, to the west across the Balkans and east to the few remaining Orthodox communities in Anatolia. The Ottoman capture of the city was, of course, significant – we shall talk about its importance in the next chapter – but there are other geographies and other chronologies that were equally consequential, if not more so, in the history of the Greek Orthodox during the early centuries of Ottoman rule. Thessaly can show us what those were.

Conquest

The fertile plain drew the attention of the Ottomans early on, even though it lay far south of the east-to-west corridor that was the main avenue of Ottoman advance. Evrenos Bey, the march lord who conquered much of the Balkans in the second half of the fourteenth century, took Larissa, the principal town of eastern Thessaly, in 1386, one year before the surrender of Thessaloniki. Just a few years later Bayezit I moved to impose direct control over the areas that had been conquered in the Balkans, including Thessaly. Tamerlane's crushing defeat of Bayezit in 1402 almost erased the Ottomans from the history books and control in the Balkans necessarily weakened, but only to a certain extent. In an agreement signed in 1403 between Manuel Paleologos II and Süleyman I, large areas of eastern Thessaly formally reverted to Byzantine control, but the situation on the ground remained unclear. The Ottoman civil wars were raging at this point and, despite the supposed return of eastern Thessaly to the Byzantines, the sources mention a Yusuf Bey as governor of "Greater Vallachia" in 1406. Further west, Turkish settlement continued apace (Savvides 1994: 40). Thessaly had to endure another decade of strife until in 1423 a large Ottoman army under the leadership of Turhan Bey returned to Thessaly and established definitive control. Turhan Bey went on to become the first governor of the province.

To understand the significance of the Ottoman arrival we must bear in mind the fact that in Thessaly the Turkish armies entered a province that, like all of central Greece, had been devastated by what one author has called the "nightmare" of the fourteenth century: "It is hard to express the debilitated misery of the Byzantine Roman empire in the fourteenth century – a period of repeated civil war, religious hatreds and foreign invasions" (Page 2008: 138). We can add to that the ravages of the Black Death and environmental problems such as the exhaustion of the soil (Matschke 2002: 82). The depopulation of the plain is evoked by the fact that the archbishopric of Larissa had been deserted for several generations by the time Evrenos Bey arrived, as successive archbishops took refuge in Trikala, further west and closer to the mighty Pindos mountains. The church itself had been taken over by outlaws (Kiel 1985: 41). Further south in Boeotia, records suggest that the entire *kaza* (district) of Thebes, an area of roughly 500 square miles, contained only one town and six villages in 1400 (Kiel 1996: 323).

Therefore, when Barak Bey, son of Evrenos Bey, established a pious foundation in Larissa (after 1423) and endowed villages in the area to build, among other things, a mosque and the famous *bedestan* (still standing) of the city, it was the first urban development that the region had seen in a very long time (Beldiceanu 1983: 112). Because of this he is rightly seen as the refounder of Larissa, henceforth known to the Turks as Yenişehir. In accordance with standard Ottoman practice, other notables established foundations of their own and the city grew by leaps and bounds. The first survey, done in the middle of the fifteenth century, recorded 421 households; seventy-five years later that number had grown to 768. Trikala, the other major city in Thessaly, also grew rapidly, from 545 to 825 households in the same period (Bedliceanu 1983: 122; Barkan 1957: 35).

Larissa was also an Ottoman creation in that it swiftly developed into a major center of Muslim urban life; in 1520, 90 percent of the population was Muslim. It resembles, then, its much better-known counterpart, Sarajevo, in that a city was created almost out of whole cloth and then peopled by members of the new faith. It is striking that even cities much further north, and thus within the main line of the Ottoman advance, were not as overwhelmingly Muslim as Larissa. Serres, for instance, was 61 percent and Monastir 75 percent Muslim. This suggests just how deserted Larissa was when the invaders arrived. Trikala, by contrast, always remained a Christian city, albeit one with a substantial Muslim (and Jewish) population, and the same is true for many other cities in the Greek lands (Sugar 1977: 51).

The survival of Trikala as a Christian city is in accordance with the historical evidence, which indicates that, by and large, the cities and villages of Thessaly surrendered peacefully, first to the march lords and then to the Ottomans themselves (Savvides 1994: 39, 43). Across the Balkans, those cities that capitulated enjoyed substantial continuity in urban life, whereas those that held out suffered devastating reprisals once they had been conquered. The clearest example of this is Thessaloniki. The city surrendered in 1387. As a result, the Ottomans contented themselves with installing a garrison at the acropolis and, from time to time, imposing the child levy or *devşirme* on the city's

Christian population. The Christian nature of the city remained intact, to the extent that a Russian monk who visited in 1401 was still dazzled by the monasteries he found there (Mazower 2004: 27). After the Ottoman debacle of 1402 Thessaloniki reverted to Byzantine control, but in 1422 the new sultan, Murat II, vowed to take it back again. This time the city resisted (despite the wishes of its population) and thus both sides had to endure an eight-year siege. When the armies broke through the gates of the city, the rules of war applied and widespread plunder and enslavement ensued. Christian life underwent a precipitous decline; by 1520 Christians were only 20 percent of the city's population, whereas in Trikala they were nearly half (Sugar 1977: 51). Larissa is the exception to the rule, a Muslim-majority city not because the inhabitants had refused to surrender but rather because the city was in ruins long before the invading armies arrived.

The Muslims who lived in these cities, whether old or new, were newcomers, Turks from Anatolia for the most part. They were a mix of soldiers – those who garrisoned the fortresses as well as fiefholders with their retinues – and officials and tradesmen. The last is important to underline as Ottoman cities in the Balkans have often been described as parasitic, places that housed a collection of functionaries who lived off the revenue from the countryside and produced nothing themselves. In fact population registers make it clear that most Muslim city dwellers, in Thessaly and throughout the Balkans, were artisans of some sort. Consider, for example, the names of some of the Muslim neighborhoods in Trikala. There was the *mahalle* (neighborhood) of Mustafa the silk worker, alongside the *mahalles* of the tanners and the butchers (Beldiceanu 1983: 121). The Ottoman conquest, then, not only rebuilt the cities of Thessaly. It also introduced an entirely new urban population.

Their Christian neighbors are a far more shadowy group. Part of this may be due to the sources. The same population register for Trikala that lists an artisanal occupation for many individual Muslims provides no such information on the Christians, who are identified only by their names (Beldiceanu 1983: 121). But the mystery surrounding Christian city dwellers in the early Ottoman period (with the exception of Istanbul) is also due to certain enduring assumptions concerning the nature of Christian life under the Ottomans. The historian Mark Mazower sums it up best when he writes: "The centre of gravity of Balkan Christianity shifted into the rural areas where monasteries, especially in Mount Athos, prospered" (Mazower 2004: 35).

This is certainly true, but it does not change the fact that a number of cities had substantial Christian populations. This was particularly the case in the Greek-speaking lands, for reasons that will be discussed shortly. The most extreme example of this is Athens, which was nearly 100 percent Christian in 1520 (Sugar 1977: 51). We know next to nothing about these urban dwellers, despite the fact that the first wave of conversions among ordinary people (as opposed to the Byzantine elites) would come from this group. In addition, as we shall see later on, Ottoman policy in Christian urban centers in this early period (as opposed to their treatment of rural monasteries) is still poorly understood, probably in part due to the relative disregard for urban Christians.

Settlement patterns suggest that the Muslim newcomers lived separate from the pre-existing Christian population. Across the Balkans, new Muslim quarters and markets were built and cities grew in new directions, away from the historic center (Argo 2008: 268). Eleni Gara's meticulous work on Veroia (Ottoman Karaferye) gives us a rare glimpse of the different feel of these new neighborhoods as opposed to the older Christian quarters. The latter remained in the old city (Veroia had surrendered to the Ottomans) where their quarters retained the medieval style of settlement, namely a cluster of houses built around a square with a church in the middle. The neighborhoods to the south where the Muslims lived had a more suburban feel with houses surrounded by gardens (Gara 2007: 57).

If we put all of these developments together – the rapid population growth; the proliferation of mosques, schools, and markets funded by the conquering elites; and the expansion outward from old city centers – it is clear that the Ottoman arrival in the Balkans heralded a major revitalization of urban life across a war-torn peninsula from Athens to Belgrade, from Serres to Sarajevo.[1] Unlike in the venerable cities of the Middle East, where the Ottomans adopted themselves to a pre-existing urban tradition, in the Balkans they created a new Balkan, urban civilization, one that bore the stamp of Ottoman and Turkish Islam.[2] The relationship of Balkan Christians to these new centers of urban civilization is still poorly understood but there is no doubt that, unlike in the case of the monasteries, the Ottomans did target the essential pillar of Christian urban life, that is the church. However, when one considers the fact that Christian populations were left essentially in place (unless the city had been taken by force), the attack on the church must have been motivated by enmity toward the patriarch and the emperor in Istanbul. The metropolitans, the bishops, and the archbishops were seen as the agents of an enemy state. It was not an attack on urban civilization per se, as it is abundantly clear that wherever they went the Ottomans were determined city builders.

The countryside

But settlement and repopulation were not a matter of the cities alone. The Ottomans were determined to restore village life – and thus their own tax base – as well. In the second half of the fifteenth century and throughout the sixteenth century the state was engaged in a great settlement drive in the Balkans and thus rural life enjoyed a great revival. A variety of mechanisms existed to establish (or re-establish) villages.

For example, any official who was willing to cultivate wasteland could gain title to the land and the peasants were settled there with a privileged status. These were the so-called *vakıf* (cash endowment) villages and there were many of them in Thessaly. Turhan Bey established foundations in Larissa that were not only the largest in the city but some of the greatest in the empire, and they were supported by revenues flowing in from the countryside. Even royalty in far-off Istanbul claimed villages in fertile Thessaly as part of their foundations; the *vakıf* of Mihrimah Sultan, daughter of Süleyman the Lawgiver, had a good deal of property in the area (Salakidis 2004: 73). Popular memory across the Balkans suggests that villagers in such places valued their connection to Ottoman royalty; even today villagers in Bulgaria and in Greece are eager to relate how their village belonged to this or that princess (Kiel 1985: 110). The attraction was not simply one of prestige; belonging to a royal foundation meant greater protection from local tax collectors and assorted troublemakers.

The Ottomans were also concerned to assure secure travel across a ravaged and underpopulated peninsula. To do so they established hundreds of so-called *derbend* villages in the high mountains and the dense woodlands.[3] These were places where villagers were charged with providing security in dangerous areas, in exchange for various tax exemptions. A rather lengthy document, a sultanic order from 1565, is worth quoting from in full, as it gives a vivid sense of how *derbend* villages were created.

> Order to the Cadi of Tărnovo: In a letter you informed us that the road over the mountains between the villages of Kilifar[evo] and Drjanovo belonging to the jurisdiction of Tărnovo, to the villages of Hümalar and Keçi Dere, belonging to the jurisdiction of Kazanlăk, is not taken in the normal manner. Because Yaylak is far off and there is no other village in the interval it is a dangerous and frightening road and a nest

of robbers where nobody can pass through. For this reason the travelers make with all possible difficulties a detour over distant places. As this road is not safe, scoundrels use it to drive stolen cattle from this side of the mountains to the other.

There is, however, in the middle of the mountains a site known by the name of Trjavna, which is suitable for founding a village there. So if it were ordered to have a village founded there, on condition of tax dispensation, in the manner of the Derbends, the travelers and all Muslim and Christian subjects, can pass in tranquillity. On this you were informed by all of the sipahis and the subjects, Muslim as well as Christian.

In this manner I order that: If the place mentioned is indeed dangerous and if there is indeed a suitable empty site to found a village, in the manner explained by you, a village that will be beneficial for the protection of the travelers, you have to bring together for three years and on condition of tax freedom, from among the non-registered people without fixed domicile those who belong to nobody (to a particular sipahi) and are not disputed and place a village there. After three years, after it has become inhabited and prosperous, you have to report how many households there are and how many fixed inhabitants and how much the production will be. On the base of these data you have to submit a petition to have it registered as a Derbend. (Kiel 1985: 99–100)

Ottoman policies, combined with the absence of war, had impressive results. In central Greece, in the Morea, and elsewhere in the Greek world the population in the villages (as well as the towns) quadrupled between the mid-fifteenth and the mid-sixteenth centuries (Zarinebaf 2005: 13).

Alongside the ordinary villagers and town dwellers of Thessaly there were also those who enjoyed a privileged status due to their willingness and ability to serve the Ottomans. Like all the early Ottoman sultans, Bayezit I was eager to absorb the pre-existing ruling class and thus, true to form, he married the daughter of one of the leading notables, a woman who had the added prestige of being a Kantakouzenos[4] (Beldiceanu 1983: 116). The Ottomans absorbed large numbers of the Christian military class. Thus in registers from mid-fifteenth-century Thessaly we find *sipahis* (fiefholding cavalrymen) and *voynuks* (a kind of auxiliary troop), in addition to the peasants and the town dwellers. Some of the *sipahis* were explicitly identified as the sons and grandsons of those who had come in with Evrenos Bey. Even at this very early date – just before the fall of Istanbul there were third-generation Christian *timar* (fief) holders in Thessaly, a reflection of how early and thoroughly the area was conquered.[5] Rank-and-file soldiers who had served in the armies of the various Balkan states found positions in the Ottoman military as *voynuks*; living in their own villages and serving in shifts, they enjoyed *askeri* (ruling class) status (İnalcık 1954: 114; Kiel 1985: 75). In Thessaly 103 *voynuks* and 203 *yamaks* (reserve soldiers) are recorded (İnalcık 1954: 114). Then there were the *derbendcis*, those peasants who lived in the *derbend* villages discussed above. No study of the *derbend* villages in Thessaly has yet been undertaken, but given their numbers elsewhere – there were at least 175 *derbend* villages in Macedonia alone – we know that they must have been numerous (Argo 2008: 275). In some cases Christians were tasked with protecting fortresses in exchange for reduced taxation; the village of Platimana (Platamon) was such a case in fifteenth-century Thessaly and its privileges were renewed in 1503 (Beldiceanu 1983: 126–7). Finally, across the Balkans there were the *martolos*, who were charged with providing security in dangerous places, in a manner very similar to the *derbendcis*, although the former were not organized in villages. Mountainous Thessaly was divided into six *armatolıks* in the eighteenth century and it is likely that *martolos* had been serving there since the very beginning of the Ottoman period (Pappas 1991: 29).

These arms-bearing Thessalians were part of a very broad swath of the Balkan Christian population that enjoyed a privileged status in the fifteenth and sixteenth centuries, due to the services they provided to the Ottomans. The enormity of their numbers is not always appreciated; Barkan estimates that out of the 832,707 Christian hearths in the Balkans in the early sixteenth century, a full 90,000 enjoyed some sort of special military status as *martolos*, *voynuks*, or *eflak*.[6] And it was not only a question of numbers. Christian auxiliary troops were also very visible because in many places they were the sole defenders of the fortresses, with only one or two Muslim officers in place. In certain places Christians represented the majority of Ottoman troops. This phenomenon has been studied most intensively on the island of Limnos, where Lowry's study of the survey registers has revealed that, out of the total of 281 military men who received *timars* in 1489, 261 were local Christians (Lowry 2002: 36).

Christians were also prominent on the Ottoman frontlines, as it were, as *sipahis* and even *akıncıs* (raiders) "who participated in Ottoman raids against other Christians, partook in the distribution of booty and received land grants (timars) in return for their services, all without having to convert" (Krstić 2011: 86). If one takes into account the *sipahis*, the *voynuks*, the *armatoles*, and all the *reaya* (tax-paying subjects) who were given tax exemptions in return for service, we see that in some areas Christians were a majority of the Ottoman forces (İnalcık 1953: 222).

Among those writing about the Greeks there is a tendency to ignore these Christians, as if by serving the Ottomans they had disappeared from history. This has had a number of distorting effects, of which I will underline the two that seem, in my view, to be the most important. First, it misrepresents the character of the conquering state that the Christian population confronted in the Balkans. Often the state was represented not by an alien Turco-Islamic foreigner, but by very familiar faces indeed. Anthony Bryer emphasized this many years ago: "In many cases the old Greek families merged, through marriage, with the leading families of the conquerors; often the same provincial governors retained their authority under the guise of a different name and not always a different religion" (Bryer 1965: 35). Commenting on this more recently, Theocharis Stavrides noted that "For this and other reasons the Ottoman/Balkan wars of the fifteenth century did not always have the clear cut Muslim versus Christian character that previous such conflicts had had" (Stavrides 2001: 105). How ordinary Christians experienced these Christian servants of the empire is one of the most intriguing questions of early Ottoman history, and it is one that has remained unexplored.[7]

Second, by writing these Christians out of the history of Christian society in the fifteenth and sixteenth centuries it is possible to argue, as Speros Vryonis has, that the Ottomans reduced the Christians of the Balkans to "an almost exclusively Volkskultur" (Vryonis 1981: 307). This is too strong. It would perhaps be too much to speak of the emergence of new elites, but there were certainly new groups within Christian society who enjoyed a degree of social privilege, and they were the result of the society that the Ottomans had created. Moreover, limited but highly significant evidence suggests that some of these privileged Christians played an important role in the Christian society that was emerging under the Ottomans. And here I am referring to the burst of monastic construction that was underway in the Balkans by the early sixteenth century, after a long period of quiescence. This is yet another sign of the vitality of Christian life; Thessaly provides some of the most notable examples.

The monastery of Dousiko sits at the base of the mighty Pindos mountains, eighteen miles west of Trikala. It was Bessarion, the metropolitan of Larissa, who founded it sometime between 1527 and 1535, on the ruins of a medieval monastery. He died in 1540 – having gone on to accomplish other good works, including a bridge outside the village of Pylos that was the only link between the Pindos mountains and the plains of Thessaly until the twentieth century – and his nephew, Neophytos the Second, also the metropolitan of Larissa, continued the development of the site (Vogiatzis 1995: 44; Triandafyllidou 1897: 59). Under his tutelage a church was built and the monastic cells were extended. An artist from the imperial capital completed the iconography of the church in 1557. In addition to the grandeur of the buildings themselves – the monastic complex was as large as those on Mount Athos – the decoration of the church, while incorporating many Byzantine traditions, broke with established convention through its use of alternating layers of stone and brick, a style that first appeared in the sixteenth century in church decoration, but that would go on to be used in other monastic churches in the seventeenth and eighteenth centuries (Vogiatzis 1995: 187). Other innovations – such as the circular base of the main dome and the large dome in the narthex – were specific to Dousiko and testify to the skill of the master builder. The influence of the monastery of Dousiko, which, due to its size, its location and its artistic and architectural achievements, must be considered the most important Christian monument in sixteenth-century Thessaly, is evident in the number of monastic churches that went on to copy many of its innovations (Vogiatzis 1995: 225–6).

Thessaly is also home to the well-known collection of monasteries known as the Meteora, whose rock formations tower above the northwestern corner of the Thessalian plane. Here, too, the sixteenth century bore witness to a remarkable burst of building, in terms of churches as well as the founding of entirely new monasteries (Alexander 1983: 96; Vogiatzis 1995: 34). All told, the sixteenth century witnessed the establishment of eight new monastic complexes in Thessaly, as well as the substantial rebuilding of the Great Monastery at Meteora, the vast majority of them at the edge of the plain where the fields meet the mountains. They spread out like a ring around the new settlements in the flatlands, both a product of the new Ottoman order (Vogiatzis 1995: 35).[8]

This explosion in the sixteenth century – which took place not only in Thessaly but across the Greek world and the Balkans – was of course dependent upon the existence of wealth within the community.[9] Where did this wealth come from? Several possibilities suggest themselves. It could have been Constantinopolitan in origin. As we shall see in the next chapter, under Fatih Mehmet a very wealthy Christian elite quickly emerged; some were the very same people who had dominated the last years of Byzantium. For example, Dimitrios Paleologos, one of the last Despots of the Morea, emerged as a tax farmer soon after he surrendered southern Greece to the Ottomans (İnalcık 1993: 387). He and men like him could well have provided funds for the construction of monasteries in their places of origin. But at this point we can only speculate, since the subject has not been investigated. Others were "new men," we can say, men who had prospered in Ottoman territory long before the fall of the city, and who then easily made the transition to the new imperial capital. Again, we know nothing of their patronage habits (Zachariadou 1996). We do know that, beginning in the early sixteenth century, the rulers of Wallachia and Moldavia were patronizing both Mount Athos and Meteora, and these ties have received a good deal of attention (Nicol 1963: 131).

The work of Machiel Kiel suggests that at least some of the wealth was accumulated within provincial society itself. It was those individuals who had secured for themselves a privileged niche within the Ottoman military system as auxiliary forces – the *voynuks*, the *derbendcis*, and others – who emerged as new patrons of the church.[10] No studies have yet been done for Thessaly but, thanks to Kiel, we know quite a bit about the Bulgarian lands. The area around Sofia is very suggestive of new patterns of patronage. Sofia and its environs are fairly bursting with churches and monasteries from the sixteenth century. Passing through Sofia in 1578 the German minister Stephan Gerlach noted that the Christian community possessed no fewer than twelve churches, as well as two religious colleges. And this despite the fact that the population of the city was overwhelmingly Muslim (Kiel 1985: 84). The ability of the Christian community to provide so handsomely for itself must be related to the fact that many Christians in this region enjoyed a privileged status within the new Ottoman order, either through their military service or as providers of sheep to the Ottoman capital. Virtually all of the villages in the district of Sofia had *voynuk* status (Kiel 1985: 76, 81). Several inscriptions in Serbian churches identify the donor as a Christian *sipahi* (Kiel 1985: 136).

Urban benefactors were important in the sixteenth century, which makes sense, given that the cities were growing. The Church of St. Petka Samardžijska in the center of Sofia was entirely rebuilt and painted at the end of the fifteenth century, thanks to the efforts of the guild of the packsaddle makers. The monastery of Strupets near Lukovit in northern Bulgaria is called the "Monastery of the Tailor's Guild" (Kiel 1985: 136). Orthodox metropolitans, urban officials par excellence, have also been overlooked in our haste to limit the church to the countryside in the Ottoman period. Zachariadou draws our attention to what she calls "the flourishing of the metropolitans" in the sixteenth century, by which she means their emergence as artistic patrons, drawing on local sources of wealth such as revenues from fairs and sacred springs, while also benefitting from low tax rates. Thus early in the century the metropolitan of Larissa resigned and went to Meteora, where he oversaw the renovations of the monastery of St. Nicholas, itself newly built at the end of the fifteenth century. He brought the renowned Cretan painter Theofanis to create the iconic program, which was completed in 1527. The metropolitans of Serres and of Veroia sponsored renovations at Mount Athos in the same period, again using renowned artists (Zachariadou 1996: 106–7).

We should note, too, that the Ottomans themselves presided over church building in the late fifteenth and the sixteenth centuries. Their determined settlement drive must have resulted in the erection of village churches, as it was impossible to imagine a Christian village without a place of worship.[11] The better-documented cities prove that this was indeed the Ottoman mentality; newly founded cities such as Sarajevo and Mostar in Bosnia-Hercegovina and Razgad in Bulgaria (founded by the grand vezir Ibrahim Pasha) all came to include Christian quarters and churches where none had been before (Kiel 1985: 193–4).

Negotiating with the Ottomans

Monasteries and churches were built within a framework determined by the new ruling authority. They were not, as some have suggested, centers of resistance that somehow escaped the tax collector (Vogiatzis 1995: 36). Although it is not longer there, the façade of Dousiko used to display a *tughra* – the sultan's seal – confirming its rights and privileges.[12] In the middle of the fifteenth century the monks of the monasteries at Meteora were in possession of *berats* (documents) that documented their privileges going all the way back to the initial conquests of Bayezit I. They did indeed have an advantageous tax status – they gave nothing for their vineyards, mills, houses, sheep, and goats – but this was the result not of resistance but of negotiations with the Ottomans. Monastic documents show that the monks of Meteora were also willing to bring the local judge, the *kadi*, into a struggle over land between the monastic establishment and four neighboring villages. With the *kadi*'s support, they retained control over land that, at least according to the monks, the villagers had been trying to seize (Alexander 1983: 96).

The privileges that the monks possessed make it clear that Meteora – and no doubt Dousiko and all the monasteries around the plain of Thessaly – was incorporated into the Ottoman system under terms very similar to those that governed the famed monasteries on Mount Athos. Due to numerous studies over the last several decades, we now have a very good picture of the agreements that were made there in the late fourteenth and the fifteenth centuries, agreements that were absolutely central in determining the nature of Christian society for centuries to come. They ensured that monasteries and monastic holdings would not only be preserved, but would also expand under the Ottomans, despite a moment of crisis in the late sixteenth century.[13]

Mount Athos emerged intact from the first Ottoman conquest of Thessaloniki (1387). The monks preserved their estates, both on the peninsula itself and elsewhere, as well as the right to collect taxes from the peasantry that worked their lands. The main tax was the *haraç*; the monks turned over one-third to the Ottomans while the remaining two-thirds stayed with them (Kolovos 2005a: 111; 2005b: 198). Despite the violence of the second conquest of Thessaloniki in 1430, Murat II confirmed the monks in their privileges in that very same year. Nobody was to enter either Mount Athos or its many rural estates without permission, and local officials did not have the right to collect taxes from them. The monks were exempt from the burden of extraordinary taxation and were free to transport to Mount Athos on their ships all the produce from their estates (Kolovos 2005b: 199). Just a few years later, however, Murat II ordered a general survey (*tahrir*) of the empire, in accordance with his program of centralization, and the monks lost many of their privileges. Most dramatically, perhaps, some of their extensive rural estates were subsumed into the *timar* system and now the tax revenue from these holdings belonged to the new military and administrative class known as the *sipahis* (Kolovos 2005a: 115). By the end of the fifteenth century, however, many of the privileges had been restored and the monks were once again collecting the taxes. In return they had to promise not to abandon their properties (Kolovos 2005a: 115).

The documents from Meteora, which date from the very middle of the fifteenth century, suggest that the monasteries escaped the centralizing drive under Murat II since they state that the monks had undergone no change in their status since the initial conquest of Bayezit I. Further research might show otherwise, but the disparity, if true, can be accounted for. Prior to the crisis of the late sixteenth century, the status of monasteries across the empire was still very much determined by a combination of custom and imperial legislation (Kermeli 2008: 190). Nevertheless, two things can be asserted without hesitation: all monastic estates in the fledgling empire enjoyed a privileged status relative to other groups, and, two, these privileges were to a great extent the result of vigorous and continuous petitioning by the monks themselves. This leads us to a larger point: the monks, like the Christians of the empire as a whole, were not simply passively incorporated into the empire. Through their own actions they helped to carve out a place for themselves in the new order (Kolovos 2005a: 116).

All of these arrangements – on Mount Athos, at Meteora and elsewhere – were worked out directly between the sultan and the monasteries in question. The patriarch in Istanbul, seems to have had little to do with what was decided. Nor did the fall of the imperial city change their status in any way. What this illustrates is that, across the Greek world (as across the Balkans more generally), the Ottomans made a series of agreements with institutions and individuals as they encountered them and these agreements, some of which (as in Thessaly) predated 1453 by many decades, would also endure long past 1453.

No discussion of the Ottomans and Christian monasticism is complete without underlining the fact that urban monasteries were in a far more precarious position. Some institutions, it is true, were able to make deals with the Ottomans. Nevra Necipoğlu has shown how the monastery of Nea Mone in Thessaloniki prospered during the first period of Ottoman rule (1387–1403), sometimes at the expense of other monasteries that did not enjoy the Ottomans' favor. In 1387 the new rulers seized some village land that belonged to the monastery of Akapniou. The land, however, was turned over not to a Muslim but rather to Nea Mone. After a difficult period of diminished revenues during the Byzantine interregnum – demonstrating how closely its fortunes were tied to the Ottomans – the monastery returned to prosperity after the final conquest in 1430 (and this despite the fact that Thessaloniki was taken by force of arms). Soon after, Nea Mone is on record leasing a linseed-oil press to a Muslim resident of the city, showing that good relations had resumed (Necipoğlu 1995: 128–9).

But Nea Mone was the exception that proved the rule. In city after city – including the imperial capital, the Balkan cities, and Trabzon in the Pontos – urban monasteries did not survive the Ottoman arrival. Of the 80 urban monasteries known to have existed on the eve of the Ottoman conquests, only 20 were still in existence after 1453. For rural monasteries the numbers were 158 and 91 respectively (Bryer 1979:

233–4). While this discrepancy has not yet been investigated systematically, the explanation must lie in the fact that the Ottomans showed far more interest in remaking the cities than they did the countryside.

If we move away from the question of Christian institutions, in this case monasteries, to the more diffuse topic of Christian individuals, the sheer intensity of the Ottoman settlement drive, on the one hand, and the vast scope of Ottoman military ambitions, on the other, created many communities that were defined first and foremost by their service to the Ottoman state, rather than by their religion. Let us return, for example, to the subject of the *derbend* villages. There were both Muslim and Christian *derbend* villages; what distinguished them from other villages was their privileged tax position and the duties they were obliged to shoulder in exchange for the privileges they had been granted. This is not to say that a Christian *derbend* village was not Christian; of course it was. But it is to emphasize that its *derbend* status must have been an essential part of what defined it as a community. Moreover, the *derbend* villages were not a fleeting phenomenon. Although their nature changed somewhat over the centuries, many *derbend* villages flourished and grew into great towns in the eighteenth century (Kiel 1985: 97). One of the most powerful Christian families in Plovdiv in today's southern Bulgaria in the early nineteenth century were recent immigrants from the village of Koprivstica, a *derbend* village in the sixteenth century. The Chalikov family, not surprisingly, made their fortune through supplying the capital with sheep (Kiel 1985: 95; Lyberatos 2009: 163).

The Ottoman Empire, like all pre-modern empires, was a patchwork of special arrangements; *derbend* villages and monasteries were only two of the most prominent islands of privileges for Christians in the Balkans. When we add to them the *vakıf* villages, the *voynuk* villages, and all those villagers charged with delivering sheep to the capital, it is clearly problematic to think of the rural population (or the urban population for that matter) only in terms of religion; individuals had a variety of rights and obligations, only some of which were connected to their religious status.

The villagers of Thessaly, then, and the monks in renowned centers of monastic life such as Meteora and Mount Athos, had worked out a modus vivendi with the Ottomans long before Fatih Mehmet entered the fabled capital of the Byzantines. Let us remember that in 1453 there were already third-generation Christian *sipahis* serving in central Greece. Of course the fall of Istanbul was an enormous symbolic loss, but it must be remembered that the conquest of the Greek world was a long and drawn-out affair, which began well before 1453 and would continue for another two centuries; the island of Crete, after all, was not taken until 1669.[14] In the Balkans, Thessaly was a very early addition to the sultan's domains, and it would remain Ottoman for half a century after the founding of the modern Greek state in 1821.

The Ottoman Balkans and the Greek lands

By the early sixteenth century the Ottomans had established the network that would supply meat to the capital for the next one hundred years. Known as the *çelepkeşan* system, it obligated certain designated tax payers to provide Istanbul with a specified number of sheep. In return for so doing, they were released from all extraordinary services as well as any other service to the state. Who were these designated tax payers? They were the residents of the ten *sancaks*, or provinces, that ran in an arc from the southeast to the northeast around Istanbul. This was the "Rumelian heartland", namely those areas in the Balkans that the Ottomans conquered first and that were firmly under their control before 1453.[15] The remaining victories in Europe would not come until after the conquest of Istanbul, and some came very much later indeed, such as Belgrade, which did not succumb until 1521. If it was in the Balkans that the Ottomans became the Ottomans – that is, with their victories there they began to separate themselves out from the multitude of *beyliks* in Anatolia – it was these ten *sancaks* that formed their base. They corresponded, roughly, to Thrace, Bulgaria, Macedonia, and Thessaly.

The geography of the *çelepkeşan* system is a useful way of thinking about the Ottoman conquest of the Balkans because it highlights, in a particularly concrete fashion, the fact that most of the historically Greek lands were on the periphery from the point of view of the imperial capital (Map 1). Thessaly was the southernmost point of the Ottoman heartland. Further south, Attica and the Peloponnese were never as tightly bound to Istanbul as the Thessalian plain; and insular Greece, of course, even less so.[16] Some phenomena, of course, were empire-wide. The rapid population growth of the sixteenth century, for example, was as much on display in Athens as it was in Trikala or Thessaloniki, as was the burst of religious building. But in terms of its place in the empire, the southern tip of the Balkan peninsula was markedly different from the Ottoman core.

This peripheral status had several consequences. First, (Turkish) Muslim colonization and, later, indigenous Muslim conversion – while

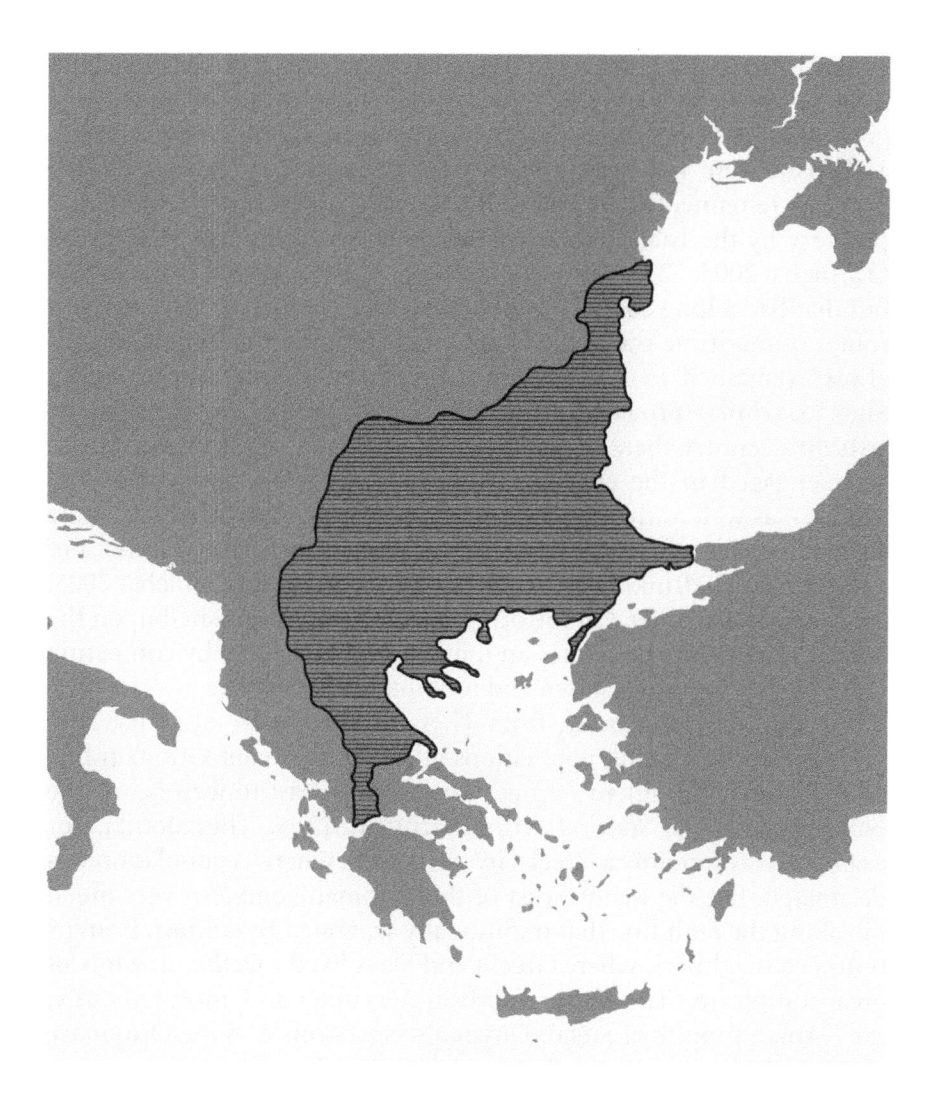

Map 1 The Ottoman heartland in the Balkans. Map created by Theocharis Tsampouras.

certainly present in the southern Balkans – was always concentrated in areas further north. In the opening decades of the sixteenth century Muslims were in a majority in the eastern Balkans, in those areas that constituted the hinterland of the capital city. Beyond that, there were significant Muslim populations in Macedonia, Bosnia-Hercegovina, and Thessaly (Sugar 1977: 51). The results of these differing settlement patterns could be quite dramatic. Monastir, Skopje, and Sofia were all towns with a Muslim majority in this period, while Larissa, with a population that was 90 percent Muslim, was almost a second Sarajevo. By contrast, the population of Athens was 99 percent Christian. Second, probably as a result of lying outside the main routes of conquest, the great Muslim foundations that figured so prominently in a place such as Larissa were not very common further south, and most church property remained in the hands of the church; the tax farming of such property by the Istanbul-based Greek Orthodox elite was widespread (Zarinebaf 2005: 22) Finally, as an area that was peripheral to the capital but that had a long coastline that figured prominently in the east–west routes of maritime trade, the Greek mainland and the Aegean islands always remained in contact with the larger Mediterranean world. Such proximity provided opportunities for profit – as early as the sixteenth century there is evidence that Ottoman *sipahis* in the Morea were engaged in the contraband wheat trade with both Spain and Venice – as well as the pleasures of the life of the outlaw. When some Venetians took refuge in a deserted fortress on the island of Euboea in 1572, a ten-day drinking party with the *reaya* ensued (Zarinebaf 2005: 29; Kolovos 2007: 52). On the other hand, the ravages visited upon the coastal inhabitants by pirates and, during times of war, by competing tax collectors are well known and too numerous to relate.

If we move north, now, from Thessaly, there were of course substantial Greek-speaking populations all along the main Ottoman line of advance, as the sultan's armies moved from east to west across the Balkan peninsula, starting with Edirne in 1365. Thessaloniki, for example, was certainly a Greek city until 1430, when its population was decimated. But the main thrust of the Ottoman conquests very much ran along the fault line that traditionally separated Byzantium from its northern neighbors, where Greeks and Slavs lived together in a mix of great complexity. The Bulgaria of Ivan Alexander and, most famously, the Serbian Empire of Stefan Duşan also succumbed to the Ottomans, along with the Byzantines. Just as they did in Thessaly, the Ottomans absorbed large numbers of soldiers, this time Serbians and Bulgarians, as they continued their march to the north and to the west. The importance of the Slav component in the Ottoman armies is suggested by the fact that the thousands of Christian native troops were known by the Slavic term *voynuk*. In addition, the recent demise of, especially, the Serbian state meant that there was a significant Serbian ruling class and this group – which preferred Ottoman to Hungarian domination – joined the Ottomans en masse as Christian *sipahis*. In this early period nearly three-quarters of the Ottoman military forces in northern Serbia consisted of local Serbs (Kiel 1985: 67). A different situation prevailed in much of the Greek world; there many Latin states, successors of the

Fourth Crusade, hung on until they were finally extinguished by the Ottomans, at which point their elites either fled or (especially in insular Greece) were retained by the new rulers for a period of time (Minkov 2004: 99). In either case, there was no Greek elite to be absorbed into the state machinery. The *devşirme* system, which forcibly took Christian peasant boys for lifelong service in the janissary corps, was concentrated in Slavic areas, although it certainly existed in the Greek lands as well.[17]

The superhighway of the Ottoman conquest of the Balkans, then, ran due west from Edirne. Over the course of the next 150 years, moreover, one sultan after another would lead his armies northward, seeking to reach the vast Hungarian plain and, beyond that, Vienna. And this was at a time when Christians still found it relatively easy to find a place for themselves in the machinery of conquest. The combination of these two aspects of the early empire meant that Slav participation in imperial governance – from the Christian *sipahi* on the Ottoman frontlines to the *devşirme* recruit in Istanbul – was very high indeed. This would have serious repercussions for the only Byzantine institution that managed to survive, albeit in an altered form, Fatih Mehmet's capture of Istanbul in 1453, namely the ancient Ecumenical Patriarchate of the Greek Orthodox Church.

Notes

1. We have already noted the rapid growth of Larissa and Trikala between the fifteenth and sixteenth centuries. This was the pattern across the Balkans. The city of Athens saw a long period of extraordinary growth and expansion. A city that had occupied only 20 hectares and housed 1,000 households in 1395 had 1,600 households in 1506 and then 3,200 in 1570. Now covering 60–70 hectares, it had become one of the largest urban centers in the Balkans (Kiel 1985: 316).
2. For example, the public bath did not exist in medieval Bulgaria. The Ottoman public bath built by the governor of Skopje in 1465/70 is three times as large as the largest non-residential monument in medieval Bulgaria. "From the point of view of urbanism Ottoman architecture was far ahead of that of Bulgaria, and indeed of all the medieval Balkan states" (Kiel 1985: 234, 236).
3. *Derbend* is from the Persian, meaning "pass" or "gate."
4. The Kantakouzenoi were one of the most prominent Byzantine noble families; several ascended to the imperial throne.
5. The register shows 203 *timars*, and 36 of these (17.74 percent) were held by Christians. Some timariots are identified explicitly as the sons or

grandsons of those who came in with Evrenos Bey. "En effet certains timariotes de Thessalie recurrent des dotations à l'époque d'Evrenos et, dans de nombreux cas, les timars resterent pendant plusieurs décennies dans une même famille." And then Beldiceanu notes that clearly *timars* went from father to son in Thessaly, "fait exceptionnel dans le système timarial ottoman" (Beldiceanu 1983: 130, 132).

6. *Eflak* was the term used to refer to the Vlachs, who also served the Ottomans as mountain soldiers (Barkan 1957: 34).
7. Bryer writes "This sort of relationship was one of many which softened the blow of Ottoman conquest," but provides no supporting evidence (Bryer 1965: 35). It seems also possible that it could have made it harder to bear. Admittedly, this would be a difficult question to explore. We do have Christian voices from this period, but they are, unsurprisingly, elite voices. More importantly, they occupy themselves exclusively with the legitimacy (or not) of the Ottomans and do not comment on the Christians serving the dynasty.
8. See Vogiatzis (1995: 35) for the number of monasteries. The reader may well ask how it was that so many new churches and monasteries were built during the Ottoman period given that this was forbidden by Islamic law. The answer is that the Ottomans found all sorts of ways around this prohibition (without ever discarding the prohibition itself), as a wealth of research has shown. For example, in the sixteenth century, as the soaring population in the capital city led to pressures to convert churches into mosques, the authorities invented the tradition that parts of the capital had peacefully surrendered, precisely to prevent the seizure of churches en masse. At the same time, the Ottomans came up with legal justifications when they wanted to seize a church and build a mosque in its place, since churches were not meant to be arbitrarily taken from the Christian community, although, in fact, they were (Necipoğlu 2005: 58).
9. In Serbia "a veritable boom in church building followed the re-establishment of the Serbian patriarchate in 1557" (Necipoğlu 2005: 58). Kotzageorgis speaks of the "mass founding (or refounding) of monasteries in the Greek peninsula in the sixteenth century" (Kotzageorgis 2011: 185).
10. Machiel Kiel would like to challenge Halil İnalcık on the demise of Christian *sipahis* by the beginning of the sixteenth century, and he includes them as patrons of Christian art in the 1500s. His evidence however, while suggestive, is very limited. Most likely some *sipahis* acted as patrons of Christian art in the fifteenth century but played no significant role in the following century (Kiel 1985: 69).
11. When Ghazi Turhan Bey started to rebuild Thessaly, ruined during the endless Byzantine civil wars of the fourteenth century, he not only founded a Turkish town (Larissa – Yenişehir) but also a Greek Christian one, Tyrnavos, where he himself provided for the church. It was still

extant in the 1930s and was still called "the Church of the Pasha" (Kiel 1985: 195). Ebussuud, the renowned Ottoman jurist of the sixteenth century, allowed new churches in *zimmi* (protected non-Muslim subject) villages without a mosque or a *medrese* (school) (Necipoğlu 2005: 523).

12. Kiel says it was the *tughra* of Selim II (Kiel 1985: 149). A 2012 visitor to Dousiko, however, was told that the *tughra* had been that of Süleyman. I thank Nikolaos Vryzidis for sharing with me his experience of the monastery (women are not allowed to enter).
13. In this way, as in so many others, the Ottomans continued trends that had begun in the late Byzantine period. The number of monastic holdings exploded in the twelfth and thirteenth centuries. See Haldon (1986: 168–9).
14. And of course if we want to include Anatolia the story begins in the eleventh century.
15. Greenwood (1988: 76). Vryonis also speaks about "the core area of Ottoman control in the Balkans" (Vryonis 1980: 287).
16. By "historically Greek lands" I mean those areas of the Balkans that were overwhelmingly Greek speaking and were firmly under the control of the Greek Orthodox patriarchate in Istanbul. Faced with the results of the Slavic invasions of southern Greece in the early medieval period, Constantinople engaged in a sustained effort to re-Hellenize the area in the ninth century, a campaign that by and large succeeded. By contrast, Byzantium was never as successful at re-Hellenizing areas further north where large numbers of Slavs and then Bulgars could not be dislodged or assimilated.
17. Hadrovics speaks of "the partial slavicization of the state" due to the prominence of Serbian *devşirme* (Hadrovics 1947: 45).

CHAPTER 2

From Constantinople to Istanbul

In 1326 Sultan Orhan and his followers starved the Byzantine city of Bursa into submission and made this verdant settlement on the slopes of Mount Uludağ their first capital. A little over forty years later another major city fell; this time it was Edirne (Adrianople) in the empire's European provinces. The Ottomans had crossed over to Europe less than twenty years earlier as part of their alliance with the Byzantine emperor John Kantakouzenos. Edirne became the new capital. When two Serbian lords attacked sultan Murat in 1371 in the vicinity of the city they both perished, and a Greek chronicle remarked "From then on the Muslims began to overrun the Empire of the Christians" (Imber 2002: 11). The Ottomans now advanced rapidly across the Balkans but behind them the city of Constantinople, although encircled on every side, remained under Byzantine control. It was nearly all they had left. And yet, remarkably, the besieged capital held on for nearly another hundred years as the Ottomans battled to cement their control over their conquests in both the Balkans and Anatolia.

Mehmet II's accession to the throne in 1451 (for the second time) meant that the war party was back in power and preparations for a final assault on the city began. The Byzantines watched with despair as the sultan assembled the stone, the timbers, and the iron needed to build the great fortress of Rumeli Hisarı on the European shores of the Bosphorus, a complement to the fortress that already stood on the Asian side. By the early spring of 1453 the Ottoman army was camped out in front of the walls of the city. The storied city of Constantinople had endured many attacks and sieges in its thousand-year history, but this time its defenders were confronted with the power of modern artillery. The ferocious cannons finally succeeded in tearing a hole in the city walls on May 29 and, one day later, Sultan Mehmet rode into his new city.

By May of 1453 Istanbul was a shadow of its former self; with a population of, at most, 50,000 "it was now in effect no more than a collection of villages" (İnalcık 1969–70: 231). Yet the enormity of Mehmet's accomplishment was abundantly clear to all. George Amiroutzes, the scholar and advisor to the last emperor of Trabzon, wrote the following to the sultan in 1466: "No one doubts that you are the Emperor of the Romans. Whoever holds by right the center of the Empire is the emperor, and the center of the Roman Empire is Istanbul" (İnalcık 1969–70: 233). As the new Roman emperor, then, what was Fatih Mehmet going to do with the old Romans, that is, the Byzantines?

When answering this question we must always bear in mind the unique circumstances of the capital city's conquest. In nearly a century of conquests in the Balkans the Ottomans had followed a very consistent policy; if a city or town surrendered, its inhabitants were left undisturbed and in possession of their properties. If they resisted, their city was destroyed and they themselves were either killed or carried off into slavery. That is why, as İnalcık notes, in newly conquered lands "the towns inhabited by Greeks are always those which had responded to the summons to surrender" (İnalcık 1969–70: 234).

Constantinople was different. We know that Mehmet's fervent wish was that the Byzantines would surrender; he was already envisioning his new imperial capital and wanted to avoid the destruction that would necessarily follow the forceful capture of the city. This was not to be, however, and therefore the conqueror had to endure the pillaging and the looting that by rights belonged to the victorious soldiers. Even so, within just a few hours of the city's fall, Mehmet showed the willingness to impose his own authority – even in contravention, some said, of the –şeriat (Islamic law) – that would come to characterize his long reign. Although the troops had the right to free rein in the city for three days, Mehmet stopped them after only one. This was to be just the first of his acts that distinguished Constantinople from all other cities that the Ottomans had taken by force. The fate of the Greeks in the city, too, would be intimately tied to Mehmet's vision.

Three issues were central: the fate of the Byzantine elite, the fate of the city, and the question of the Ecumenical Patriarchate. Let us take them one by one.

The Byzantine elite

The emperor, Constantinos Paleologos, lay dead but the question of the city's elite remained. Here Mehmet's policies were not particularly distinctive. In the weeks, months, and even years that unrolled after the conquest, the conqueror availed himself of the same options that his predecessors had used. Those who were deemed disloyal – most notoriously Lucas Notaras – were executed. Others – most often the sons of the nobility – were taken into the palace and converted, often to emerge later on at the very highest levels of the government. Two grand vezirs who served toward the end of the century – Rum Mehmet Pasha and Mesih Pasha – began their lives as Byzantine nobles (İnalcık 1969–70: 240). The latter was the nephew of Constantine XI Paleologos and, considering that Constantine died childless, he might well have gone on to become the next Byzantine emperor if the empire had survived. Their life histories, then, were not so very different from that of the grand vezir Mehmet Pasha Angelovic, who had been snatched on the road between Novo Brodo and Smederevo many decades prior. The descendant of a Byzantine aristocratic family resident in Serbia, he entered the palace as a child, and exploded onto the scene in 1458 when he led the Ottoman conquest of his homeland.[1] Finally, it is clear that other members of the elite were allowed to continue living in the city, as Christians, and some of these prospered under the sultan just as they had under the emperors of Byzantium. Demetrios Paleologos, for example, the last despot of the Morea, soon emerged in the capital city as a tax farmer of Ottoman state monopolies while other members of the Paleologan dynasty were farming the extremely lucrative customs tax farm around 1470 (İnalcık 1998: 381, 384). Remarkably, some Byzantine notables were even given houses to settle in (İnalcık 1998: 235). This lenient policy toward a political class that had, in the end, fought the Ottoman armies tooth and nail was of course not characteristic of Ottoman policy prior to the capture of Istanbul. It can only be explained through Mehmet's ambitions for his new capital. The treatment of the elite, in other words, was inextricably linked to the second issue, namely the fate of Ottoman Istanbul itself.

The city

There is no question that Fatih Mehmet was determined to build a great and glorious capital for himself out of the ruins of the Byzantine city. He knew the city's history and was well aware of the prestige that he had gained for himself and for his empire by capturing it. Nevertheless, by the time the looting and the enslavement were over, he was the ruler of a completely deserted city. As one chronicler put it, "There was not a person, nor an animal, nor even a bird to sing" (Zachariadou 1996: 46). Therefore he began a relentless drive to repopulate the city, a campaign that lasted many years. As we have seen earlier, the Ottomans were always great urbanizers. What made the case of Istanbul different was that the sultan was very willing – some might even say eager – to repopulate the city with Greeks, even though by rights they should have been excluded from the city due to their refusal to surrender. He pursued this goal through various means.

First, there was the lenient treatment of the Byzantine elite, as mentioned above. Second, he settled his own Greek slaves (the one-fifth share that he was entitled to as ruler) along the shores of the Golden Horn and paid them good wages for their work on the various projects of reconstruction going on in the city. In this way rebuilding would be advanced and the slaves would be able to ransom themselves with their earnings. Mehmet encouraged ransomed slaves to live in the city as free men and gave them various incentives to do so (İnalcık 1969–70: 235–6). Finally, the long-standing policy of *sürgün* – forced relocation – was applied with great vigor in order to build up the city's population. Very shortly after the conquest, the sultan sent out an order that Christians, Muslims, and Jews should be sent to the city from every territory in his domains. This, too, had the result of increasing the city's Greek population, as did subsequent measures along the same lines such as the order, sent in 1459, that Christians who had left Istanbul as slaves or refugees to live in other cities should return (İnalcık 1969–70: 236, 238). As we trace the history of Istanbul in these early years, we must also keep in mind the commercial center of Galata right next door. Prior to the siege some Greeks had taken refuge there. Unlike Istanbul, it had surrendered and thus its population was spared. Mehmet was intent on keeping this valuable commercial center intact and thus the Greek population in Galata benefitted in two ways: from the surrender and from Mehmet's regard for this crucial area (İnalcık 1993: 384).

The end result of Mehmet's determination to implement his vision of the city was remarkable; despite the city's refusal to surrender in 1453, in 1477 the Greek Orthodox still constituted over one-quarter of Istanbul's population. In Galata they were actually a majority. All the other non-Muslim communities combined – Armenians, Latins, and Roma – did not equal the number of Greek Orthodox in Istanbul alone (İnalcık 1969–70: 247).

In the fifteenth-century Ottoman Empire, when proximity to the ruler was the very metric of political power, there is no question that Mehmet's policies put the Greek Orthodox in a powerful position, a position all the more striking considering that they could be considered a defeated population. Out of that power came prosperity, as they developed a strong presence in the guilds, in trade, and, probably most visibly, as some of the most prominent tax farmers in the empire.

The high visibility of the Greeks is made clear by the resentment expressed toward them by some segments of Muslim society in Istanbul. There were complaints that Greeks (and Jews) were favored when it came to tax-farming bids. It did not go unnoticed, for example, that members of the Paleologan family obtained the extremely lucrative customs tax farm at a time when two high-ranking pashas were also members of that family (İnalcık 1998: 386). And then there was the long-simmering question of rents. As part of his efforts to revive the city, Mehmet granted houses rent-free to the newcomers, both those who came on their own and those who were forcibly resettled. Yet on several occasions over the following decades, once the repopulation efforts had met with success, he attempted to impose rent on these very same properties. The response was always swift and vociferous opposition. Most interesting for our purposes is the fact that anti-Greek rhetoric was a reliable part of this reaction. The Ottoman chronicler Aşıkpaşazade, in writing about a particular episode from 1471, foregrounded the role of the grand vezir, Rum Mehmet Pasha, who was of Greek origin. He described him thus: "There came to the Sultan a certain vizier who was the son of an infidel and had won high favor with the Sultan. The former infidel inhabitants of this city of Istanbul had been friends of this vizier's father." It was Rum Mehmet Pasha, he wrote, who wanted to reimpose the rents, and his reason for so doing was to drive the Turks out of the city (İnalcık 1969–70: 244). More generally, Mehmet's several attempts to collect rent from the city's population was blamed on the fact that he had been led astray by the Greeks.

The theme of anti-Greek and anti-Christian resentment on the part of at least some in the Muslim community will be with us from time to time throughout our story. The saga of the rents is a felicitous conflict, if one may say that, with which to introduce the topic. This is because it shows clearly that such negative rhetoric never exists in a vacuum and must not be interpreted first and foremost as some sort of unchanging impulse on the part of Muslim society. Instead it is always part of a larger social and political struggle and any explanation must take the particular historical context into account. In this case there was a long-standing critique of Fatih Mehmet as an absolutist ruler who failed to grant the *şeriat* the authority that it was due in a Muslim society. From his decision to deny his soldiers the three days of looting that they should have enjoyed after the fall of Istanbul, to his liberality toward the Greeks despite the fact that the city had been taken by force, Fatih seemed to many to be intent on ruling the empire without any constraints on his authority at all. What would be unchanging, however, throughout the long centuries of Ottoman rule was the fact that, officially, society was divided along religious lines and non-Muslims were inferior, both de facto and de jure. Therefore, social tension tended to be expressed in religious terms (Kolovos, Sariyannis, and Anastasopoulos 2008: 33).

We can illustrate the importance of context by considering the example of Mehmet Pasha Angelović, another member of an elite Byzantine family who entered the palace as a young boy and then emerged, decades later, to lead the final Ottoman conquest of Serbia and to serve as grand vezir from 1455 to 1468 (İnalcık 1989: 95). As the scion of an illustrious family, it is not surprising that he encountered his relatives as he swept across the Balkans.[2] What is interesting is that Ottoman chroniclers themselves drew attention to his family connections and noted how they helped in the conquest of territory. The historian Saadeddin, for example, noted that Angelović negotiated with his own brother, Michael Angelović, for the surrender of the fortress of Smederevo (Stavrides 2001: 104). Whereas in the awarding of tax farms connections between vezirs of Greek origin and successful Greek Orthodox bidders were viewed as a source of corruption – with all the attendant anti-Christian rhetoric then following – the family relationship between Angelović and his brother as it related to the fall of Smederevo was viewed in a far more positive light. This is not surprising. In Saadeddin we have a chronicler of the Ottoman dynasty who is recording the addition of yet more territory to the domains of the sultan. In this happy instance, there would be no reason to begrudge the family relationship between a convert to Islam and his Christian brother.

Muslim resentment of the grand vezir Rum Mehmet Pasha for his perceived favoritism toward the Greek community brings up an important point that is often neglected when it comes to the history of the Greeks in this early period, namely the nature of the relationship between them and the many prominent converts of Greek origin. Were the converts serving their former community in some way?[3]

Here we must bear in mind a distinction that has been pointed out by Heath Lowry; not all converts serving the sultan in this early period were *devşirme*, which is the term used to describe the forcible Ottoman levy of Christian peasant boys that came into being at the end of the fourteenth century. These boys would be converted to Islam and enter into a lengthy period of training, after which they would enter the elite janissary corps. Famously, some rose from the corps all the way to the highest offices in the bureaucracy, including the grand vezirate.

But other Christian converts who came to hold the office of grand vezir were not of peasant stock at all; instead they came from the very highest levels of the Byzantine aristocracy or its regional variants, as in the case of Mehmet Pasha Angelović, discussed above. These individuals were of course well known in the Greek community and indeed often had ties of kinship that crossed religious boundaries. It would not be at all surprising if the pull of family continued to shape both attitudes and actions, and we know numerous instances where it did. One quite notorious case involved, once again, Mehmet Pasha Angelović.

George Amiroutzes was a Byzantine scholar and aristocrat who served David Komnenos, the last emperor of Trabzon. It was Amiroutzes who negotiated the surrender of the city to his cousin, Mehmet Pasha Angelović in 1461(Lowry 2003: 61). Amiroutzes then went on to serve as an advisor in the palace and was granted some land by the sultan as well. During this period, he fell in love with the widow of the last duke of Athens, from the Acciaiuoli family. He wished to divorce his wife and to marry the widow but the patriarch, Iosaf, refused to go along with his request. His cousin, infuriated, stepped in. Mehmet Pasha had the patriarch's beard cut and then threw him out of office (Stavrides 2001: 89).

The chronicle of Theodore Spandounes – who was the grand-nephew of Mara Branković, the Serbian princess and widow of Murat II – provides further evidence of ongoing, and friendly, ties between Byzantine elites and their now Muslim family members. At one point he mentions the following meeting: "I was able to consult two of the nobility who were on most intimate terms with the Emperor of the Turks; they were among my closest friends and my relations, men of rare talent and great knowledge of these matters" (Lowry 2003: 123). The two men in question were Grand Vezir Mesih Pasha, Spandounes' great-uncle, and Grand Vezir Hersekzade Ahmet Pasha, to whom he was related by marriage.

Post-Byzantine Istanbul, then, was a remarkably Greek and even Byzantine city, when one considers the fact that Fatih Mehmet had just taken it from his Greek-speaking Byzantine adversaries. It was Greek in the sense that large numbers of Greeks were settled in the city through the policy of *sürgün* and it was Byzantine in that the elite families of the conquered empire – the Kantekouzenoi, the Paleologoi – not only remained in the city, but also continued to enjoy positions of power, some as Christians, others as Muslims.

The Ecumenical Patriarchate

The Byzantine Empire had always rested on two pillars: the emperor and the patriarch. Now the emperor was dead and there was a new emperor, a sultan. What would happen to the patriarch?

We know the following about the early, chaotic days after the fall of the city. Fatih Mehmet made inquiries and discovered that the prominent and learned anti-Unionist monk Gennadios had been enslaved, along with so many others. He was in Edirne and it was in Edirne that Mehmet issued the *berat* that made Gennadios patriarch, after having released him from slavery. Some months later, in January of 1454, a ceremony of investiture took place in Istanbul and the Holy Synod elected him patriarch. Gennadios took up residence at the Church of the Holy Apostles. It is generally agreed that Mehmet's motives combined the more immediate goal of repopulating the city – including giving encouragement to Christians, as has been discussed – with the long-term policy of favoring the Greek Orthodox Church over the Latin enemies.

Much has been hung on these events. Until very recently, scholars constructed from them four hundred years of communal autonomy for the Greek Orthodox community, enshrined in law. As leader, the patriarch enjoyed religious, legal, and jurisdictional rights over the community. This was the famous *millet* (autonomous self-governing religious community) model of the empire. No longer widely adopted by Greek and Ottoman scholars, it is still the standard approach in treatments of the Ottoman Empire written for a general audience.

Now it is clear that much less was granted to Gennadios in those immediate pre-conquest days than had been previously assumed (Konortas 1998: 295). Starting from a more modest position, we know that the sultan must have given Gennadios a *berat*, a grant of privilege, to hold an office, although the actual *berat* has not survived. We know this because long before the conquest of Istanbul, the Ottomans were already in the habit of issuing *berats* to metropolitans that they had appointed in the Balkans. Therefore, it is inconceivable that they would not have done the same with Gennadios (İnalcık 1991: 203).

The earliest patriarchal *berat* that has come to light dates from 1483 and was given to Symeon by Bayezit II. A consideration of this document, combined with other *berats* granted to Orthodox clergy in the fifteenth and sixteenth centuries, allows us to draw the following conclusions. First, the patriarch's jurisdiction was defined as jurisdiction over a specific number of metropolitan sees, not as authority over a religious community, however defined. In the case of the *berat* of 1483 there were fifty-seven such sees, corresponding, roughly, to the following areas: Thrace, the western shores of the Black Sea, Macedonia, central and southern Greece, the eastern Black Sea, northwestern Asia Minor, Ankara and Amaseia, the Aegean coastline of Asia Minor, and the islands of the eastern Aegean (Zachariadou 1996: 114–15). Despite this rather extensive sweep, the most common Ottoman title for the patriarch in this early period, and continuing through the seventeenth century, was "the patriarch of Istanbul and its surroundings," which indicates that the sultans did not see the patriarch as the head of the Orthodox community contained within the borders of the empire (Konortas 1998: 301) Moreover, this jurisdiction was shifting. Amaseia, for example, appears in the *berat* of 1483 but has disappeared from the list given in the 1525 *berat* (Zachariadou 1996: 116) (Map 2). As we shall see, by the second half of the eighteenth century the patriarch had become head of the entire Orthodox *millet* in the empire, but this was a process that took three hundred years to accomplish; the first step was taken in Istanbul in 1453, but it was a small one.

The privileges granted to the patriarch were four. He had the right of appointing and dismissing all hierarchs; he had ultimate control

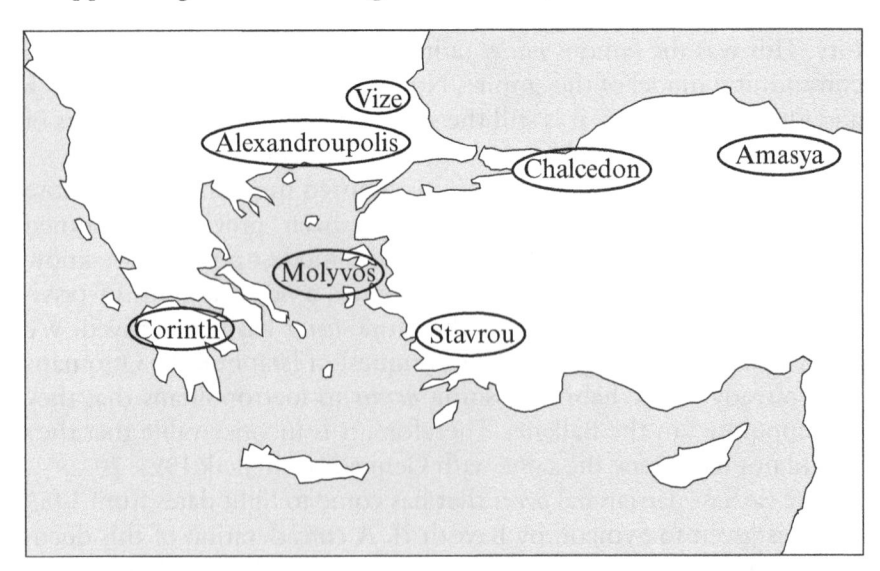

Map 2 *Between 1483 and 1525 seven metropolitan sees disappeared, according to Ottoman documents issued to church authorities (Zachariadou 1996: 117). Map created by Theocharis Tsampouras.*

over all church and monastic property; he had authority when it came to issues of family law such as marriage, divorce, and inheritance and, finally, he had the right to collect taxes from his flock (Zachariadou 1996: 116).

Yet every single one of these privileges must be qualified. In the first place, all of them – like all privileges granted by the sultan to anyone – were personal, that is, they were granted to the patriarch as an individual, rather than to the church as an institution (Kermeli 2007: 176). Moving on to the first privilege, that of appointment, we know that from time to time the sultan forced the patriarch to accept a candidate whom he, the sultan, favored for whatever reason; occasionally he even appointed someone without consulting the patriarch. He could do this because it was the sultanic *berat* that made someone a bishop, a metropolitan, or a patriarch. The Holy Synod would then elect the candidate and thus confirm the choice. The patriarch had no power to issue a *berat*; rather each and every hierarch lower down the scale had to receive his *berat* from the sultan.[4]

Control over monastic and church property was, of course, a huge privilege. It was the source of the very considerable wealth of the patriarchate in Istanbul. A portion of the revenues that derived from the vineyards, the orchards, the sacred springs, the fairs, and the landed property that was under the control of the churches and the monasteries made its way to Istanbul. Yet here, too, the patriarch was not in a position to decide on the ultimate status of the land. At the end of the fifteenth century some monasteries, such as Vlatathon in Thessaloniki, enjoyed full property rights over their landed property while, in the same period, several of the establishments on Mount Athos had the right only of *tesarruf* – they had full use of the land but could not sell it or give it away (Zachariadou 1996: 104). And, as we shall see later on, a crisis at the end of the sixteenth century threatened the very existence of Mount Athos, although ultimately the crisis was averted.

The limits of patriarchal authority are most striking when it comes to the final two privileges, both of which concern jurisdiction over Orthodox Christians more generally. Although the patriarch (and the clergy more generally) had authority in matters of family law, a now fairly abundant literature makes it crystal clear that they were not granted, and did not have, exclusive authority. Orthodox Christians did not hesitate to turn to Ottoman authority when it suited them, and this included even matters intimately connected to religion. Nor did the Ottomans turn them away. The sultans insisted on "the individual judicial freedom of its subjects to submit to the arbitration body of their choice" (Kermeli 2007: 176). One of the more striking examples concerns Maria-Eleni, the granddaughter of the last despot of the Morea, Thomas Paleologos, and widow of the last king of Bosnia. She applied to the Islamic court in order to ensure that she could inherit from her equally illustrious aunts, Mara and Katerina Branković (Zachariadou 1996: 95). This was by no means a matter only of elite behavior. When it comes to marriage and divorce, the evidence for Christian recourse to the Islamic courts is too overwhelming to enumerate. Suffice it to say that, after 1453, we see a steady growth in the flexibility of the Orthodox Church with regard to divorce. In the Byzantine period there had been grounds for divorce – such as a husband's impotence for a period of more than three years – but now the husband's absence for an extended period, the non-virginity of the bride, insanity, and epilepsy could also be a basis for divorce. In 1717, in a dramatic departure from tradition, the church accepted divorce by mutual consent. The reason for this, and all the other concessions, is clear: Orthodox women and, to a lesser extent, men were going to Islamic courts and obtaining divorces (Laiou 2007: 246).

It is when we come to the final privilege – the right to collect taxes from the Orthodox Christian population as a whole (as opposed to those who happened to live on property belonging to a church or a monastery) – that we see the sultan at his most ambivalent. Although the exact nature of the taxes that were collected from the Christians at this early date is somewhat unclear, the most common justification for the taxation was the payment of the *peşkeş* and the *haraç*. Both of these were sums paid to the sultan by the Orthodox clergy and both came into being at some point in the last quarter of the fifteenth century, in circumstances that I shall discuss shortly. What is important to emphasize here is the rather extraordinary fact that the contribution of ordinary Christians to these taxes was voluntary. In the two patriarchal *berats* (1483 and 1525) Christians are encouraged to contribute, if they would like and in accordance with their established customs; however, no one is to be forced to pay through violence or pressure. In fact, very shortly both of these taxes became obligatory, as one would expect (Zachariadou 1996: 100). Nevertheless, the question remains: why would the sultans issuing these *berats* make such a statement?

As Halil İnalcık forcefully shows in his article on the status of the Greek Orthodox patriarch under the Ottomans, no Muslim sovereign was ever willing to give up his rights over his non-Muslim subjects (İnalcık 1991: 204). The right to tax, of course, was intimately linked with sovereignty. On the other hand the income from the *haraç* and the *peşkeş* was certainly useful and was much less likely to be forthcoming if Christian subjects did not have to pay it. The language in the *berats*, I believe, shows this hesitancy between fiscal realities and the prerogatives of sovereignty. There is no such hesitancy when it comes to granting the patriarch the authority to collect taxes on church and monastic property (at some point he even gained the right to cut the beards of clergy who did not pay up); tax farming, after all, was one of the most routine of privileges regularly granted by the sultan to members of the elite (Zachariadou 1996: 97). The difference in language is yet a further indication that neither Bayezit II nor Süleyman (nor anyone else) ever intended to grant jurisdiction over the Orthodox Christians, as Christians, to the patriarch.

In return for these privileges the patriarch had obligations, of course, toward the sultan. He was to pay the *haraç*, on a yearly basis, and the *peşkeş* when a new sultan came to the throne. He was to ensure that the clerics below him collected the revenues that were due on the vast property belonging to the churches and the monasteries and he was, of course, to turn over a portion of these revenues to the sultan. The overwhelming emphasis in the *berats* is on these economic transactions. This is not a surprise if we realize that the goal was never to grant the patriarch political privileges over the Orthodox Christians as a kind of self-rule. It was rather to allow the church hierarchy to survive and to reproduce itself so that the metropolitans, the bishops, and other members of the clergy could continue to collect the revenues from the very substantial property that the church possessed. There was an extensive and ready-made bureaucracy, in other words, which the sultan found it expedient to use (Papademetriou 2001: 17).

The preponderance of fiscal concerns in the *berats* has raised the question as to whether, in fact, the sultan viewed the patriarchate as no more than a tax farm and the patriarch as a, possibly rather peculiar, tax farmer. In addition to the *berats*, there are other good reasons to suggest that he did. The patriarch received his privileges through a *berat*, as did all tax farmers, and the office that dealt with the patriarchate was part of the Financial Service.[5] In the 1483 *berat* the patriarch was identified explicitly as a tax farmer (*mültezim*) (Papademetriou 2001: 17).

Nevertheless, I do not think it is correct to say that the sultan's view of the patriarch can be entirely captured through the institution of tax farming, although the relationship certainly had those aspects. Rather it was a hybrid institution, and not only because of small, but significant details such as the fact that only Christians could farm this tax (Konortas 1998: 342, 348) The sultan's willingness – however ambivalent – to allow the patriarch to tax all Christians as Christians (or, at least, those within his territorial jurisdiction) indicates a limited authority of the patriarch over the empire's Christian Orthodox population that made him something more than a tax farmer. It is highly significant that the sultan refers to adherence to "custom" (*ayın*) or "law" (*kanun*) only when justifying the taxation of ordinary Christians, indicating that he was willing to incorporate this inheritance from the Byzantine past (Konortas 1998: 323; Zachariadou 1996: 100).

Whether the patriarch was a tax farmer or something more, the research of recent years has made it absolutely clear that the sultan granted him his privileges as an individual. There was no institutional recognition of either the Orthodox Church or the patriarchate until the nineteenth century, and thus no autonomous Greek Orthodox community under his authority. The relationship between each sultan and each patriarch was a personal one that had to be re-established every time there was a new patriarch or a new sultan (Zachariadou 1996: 91; Konortas 1998: 317). Insufficient appreciation of this fact has helped perpetuate the impression of Ottoman policy toward the church as arbitrary and even lawless. For example, when the Ottomans took the monastery of Pammakaristos away from the patriarch in 1587 and converted it into the Fethiye mosque, the Ottoman view was that the old *berats*, which had given it to the patriarch as his private residence, no longer applied (Zachariadou 1996: 92). This is not to exclude the possibility of aggressive intent on the part of the Ottomans. Nor is it to deny that the Orthodox clergy saw things differently. An Orthodox narrative account of the events around Pammakaristos describes how the clergy produced the *berats* of Fatih Mehmet and Bayezit II, with the clear conviction that these documents should have granted the church to them in perpetuity (Zachariadou 1996: 92). If we can understand the church's position, we must also be informed on what an Ottoman *berat* meant, since it was through a *berat* that each and every member of the Orthodox clergy exercised his authority (Konortas 1998: 318).

Thus far we have been speaking only of certain key Ottoman decisions vis-à-vis the Orthodox Church in the decades after the conquest. But, as we have seen earlier, early Ottoman Istanbul was a city where elite Greeks enjoyed (or suffered from) a very high profile. We would expect these individuals to take a keen interest in the fate of the church and to have some influence in shaping its new place within the Ottoman system, and in fact they did.

The ex-Byzantine elite were not the only powerful Greeks in the society that was emerging. Just as the monasteries came to their own arrangements with the Ottomans long before the fall of Istanbul, so too did other Greeks find opportunities for themselves, in Bursa, in Edirne, and in other important Ottoman centers before 1453. For example, it was two Greeks who ransomed Gennadios in Edirne and then arranged for him to meet Fatih Mehmet. They were well placed to do so. Dimitrios Apokavkos and Thomas Katavolinos were both secretaries to the sultan who undertook important missions on his behalf, both before and after 1453. The partial correspondence of an extremely wealthy Greek, also from Edirne, has come down to us and many of the names that appear in it are connected to the history of the patriarchate once it was established in Istanbul. This wealthy individual, Nikolaos Isidorou, was already a powerful tax farmer before 1453, farming the extremely lucrative salt tax from Edirne, with partners in Thrace, in Macedonia, and along the Black Sea coast. Nor was he the only one. Concentrated in Edirne, Plovdiv, Gallipoli, and Bursa, these "early notables" all got rich farming Ottoman monopolies, and they used that money to buy their way into church affairs (Zachariadou 1996: 63–4). Early on, there was intense competition over the buying of church offices, including the office of patriarch itself. The chronicles preserve the vivid image of Mara, the Serbian princess and stepmother of Fatih Mehmet, appearing before her stepson with 2,000 florins on a silver disk, asking that Dyonisios Filipoupoleos be appointed patriarch (Zachariadou 1996: 69–70).

Through their competition, these elites managed to drive up the asking price of all clerical offices, but that wasn't all. The arrival of the Trabzonites in Istanbul after the fall of the Empire of Trabzon (1461) illustrates the active role played by the Christians in shaping the terms under which the Orthodox Church would take its place in the Ottoman Empire. Having been the proud servitors of the last independent Greek Empire, it is not a surprise that the Trabzonites had their own views about their rightful place in Istanbul's Christian community, and this included having their own candidate as patriarch. To that end they offered the sultan 1,000 florins in order to appoint Symeon, who was from Trabzon. It was in reaction to this that Mara offered the 2,000 florins to Fatih, as mentioned before, and from then this payment became institutionalized as the *haraç*. The sources are all in agreement that no such payment was required until that point; the impetus for the *haraç*, in other words, came not from the sultan but from the factional fighting of the Christian community in Istanbul (Zachariadou 1996: 83–4).

We have seen that the monks of Mount Athos and Meteora helped to institutionalize and legalize their relationship with the sultan both through their ongoing negotiations and by their willingness to bring their disputes to him. The same can be said for the patriarchate and, in fact, the entire clerical hierarchy. The advent of the *haraç* is perhaps the most dramatic example, but just as importantly the patriarch, and metropolitans and bishops, turned routinely and repeatedly to Ottoman authority whenever they faced resistance to their authority, whether that resistance was coming from other Ottoman officials, members of the clergy, or the Christian laity (Konortas 1998: 329–30). Both sides shared an interest in establishing the parameters of the relationship.

In the treaty that Fatih Mehmet signed with Venice in 1454 the sultan tried to ensure patriarchal revenues from Latin-held territory (Zachariadou 1996: 59). He even asked that the patriarch be given jurisdiction over the Greek Orthodox community in Venice, a request that he was clearly making on the patriarch's behalf (Zachariadou 1996: 47). At the end of another Ottoman–Venetian war, in 1479, Fatih once again brought up the issue of church revenues, this time singling out the island of Crete (Zachariadou 1996: 59).

If in the previous section I have emphasized the limited jurisdiction of the patriarch, particularly relative to the assumptions of the *millet* model, here we must acknowledge the importance of 1453 as the first step in the long-term expansion of the Orthodox patriarchate. The Ottoman conquest of Istanbul, after all, was a defeat not just of Byzantine power, but of Italian as well. The extremely favorable position that, especially, Genoa and Venice had enjoyed in the Byzantine Empire was to be no more as the sultan negotiated new treaties that got rid of their commercial privileges. As Traian Stoianovich pointed out years ago, the beneficiaries of this were local merchants, including the Greeks, who had long suffered from the effects of Italian competition (Stoianovich 1960: 240). The church, too, was a major beneficiary because of course Italian power also meant the Catholic Church. We see this almost immediately in Fatih's negotiations with Venice in 1454, and the pattern will repeat itself for more than two centuries to come. As the Ottomans expand into the Mediterranean world, Catholic bishops will fall to the wayside and Orthodox metropolitans will hurry to take their place.

This Orthodox victory requires that we modify somewhat our description in the previous chapter of southern Greece – this time including the Aegean islands – as a peripheral area. It was peripheral to the Ottomans, but not to the Greek Orthodox Church. The island of Andros nicely illustrates this dichotomy. When the Ottoman admiral

Hayreddin Pasha conquered the smaller Aegean islands in the middle of the sixteenth century the Ottomans did little to consolidate their rule over these rocky outposts. The islands lacked strategic importance and had no agricultural value at all. They did not even bother to survey the smaller islands until late in the seventeenth century.

The response of the Orthodox, both local and in Istanbul, was very different. No sooner did the Ottomans conquer the islands than the Orthodox patriarch began to send bishops to them (Kolovos 2007: 55). Four monasteries were founded on the island of Andros in the sixteenth and seventeenth centuries, the very first Orthodox monasteries that had been built on the island since the Fourth Crusade of 1204 brought Latin rule to so much of the Greek world. One of them became the largest landowner on the island. When Joseph Nassi died in 1579 the sultan – as part of his consolidation of the islands' administration in the wake of the defeat at Lepanto – handed over the island of Naxos to the Kapudan pasha, Kılıç Ali. In that very same year the patriarch asked Sultan Murat III to issue an order on behalf of the monks of the (Orthodox) monastery of Hagia on Andros. Apparently Franks on Andros and on Naxos had been impeding the collection of revenues due to the monastery; they were told in no uncertain terms to cease and desist (Kolovos 2007: 57–8).

This pattern of Ottoman expansion, followed by Orthodox profit at the expense of the Catholics, would continue for a long time. Even before their final victory in Crete in 1669, the Ottomans had installed an archbishop on the island with seven bishops under him. In so doing they reversed almost five hundred years of Venetian policy, which had not even allowed for the presence of an Orthodox bishop on the island (Greene 2000: 175, 178).

The Ottoman view of the patriarch's jurisdiction is laid out clearly in the list of metropolitan sees included in the *berats*.[6] The patriarchate kept its own lists, of course, known as the Notitiae. Fortunately, a Notitiae from 1500 has come down to us, a date that comes almost in the middle of the earliest two patriarchal *berats* (1483 and 1525). This allows for a comparison of the sees already within Ottoman borders to those to which the patriarch still aspired. In the list of 1500 there were eight that fell outside the borders of the empire, and six of these were in territory – in southern Greece and the Aegean – long held by the Latins. Within the next century the Ottomans would conquer all of them (Zachariadou 1996: 118).

The other two – Moldavia and Hungary-Vlachia (Ουγγροβλαχία) – turn our gaze away from the Mediterranean and toward the Slavic world to the north. When we do this, 1453 is much less of a clear-cut victory for the patriarch. It is also less distinct as a turning point.

It is often remarked that the Ottoman sultans (and indeed many Muslim rulers before them) favored the Orthodox Christians over the Catholics. This is true but inadequate, as it fails to distinguish between different Orthodox Christians and different Catholics. If the main Catholic enemy in the Mediterranean world were the Italians, and the Greek patriarch the obvious beneficiary of their defeat, in the Balkans it was the Hungarians who presented the greatest threat to the sultans' expansion. And the Orthodox Christians on the ground were, for the most part, not Greeks but rather Bulgarians and Serbs. Successive Ottoman sultans of course had good reason to favor the Orthodox over the Catholics but the situation was not so obvious when it came to choosing between different Orthodox populations. The result of this was that the late Byzantine dynamic in the Balkans – where Serbs, Bulgarians, and Greeks battled each other for dominance – continued into the Ottoman period; this time the sultan was the arbiter.

In 1393 the Ottomans captured Tarnovo and extinguished the already very feeble Second Bulgarian Empire.[7] Nearly two hundred years prior, the Ecumenical patriarch had vigorously protested the Bulgarian establishment of their own patriarchate at Tarnovo. What would happen now that the Ottomans had captured the city and banished the Bulgarian patriarch Euthymius to a monastery further south? It is not clear what happened in the decades immediately following the fall of the city, but in 1439 we know for certain that this bishopric had come back under Byzantine control, now as a metropolis, because one Archbishop Ignatius of Tarnovo was present at the Council of Florence to discuss the unification of the churches. At least in the case of Tarnovo, then, the Ottoman advance into the Balkans meant a victory for the patriarch in Istanbul over the Bulgarian church.

Other new arrangements were less favorable to the Byzantines. Bayezit gave much of the territory that had belonged to the patriarchate of Tarnovo to the autocephalic archbishop of Ohrid, based in the Macedonian city of the same name. This might seem to be not such an affront to the Ecumenical patriarch; the Byzantines themselves had agreed to the autocephalic status of Ohrid early in the eleventh century, and over time Greeks managed to dominate its higher ecclesiastical offices. Nevertheless, it had been a grudging compromise and the Byzantines would certainly have preferred it if the Ottomans had extinguished, rather than maintained, Ohrid's privileges.

The Serbs held on until the middle of the fifteenth century when, as mentioned earlier, Michael Angelović negotiated the surrender of the fortress of Smederevo with his own brother, Mehmet Pasha Angelović, in 1457. Like the Greeks, the Serbs too had a choice between a Catholic and a Muslim power and Michael Angelović belonged to that section of the Serbian nobility that was pro-Ottoman. As a result of his choice he subsequently found favor in the Ottoman court (Stavrides 2001: 105). Although the southern Serbian lands, conquered earlier, had also been handed over to the archbishop of Ohrid, Fatih Mehmet allowed the territories surrendered by Michael Angelović to remain under their own ecclesiastical leaders.

The patriarch in Istanbul, then, made some gains with the Ottoman conquests but had to tolerate both the autocephaly of Ohrid and limited Serbian ecclesiastical autonomy. The Bulgarian Church was extinguished, yes, but it had been on its last legs anyway by the time the Ottomans took Tarnovo.

The ability of the Serbs to hang on to at least some remnant of their church was no doubt related to their significant presence in the Ottoman state, a presence that the Bulgarians never enjoyed.[8] A dramatic demonstration of Serbian power came in the middle of the sixteenth century. This was when the Bosnian-born Grand Vezir Mehmet Pasha Sokollović, backed by the Serbian nobility and the extremely numerous Serbian forces serving in the sultan's armies, managed to restore the patriarchate of Peć, symbol of the glory of Tsar Dušan's Serbian kingdom. Not only that, but Ohrid was forced to relinquish some bishoprics, and the vast sweep of newly conquered lands in Hungary was granted to the Serbs as well (Fodor 2001).

From this review of the reshuffling of ecclesiastical boundaries, stretching from the late fourteenth until the middle of the sixteenth century, the following points with regard to the Greeks emerge. First, it is a further demonstration of the argument made earlier that the sultans were deeply involved in the internal affairs of the Orthodox Church (or churches). Second, the arrival of the Ottomans did not extinguish other Orthodox patriarchates. By the middle of the sixteenth century the Serbs had managed to carve out an independent ecclesiastical structure for themselves; it was certainly much more limited than that which the Greeks controlled, but it was impressive never the less. The consequences of this are still with us today. Third, even when it comes to the Ecumenical Patriarchate, lodged of course in Istanbul, the importance of 1453 must be qualified. Rather than a momentous encounter between sultan and patriarch in the spring of 1453 as the two confronted each other for the first time, contacts between the Ottoman sultans and ecclesiastical authority in Istanbul pre-dated the fall of the city. Nor did the assumption of Ottoman control in the former Byzantine capital mean that a blueprint for the Orthodox Church from that date forward was hammered out. Instead the *berat* that Fatih Mehmet presumably gave Gennadios was one of a series of arrangements that had been made, and would continue to be made, with representatives of the clergy across the Balkans.

This view of the importance of 1453 is at variance with the influential argument (which also makes intuitive sense) that the capture of the city was a watershed moment in the relationship between the church and Ottoman authority. Briefly, prior to this the Ottomans viewed the church, which after all was an arm of the Byzantine state, as an enemy and every bishop as an agent in the service of that state (Vryonis 1971: 349). Subsequent to that date, Fatih Mehmet "reconstituted" the patriarchate, with far-reaching and positive effects on the Christians of the empire, who had previously been under siege. Critically, it helps to explain why conversion in the Balkans remained a limited phenomenon, as opposed to what happened in Anatolia (Vryonis 1971: 498–501).

We have already seen that it is problematic to say that Fatih Mehmet reconstituted the patriarchate in 1453. What remains, then, is an assessment of Ottoman policy in the Balkans in the seventy-five years preceding the fall of the city. Was there an assault on the Christian community, with bishops and archbishops and metropolitans in the cities treated as the enemy?

In certain cities there is no question that the Ottoman conquest brought about an end to the Christian community there. Gallipoli, for example, was conquered in 1354, and it never again appears in the lists of the synod (Vryonis 1980: 289). In many other cases the evidence is contradictory. For instance, when the town of Serres surrendered in 1383 the terms of the treaty guaranteed to the Greeks their churches and their quarters; no Muslims were to be allowed to live in the center of the walled city. These arrangements proved to be enduring. In the middle of the sixteenth century Christians were still living in the city center and no churches had been converted (although from time to time some churches were attacked or even destroyed) (Petmezas 1996a: 438–40). On the other hand, the metropolitan of Serres was captured and held for four years before being ransomed; he then appeared before the synod in Istanbul but was not able to go back to Serres (Vryonis 1980: 289). Prior to 1453, however, the ecclesiastical hierarchy had been re-installed. A metropolitan of the city, Makarios, appears in Ottoman documents from 1440 (Zachariadou 1996: 123).

Edirne, which became the new capital of the empire in 1361, had even greater difficulties. The metropolitan was seized and, despite the strenuous efforts of the patriarch, it is not clear that another metropolitan was able to enter the city for nearly another century, that is, until 1453. Confiscation of church properties and revenue took place on a massive scale (Vryonis 1980: 294). On the other hand, at least some of the Christian population was allowed to stay. There is no question that Christian life in Edirne suffered a great decline after 1361, but Ottoman policy in this period seems not to have included the systematic displacement of Christian populations. In addition, as our previous discussion of the patriarchate showed, by 1453 some very powerful Greeks were established in Edirne; Dimitrios Apokaukos and Thomas Katavolinos, secretaries to Fatih Mehmet, were the wealthy residents of Edirne who ransomed Gennadios. In the same period another wealthy Greek of Edirne, Nikolaos Isidorou, held the extremely lucrative salt tax farm, as mentioned earlier in this chapter.

A recent study of conversion in this early period provides a tantalizing glimpse into life around Edirne in the late 1430s. Many Christians fighting for the Ottomans took Christian captives into their households, with the proclaimed goal of saving them. What this meant exactly is unclear; our source speaks of this practice as persecution and it is possible that these Christian soldiers were enslaving their Christian captives. On the other hand, given the well-known mechanisms of social mobility in Ottoman society at this time, it is not unreasonable to see this process as the first step in bringing the captives into networks of Ottoman patronage. This practice on the part of local Christians was opposed by ecclesiastical circles (Krstić 2011: 104). This story suggests that despite (or because of?) the absence of a metropolitan in cities such as Edirne, Christian urban society underwent important transformations in the century before 1453, and the subject deserves more study beyond the binary of survival or destruction. This is particularly the case because wide-scale conversion to Islam in the Balkans, when it began in the sixteenth century, began in the cities.

To return more directly to the question of Ottoman policy, there are other cities where the Ottomans themselves undertook the appointment of a metropolitan. In 1399 Bayezit I provided a metropolitan for the Christian community of Antalya, just eight years after the city was taken. Several decades later Murat II did the same for the city of Berat in Albania (İnalcık 1991: 197). Despite the brutal treatment of the city's population after it fell in 1430, there was a metropolitan in place in Thessaloniki just two years later (Zachariadou 1996: 124).

We have already discussed the case of the city of Tarnovo, seat of the Bulgarian patriarchate, which Bayezit I took in 1393. We know that a metropolitan was in place in 1439, so here too is another example of a Balkan city where the Ottomans reconstituted the clerical hierarchy, at least to a certain extent, prior to 1453. Tarnovo is a particularly valuable example because it demonstrates, beyond a shadow of a doubt, that the patriarch in Istanbul and the sultan, in this case Murat II, were in contact. This is because Archbishop Ignatius participated in the Council of Florence, held, ironically enough, with the goal of obtaining Catholic support against the Ottomans. Obviously he could not have been there except as a representative of the patriarch. Along the same lines, Ignatius of course only held his position in Tarnovo with the sultan's permission.[9]

To conclude: it is difficult to identify a consistent Ottoman policy toward the church before 1453. In some cases the sultan and the people around him led an all-out assault on metropolitans and the property that sustained urban Christian life, but we also see the Ottomans installing Christian clerics on more than one occasion. After 1453, as the Ottomans pushed deep into Serbian territory, they continued to make and remake the jurisdiction of the various Orthodox authorities. What is consistent over time – including both before and after the fall of Istanbul – is the willingness of the Ottomans to intervene quite dramatically in church affairs. On rare occasions we have a clear idea of what drove their choices. Here I have in mind, of course, the famous restoration of the patriarchate of Peć, an initiative taken by the Bosnian-born Grand Vezir Mehmet Pasha Sokollović in order to benefit his (Christian) family in the Balkans.[10] The reasons behind Bayezit's generous treatment of the archbishop of Ohrid at the very end of the fourteenth century are much less well known, but in that instance too personal relationships may well have been decisive. It is a broader question that still awaits its researcher (Kiel 1985: 289).

Greeks

Thus far we have spoken at length about Greeks, Serbs, and Bulgarians and their joustings with each other within the framework of ecclesiastical politics. In the previous chapter, I talked about the Greek lands and what made them distinctive vis-à-vis the areas where Slavic populations were in the majority. Here we must pause and acknowledge that the use of these terms is problematic, both because their modern use does not reflect how they were understood in earlier centuries and because the Ottomans did not use them in the organization of their subject Christian population. The Ottomans, as is well known, classified people, for purposes of taxation and general regulation of status, strictly along religious lines. The sultan's subjects were Muslims, Christians, and Jews, not Serbs or Arabs or Greeks or Albanians. This is not to say that they were not aware of differences; their deep involvement in the re-arranging of ecclesiastical boundaries, discussed above, shows a keen sense of Christian difference and a willingness to work within that framework, at least to a certain extent. But the official position was clear.

What about the Christians themselves? How did they think of themselves within the new framework? Put differently, how did older identities navigate the transition to Ottoman rule? We will concentrate of course on the Greeks but other groups, particularly the Serbs, will necessarily come into the picture, since identity is always formed in relation to others. We will, also, move back out of Istanbul and into the provinces again.

To raise the question of Greek identity is to walk into a hornet's nest. The question staggers under the burden of several legacies. First there is the violent history of Balkan nationalism as, during the course of the nineteenth and twentieth centuries, populations that had always lived under one umbrella struggled to sort themselves out (or, more likely, to be sorted out) into distinct national populations. Then there is the equally hotly contested debate over the relationship between the Byzantine Empire and the Greek people, however defined: was Byzantium in some fundamental way a Greek empire? In addition, we must deal with the awkward fact that the people we have in mind when we refer to the Greeks do not even refer to themselves this way today. The preferred term is Hellene (Έλληνας), which is itself an assertion of a link to Greek antiquity. During the Byzantine period, by contrast, a Hellenic identity would have been strenuously rejected; then the operative word was "Romios" (Ρωμιός), by which they meant Roman, even more confusing for the western reader. And, of course, the Byzantines were deeply, profoundly Christian, a commitment that, seemingly, would downplay ethnic differences among the believers.

All of these conundrums will not be solved here. Instead only the most immediate question will be addressed, and even that is a formidable task. How did late Byzantines identify themselves and think about their state, and what changed with the coming of the Ottomans?

"A Byzantine could be simultaneously a Roman, a Christian and a Greek" (Kaldellis 2007: 362). Historians agree that all three identities were always in play; it is less easy to agree on the relative balance at any one time, let alone for a thousand years. All historians, however, are in agreement that the Fourth Crusade represents a major break in Byzantine history and most subscribe to the opinion that, after 1204, Greek Orthodoxy grew in importance, both institutionally and in terms of individual identification. So let us start with Byzantines as Christians.

The Fourth Crusade took the Byzantine capital and thus dislodged the emperor from his throne. New states, the successor states, would gradually be formed, but their existence, ironically, served to underline the reality that the Byzantine ethos of one emperor, one state, no longer applied. What remained was one Orthodox community, with the patriarch at its head. The church's growing importance was material as well. The twelfth and thirteenth centuries saw an explosion in the area of monastic holdings as both the poor and the rich donated their lands. They had a number of reasons for doing so but one was to contribute, in a concrete way, to the concept of the Christian *oikoumene* now that the state was in decline (Haldon 1986: 168–9).

The Fourth Crusade also deepened an identification with Greek Orthodoxy on the part of ordinary Byzantines, as they became aware of the religious differences between themselves and the hated Latins. It was no longer sufficient to simply be Christian, as the Latins were Christians as well.

The growing importance of Greek Orthodoxy takes on a special significance when one considers the question of the transition to Ottoman rule. If the church was indeed becoming more prominent in the centuries after 1204 then this period can be seen as a dress rehearsal for what followed in 1453. This is an argument that has been made; the emergence of the patriarch as the new leader of the Christian community in the Ottoman Empire was but the final extension of the power of the church that had been growing since 1204. In light of what I have said above, this analysis does not hold because it turns out that the Ottomans did not hand over leadership of the Orthodox community to the patriarch. Nevertheless, the question remains as to whether or not the Christian *oikoumene* was the most powerful "imagined community" in the late Byzantine period. If so, then perhaps the advent of Ottoman rule would not alter the terms of identification so dramatically; of course the emperor was gone but the Orthodox community endured and, moreover, by the middle of the sixteenth century it was united under one political roof.

Anthony Kaldellis (2007) has taken aim at the supposed Christian *oikoumene* of the late Byzantine period, and this brings us to the second component of Byzantine identity, namely Roman-ness. In Kaldellis' view, historians have not taken seriously enough the Byzantine commitment to their Roman identity. From beginning to end the Byzantines were committed to their state and to their emperor, and this has been neglected, he argues, due to the conviction that Greek Orthodoxy was the real glue that held the empire together, particularly in the later centuries. In Kaldellis' view, the revolts against the Latins in the wake of 1204 were just as much pro-imperial as they were pro-Greek Orthodox, and people continued to refer to themselves as Romans.

The Byzantine attitude toward barbarians – the pre-eminent Other prior to the Latin conquest – is also revealing of Roman identity and how it evolved over time. In the sixth-century Byzantine Empire, Roman-ness was unproblematically political. The empire's greatest accomplishment was the state itself and all subjects of the emperor were Roman. They were helped along in this conviction by the fact that by then the less Romanized parts of the empire had been lost (Kaldellis 2007: 48). Over time, however, this political identity became harder to sustain as so many barbarians came to be living within the borders of the empire. Large groups, such as the Bulgarians, presented real problems of categorization. They were Roman subjects, they had converted to Christianity, more or less, and yet it was hard to feel that they were truly Romans. We see this Byzantine ambivalence in the fact that the Bulgarians were called *mixovarvaroi* (μιξοβάρβαροι), or semi-barbarian (Page 2008: 48). This appellation, plus the well-known Constantinopolitan horror of life in the provinces, does suggest that the ideal of a larger Christian community only went so far. Although the Byzantines never articulated an idea of common ethnicity as happened in the west, over time being Roman did come to have more of a cultural definition, since not all those living within the empire could be accepted as fully Roman. Romania, Kaldellis writes, "was the nation-state of the Romans that happened at times to include a number of partially assimilated minorities within its borders, as have all modern nation-states" (Kaldellis 2007: 97).

The provocative use of very modern terms is deliberate on Kaldellis' part. In a break with most views on the late Byzantine Empire, he disagrees vehemently with those who describe it as a multi-ethnic empire whose subjects were loosely united by religion and loyalty to the empire. Rather, it was a tightly knit nation, like a modern nation, and minorities (such as the Bulgarians) were simply that: minorities. The majority, the Romans, were united not so much by ethnicity as by a common devotion to their state (Kaldellis 2007: 75). Here Kaldellis, by his own admission, is taking direct aim at Dimitri Obolensky and his classic work *The Byzantine Commonwealth: Eastern Europe 500–1453*. As the title implies, Obolensky laid great emphasis on the culture that the Balkan states and peoples came to share with the Byzantines, as they learned art, literature, law, and religion from the venerable empire.

Kaldellis is having none of this. The Orthodox who were barbarians were not Romans, and being Roman was what mattered most. Even Romans outside of Rome (that is, Byzantium) did not stay Roman for long. He cites a Byzantine historian's comment on Emperor Ioannes Komnenos who encountered in 1142 some former imperial subjects in Asia Minor. While still Christian, they had come to an agreement with the Turks and "looked upon the Romans as their enemies" (Kaldellis 2007: 76).

This argument, too, is vital for how we interpret the transition to Ottoman rule. It would imply a more dramatic shift in self-understanding and in the meanings of terms, and this is just what Kaldellis argues. Roman identity, he writes, survived the fall of the empire but under the Ottomans it was a very different thing. Whereas in Byzantium the Romans were a highly unified nation, under the sultans they were redefined so as to encompass a multi-ethnic and linguistically diverse community (Kaldellis 2007: 44).

An essential part of being Roman was speaking the Greek language, and this brings us to the third component of Byzantine identity: Hellenism. Here we must understand what Hellenism meant to the Byzantines; it referred either to paganism, and was therefore very negative, or to the intellectual inheritance of antiquity, which only some members of the elite – those who were educated in ancient Greek – could access. This Hellenism was positive, although somewhat risky. The yawning divide in status between ancient Greek and the demotic Greek spoken by ordinary people cannot be emphasized enough. Among many possible examples, we can cite the tenth-century epigram written in Constantinople that said "Not the land of the barbarians but Hellas itself has been barbarized in speech and in manner" (Kaldellis 2007: 70). Whereas ability in ancient Greek conferred high social prestige, no particular significance was attached to speaking the demotic form of the language. A very low estimation indeed of demotic Greek is implied in a 2008 study where the author argues that, by the twelfth century, the Constantinopolitan elite saw little difference between ethnic others and provincial Romans (Page 2008: 66). We shall turn to the subject of the provincial/imperial divide shortly.

In the twelfth century the Komnenian dynasty prompted a revival of Hellenic literature among the elite; pagan myths enjoyed a new popularity and classicizing tendencies are prominent in Anna Komnena's *Alexiad*. When the Latins invaded in 1204, this aristocratic pastime turned into something more urgent; for the first time some Byzantines begin referring to themselves as Hellenes. Rather than simply being an admired ancient people, the Hellenes become possible ancestors. This turn reflects the tremendous ideological destabilization of the period; the Byzantines had always called themselves Roman, but this term was newly problematic when actual Italians were occupying the imperial capital (Kaldellis 2007: 338). In addition, the Latin Christians spoke a different language and thus speaking Greek assumed a significance that it had not had before.

Given this "Hellenic turn," some modern Greek historians date the origin of the modern Greek nation to the aftermath of 1204. The shock of the events produced a move away from the universalism of the Roman ideal to a narrower identification with "Greekness," defined by religion and by language.

This interpretation must be rejected. First, the Greek language did not operate as a unifier in any sort of national sense; in fact with the archaizing turn in Constantinople under the Komnenoi one could argue that the already existing situation of diglossia only got worse. Second, the flirtation with the idea of descent from the ancient Hellenes was a phenomenon of the capital only. In the provinces the "Hellenes" continued to be what they had always been: a mythical race of giants from a distant past (Page 2008: 66). The restricted nature of the phenomenon brings us to the final point: Hellenism was always the most rarefied of the identities that a Byzantine could adopt and it pales in comparison to the Byzantine investment, both symbolic and material, in state and church.

By his own admission, Kaldellis' work is a study of the Constantinopolitan elite. When that is taken into account, we can see why loyalty to the Roman state and to the emperor figures so prominently in his assessment of Byzantine identity. Things were different in the provinces, so much so, in fact, that regional identity came to rival the sense of being an imperial subject.

Due to a relative abundance of sources, the Peloponnese provides a good sense of a provincial identity that was Byzantine yet clearly divorced from the Constantinopolitan milieu. Here, the (relative) leniency of the Franks vis-à-vis the Orthodox population helped to create a new and distinctive regional society. The Franks who came to southern

Greece made room for the local nobility in terms of land-holding and the continuation of Byzantine laws of inheritance. In return for their privileges the nobility was required to serve in the army and thus a mixed military force emerged; it was probably bilingual and *The Chronicle of the Morea* refers to it as a "Moreot" army. Its enemies' armies, such as that of the despotate of Epirus, are similarly described in regional terms. *The Chronicle of the Morea* itself, of course, is a testimony to this ethnically mixed society; if it was written by a Greek, it shows a distinct sympathy for the Franks; if the author is a westerner, he had learned very good Greek and used words in their local sense. Unlike the Latins in Constantinople – who insisted on calling the Byzantines *Graeci* – the author of the *Chronicle* called the Orthodox what they called themselves: Romans.

Although the Franks certainly subordinated the Orthodox Church, religious boundaries proved permeable just the same. Some Byzantines accepted the Latin rite, thus becoming Franks in accordance with the understanding of the day, and repeated papal scoldings make it clear that Franks attended Orthodox church services. If Greek soldiers fought in Frankish armies, some Frankish knights chose to serve the Byzantine despot at Mistra in the fourteenth century. Given this situation, it is not surprising that *The Chronicle of the Morea*, along with other Greek sources produced at the same time, displays far less ethnic chauvinism toward the Franks than do Constantinopolitan texts from the same period.

Even more interesting for our purposes is the content of Roman identity in the Peloponnese. We know that it survived because in all of the literary sources society consists of two groups: Franks and Romans. In *The Chronicle of the Morea* being Roman is associated primarily with speaking Greek, with the Orthodox religion, and with Roman (Byzantine) law. Assertions of Roman superiority, however, are far more muted than they are in the capital and the idea that allegiance to the Byzantine emperor was a necessary component of Roman identity is entirely absent.

This last point is crucial. It stands in direct contrast to Kaldellis' assertion that the Romans were united by a common devotion to their state. On the other hand, the view that Kaldellis rejects – that the Byzantine Empire was a multi-ethnic empire whose subjects were loosely united by religion – does not seem to capture the reality of the late medieval Morea either. The sense of belonging is distinctly local, or regional, rather than imperial. Both Frankish and Byzantine outsiders were equally scorned (Shawcross 2013: 242). One author even goes so far as to speak of a "unique Moreot identity in which Greeks and Latins could equally have a share" (Shawcross 2009: 25). Along these same lines the classicizing tendencies of Constantinople did not translate to the Morea. In the south of Greece Turks were always called Turks, whereas in the capital they were "Persians" (Page 2008: 222).

Regionalism is, I think, the key that can reconcile Kaldellis' argument about Byzantine identity with the very different society that developed in southern Greece. And not just there; although 1453 is the official date of the end of the Byzantine Empire, Byzantine historians are increasingly making the argument that, in the wake of the Byzantine conquest of Constantinople in 1261, it is misleading to think of an empire confronted by numerous enemies. Despite the imperial dreams well documented by Kaldellis and others, the reality was "a proliferation of power bases, each with its own interests to uphold" (Shawcross 2009: 255). From Latin duchies to Turkish *beyliks* and Greek despotates, the eastern Mediterranean from the thirteenth through the fifteenth centuries was a checkerboard of small states, of which the Byzantine Empire, despite its name, was only one, albeit a particularly illustrious one.

To ask, then, about the balance of religion, identity, and state in late Byzantine identity is insufficient. Far more significant was the fragmentation of Byzantine identity into different regional loyalties. Each regional center developed its own identity and it is not surprising that attachment to the state of the Romans was strongest in the particular state – that is, the Byzantine Empire – that had managed to hang on to Constantinople. We can view this as the expression, par excellence, of their own brand of regional identity, just as an attachment to the Morea, regardless of religion, was the essential component of aristocratic identity in southern Greece during the same time period. Some of these aristocrats were Romans, but they were not Roman in the same way as the residents of Constantinople. The transition to Ottoman rule must be seen within the context of the extreme fragmentation of the Greek Orthodox world. It was not one, but many Greek Orthodox societies that came under Ottoman sovereignty.

Therefore, although Kaldellis argues that under the Ottomans the meaning of Roman-ness was transformed into a pan-Christian identity that was multi-ethnic and multi-linguistic, it seems unlikely that that ever happened in Istanbul. An attachment to Hellenism, and specifically a mastery of the Greek language, appears to have remained as strong as ever in the decades after 1453. Almost all of the fifteenth- and sixteenth-century patriarchs were Greek speakers and had had a Greek education and most were from Istanbul. One of the few non-Greek speakers, the Serbian Rafael (1475–6), did not fare well; admittedly he suffered from alcoholism but the sources also never failed to mention his ethnic background as well. He was mocked for his inability to pronounce diphthongs. When it came time for him to pay the monies owed to the sultan, none of the Greek notables of the capital would come to his assistance, and thus he was thrown in jail.[11] Elsewhere it seems unlikely that Hellenism was relevant at all – it had not been prior to the Ottomans either – and some Greek Orthodox communities, such as those in Cappadocia, were not even Greek speaking.[12]

The more intriguing question concerns the fate of a Roman, as opposed to a Christian, identity. It is well documented that, from the eighteenth century onward, the Greek Orthodox called themselves – and were called by others – Romans (Ρωμιοί). The Turkish word *Rum*, after all, is still the official term today for Greeks who are Turkish citizens, as opposed to the Greeks of Greece, who are *Yunanlılar*. Therefore, it is sometimes assumed that this term was operative throughout the entire Ottoman period; there are frequent references in the literature to the *Rum Millet*, meaning the community of Greek Orthodox Christians, whether the writer is referring to the sixteenth or to the nineteenth century.

But it is not at all clear that this term was in consistent use from the end of the Byzantine Empire straight through until the downfall of the sultans in the early twentieth century. The Ottomans, for one, only began to use the term *Rum* for the Greek Orthodox at some point in the late seventeenth century. Prior to that, official documents always referred to the patriarch as "Patriarch of the infidels of Istanbul and its surroundings" (Konortas 1998: 301).

This shift in Ottoman terminology suggests that, if it didn't disappear altogether, the use of the term "Roman" for the Greek Orthodox of the empire declined at some point after 1453, relative to the term "Christian." An explanation for this would be the gradual extinction of the aristocratic groups – such as the nobility of the Morea – that had referred to themselves in the former way. This correlation is strengthened by the fact that the return of the Roman appellation in the late seventeenth century is closely linked to the rise of the new Greek Orthodox aristocracy, the Phanariots.

Finally, the divergence between the Greek Orthodox and the term "Roman" is also suggested by the fact that, beginning in the thirteenth century, the term "Rum" began to be used in a completely different context. The word starts to be adopted by, and to refer to, Muslims living in the lands of the "Rum," that is, the Romans or the Byzantines. Never an official category used in bureaucratic documents, its rise was due rather to the need to describe the new urban class of cultivated Muslims who inhabited the towns and cities of Anatolia and the Balkans under Ottoman rule. Its most common binary was "Acem," by which was meant the Persians, but not in an ethnic sense (Kafadar 2007: 15). Rather, because it was a cultural discourse, biographical dictionaries, for example, would speak of the "poets of Rum" as opposed to the poets from Acem, or the poets of the Arab lands.[13] It was a word that testified to the increasing cultural confidence of Ottoman literati. The Moroccan ambassador to Istanbul in 1589 was alert to the way the meaning of the term had shifted.

> That city was the capital of the lands of Rum and the seat of the empire, the city of caesars. The Muslims who live in that city now call themselves Rum and prefer that origina to their own. Among them, too, calligraphy is called *khatt rūmī*. (Kafadar 2007: 16)

And then, toward the end of the seventeenth century, the term began to fall out of use with reference to this social and cultural milieu, just at the time that it began, once again, to refer to the Greek Orthodox (Kafadar 2007). These two shifts could hardly have been coincidental, but the matter still awaits research.

From this review we can conclude the following about the Byzantine mix of Hellenism, Christianity, and Roman-ism and its fate in the Ottoman years. The change was at one and the same time greater and less than what Kaldellis proposes. After 1453 the Greek Orthodox came to identify themselves primarily as Christians, not Romans, and this was probably linked to the extinction of an Orthodox Christian aristocratic class. By the end of the seventeenth century the appellation "Rum" began to make a comeback, but it should not be assumed that this eighteenth- and nineteenth-century reality held true for an earlier period. "Rum" was not a continuous identity but rather one that broke down and then was reconstructed again. The term itself, in other words, is part of the history of the Greek Orthodox community in the Ottoman Empire, not simply a description of it.

If the end of the Byzantine Empire meant the temporary eclipse of the term "Rum" for the Greek-speaking Christians – and this was a major shift brought about by Ottoman rule – in another way the meaning of Roman-ness (at least in so far as it referred to Christians) showed a remarkable stability. I do not agree with Kaldellis that under the Ottomans "Rum" was redefined to mean a multi-ethnic community including many different linguistic groups. Instead, when the word made a comeback it was inextricably linked to the rise of a new Greek-speaking aristocracy in Istanbul with strong Hellenizing tendencies. In 1700, as in 1400, or 1300, "Rum" had something Hellenic about it – in the sense both of language and of civilization – that was not synonymous with the Christian Orthodox world as a whole.

At the same time, debates over the mix of Roman-ness and Christian identity that followed the Greek Orthodox into the Ottoman period should not be allowed to overshadow the more important, in my view, inheritance of the late Byzantine period, which was a proliferation of strong regional identities and loyalties. This is, I think, how we should interpret the actions of the Trabzonites, discussed earlier, as they poured into Istanbul after the collapse of their state in 1461; they wanted the patriarchate to be in their hands, by which they meant not the Greek speakers of the Ottoman Empire but rather the community of Trabzon.

Here we must duly note the fact that the Trabzonites wanted to capture the patriarchate for themselves. The institution remained powerful, both materially and symbolically. The decision of Fatih Mehmet to appoint a patriarch, combined with the eagerness of Greek elites from all parts of the empire to compete to control it, sowed the seeds for the steady rise in the power of the patriarchate, and of Istanbul, over the far-flung Christian communities of the empire, a process that would peak in the eighteenth century. It bears repeating that Mehmet did not simply hand this power over to Gennadios in the winter of 1454; his action rather began a long historical process. In the words of Socrates Petmezas,

> La formation d'un corps formel de prérogatives et de "privilèges" du patriarche grec-orthodoxe, reconnu par la Sublime Porte, ainsi que la consolidation et l'élargissement de son pouvoir sur ses suffragants ou ses pairs (les autres patriarches et archevêques autocéphales de l'Orient) ont été *l'oeuvre patiente de trois siècles*. (Petmezas 1996a: 490; my emphasis)[14]

The historical trajectory of the patriarchate is bound up with not only the history of Christianity under the sultans, but also the history of Hellenism. As we have seen above, it is unlikely that the elites in and around the church in Istanbul ever abandoned their Hellenic biases and even if these sentiments were somewhat attenuated in the sixteenth and seventeenth centuries, they came roaring back in the eighteenth with the rise of the Phanariots. Therefore, as we go forward we shall keep in mind the Hellenizing tendencies of the patriarchate and of the Istanbul elites. This configuration of power under the long centuries of Ottoman rule means that the boundaries of the Hellenic world, the Greek world, were necessarily indeterminate. This was because anyone who was an Orthodox Christian was potentially available for a Hellenizing project. Now from the vantage point of the early twenty-first century, we know where the Hellenizing project succeeded and where it failed; there is a temptation, then, to include western Asia Minor in a history of the Greeks and to exclude the Bulgarian lands. This is, however, anachronistic and should be avoided. The approach in this book will be to treat Hellenism as a project rather than a reality, and to consider where it failed as well as where it succeeded. And we will bear in mind that it was just one of many projects that emanated from the patriarchate in Istanbul.

Conclusion

In Ottoman historiography 1453 is a turning point of the most dramatic kind. With the conquest of the city, Mehmet now ruled over a true world-empire, and he made changes accordingly (İnalcık 1989: 29). He set about constructing an imperial image for himself that was a dramatic departure from that of his predecessors. He introduced the imperial-apple motif, symbol of universal sovereignty, into Ottoman ceremonial and this was part of a more general increase in royal splendor and pomp. His imperial mosque changed the skyline of the city while the new royal palace, the Topkapı, was designed to increase imperial seclusion. Between 1477 and 1481 he drew up a new dynastic law code to regulate life at the palace. Necipoğlu speaks of "the new vision of centralized government" envisioned in the dynastic code, and how the rules it prescribed stayed in place throughout the following two centuries (Necipoglue 1991: 16). Outside the palace, Mehmet used the occasion of his victory to move definitively against potentially independent centers of power within Ottoman society. He executed the grand vezir, Çandarlı Halil, whose family had been providing vezirs to the sultan since 1385. From now on the vezirs would be drawn from ranks of presumably more pliable Christian converts, whether *devşirme* or captives.

Viewed from the perspective of the sultan's Christian subjects, the dramatic fall of the city should not be allowed to obscure certain continuities. Istanbul continued to be a city with a large Greek population and many members of the Byzantine elite – whether Christian or now converted to Islam – were still influential residents of the city. Much, if not most of this, was due to Fatih Mehmet's willingness, perhaps even eagerness, to come to terms with his Christian subjects. The reasons for this have been much discussed among historians of the Ottoman state; here I have tried to outline what the prominence of the Greeks meant for the Greek Orthodox of Istanbul and, by extension, the empire.

This prominence was, necessarily, a temporary phenomenon. The descendants of the converts belonged firmly in Islamic society and Byzantine royalty died out. And then two critical events in the early sixteenth century – the battle with Safavid Iran and the Ottoman conquest of Syria and Egypt – put the empire on a more Islamic course. The next two chapters will consider the fortunes of the empire's Christians, and particularly the Greeks, in light of these new circumstances.

Certain continuities in pre- and post-1453 Istanbul return us to the question of alternative chronologies that I raised in my discussion of Thessaly. Let us conclude these two chapters on the conquest of the Greek world by the Ottoman sultans with a more explicit consideration of periodization, keeping in mind the goal of bringing into dialogue the master narrative on the empire and the experience of the sultans' Christian subjects.

Unfortunately the two tend to run along separate and parallel paths which do not often intersect. The story I have told about Constantinople/Istanbul is, I think, relevant to broader themes in Ottoman history, most particularly the importance of 1453. Among Ottomanists Fatih Mehmet's reign is seen as a radical break with much of Ottoman tradition. And, of course, in many ways it was. But he looks less radical when considered from the point of view of his Christian subjects. In some areas – such as palace life – Fatih Mehmet was determined to break new ground, but in others – such as the Orthodox Church – the ad hoc policies of the past would continue to be preferred. Similarly, while the conqueror moved ruthlessly against some sectors of Muslim society, he appears to have been remarkably tolerant toward Greek elites. I should emphasize that I am not speaking here only, or even principally, of the well-known turn toward the *devşirme* for the staffing of offices such as the grand vezirate, but rather of ex-Byzantine elites, as well as those men who served Mehmet in Edirne and continued to serve him in Istanbul – all those, in other words, whom Zachariadou has called, with deliberate paradox, "the powerful losers."[15]

Notes

1. Here we should take note of the point that Stavrides makes: neither Angelović, nor any other member of the Christian aristocracy, entered the palace as *devşirme*. The *devşirme* were recruited exclusively among the peasantry (Stavrides 2001: 109).
2. Babinger, who calls him "the half-Serb, half-Greek Mehmed Pasha," pointed to the fact that he had relatives throughout Greece and this allowed him to make "himself extremely useful to the sultan" (Babinger 1978: 196).
3. İnalcık is agnostic on this point. He merely writes (of Rum Mehmet Pasha) "It may be that the Pasha's descent inclined him to favor the Greeks and that at this period Greeks exercised some influence in the Palace and in state affairs" (İnalcık 1969–70 : 245).
4. This is a controversial point. Zachariadou points out that accounts of the election of the first patriarch, Gennadios, present it as if he was formally elected in Istanbul and then accepted by the sultan. This would be more in accordance with traditional church practice. As Zachariadou shows, it was, in fact, the other way around (Zachariadou 1996: 46).
5. The office was called thed *Piskopos Mukata'a Kalemi*, literally the office of the patriarch's tax farm (Konortas 1998: 346).
6. It is interesting to note that that the Ottomans did not use ecclesiastical language to refer to the metropolitans sees. They called them, simply, *vilayets* (Zachariadou 1996: 113).
7. This account draws heavily on chapter 8 of Kiel (1985).
8. Only one Bulgarian-born Muslim ever became grand vezir, and this was in the eighteenth century (Kiel 1985: 292).
9. İnalcık writes that there is every reason to believe that "the Ottomans established close ties with the Patriarchate in Istanbul before 1453." Tarnovo is a valuable piece of evidence in support of İnalcık's argument (İnalcık 1998: 197).
10. There must also have been the desire the please the ironworkers of Samokov, probably the largest iron-producing area in the Ottoman Empire. The workers were Orthodox Serbs for the most part (Kiel 1985: 123).
11. And there were signs of disapproval even before he began to serve. Most patriarchs at this time were ordained by the metropolitan of Herakleion but in Rafael's case it was the metropolitan of Ankara (Zachariadou 1996: 74).
12. And Matschke notes that in the Ottoman period "Mt. Athos was opened to the propertied classes of both the Greek and the Slavic Worlds" (Matschke 2002: 110).
13. It is striking how much Cemal Kafadar's definition of "Rum" coincides with cultural definitions of Roman-ness in the Byzantine Empire, where

speaking Greek and living a cultivated life were essential aspects of being Roman. He writes "Rumi in its new meaning was used in large measure to designate a novel social and cultural constellation, namely the identity of those from a variety of backgrounds but with a shared disposition toward a certain style of expression in the arts as well as quotidian life" (Kafadar 2007: 11).

14. The Sublime Porte was, in European languages, the conventional term when referring to the Ottoman bureaucracy, as opposed to the person of the sultan.
15. The phrase she uses translates literally as "the strong subjugated," "οι ισχυροί υπόδουλοι." My translation is somewhat freer in order to convey the paradox that she intends (Zachariadou 1996: 63).

CHAPTER 3

Christians in an Islamic empire

Sultan Süleyman came to the throne in November of 1520. Sometime soon after – most likely in the winter of 1521 – the *ulema* (religious scholars) pressed him to allow the seizure of Christian property in the capital city. This event has famously been described in a sixteenth-century church chronicle. The Islamic scholars produced a *fetva* (legal opinion) saying that, since Mehmet II had conquered the city by force, all the churches still existing in the city should be seized and destroyed. The patriarch then paid a visit to the grand vezir, the chronicle continues, and the two agreed to a plan to save the city's Christian patrimony. They appeared before the sultan with two aged janissaries who testified that, at the very last minute, the city had capitulated. Thus, the churches must be spared.

This story is very likely a fiction. Nevertheless, it is clear that the seizure attempt was made. Ottoman sources mention it and news of it trickled in from the Levant to Venice, where the chronicler Marino Sanuto recorded it. Sanuto received a letter dated April 14, 1521, from a Venetian official in Corfu, in which he said that a monk had arrived from Istanbul. This monk said that "il Signor Turco" had decreed that no Christian was allowed to wear "Turkish dress," and that all Christian churches would be destroyed. Other reports went so far as to say that the sultan planned to convert all the Christians in the city and to kill all those who refused (Patrinelis 1966: 567–72).

These events took place just a few years after the Ottoman conquest of the Middle East and the battle of Çaldiran, in which the Sunni Ottomans defeated the Shi'ite Safavid dynasty of Iran. Both of these events have been credited with setting the formerly eclectic Ottoman Empire on a more Islamic path. Should we infer a link between the two? In other words, did the increasing emphasis on Islam mean more difficulties and restrictions for the empire's Christian population?

In the previous two chapters I suggested that 1453 cannot support all the historical significance that has been piled onto it. In the Balkans new arrangements had already emerged, which the fall of the city did not disturb. The relationship between the sultans and the church continued to be a work in progress, both before and after 1453. In this chapter we will ask if the early sixteenth century is, instead, the more significant turning point. In so doing we will consider the history of the Greeks in light of a historiography that has been developed by Ottomanists, a historiography that emphasizes the twin themes of Islamization (or, alternatively, Sunnitization) and a state increasingly bent on social discipline. There is no countervailing narrative when it comes to the empire's Greek population, although particular incidents – such as the seizure of the churches discussed above – have received a fair amount of attention. In my opinion this reflects that fact that Greek historians have concentrated their attention on the seventeenth and eighteenth centuries, seeing in these two centuries the recovery, or the rebirth, of the nation. This is not to say that there have not been very important studies on the earlier centuries, because there certainly have, but no larger narrative has yet emerged.

At the same time, Ottoman scholars writing on the more ideological state of the sixteenth century have concerned themselves mainly with the consequences this had for the empire's Muslim population. This is in accordance with long-standing assumptions, usually implicit, about the empire's character that tend to marginalize the non-Muslim populations.

By bringing the Greeks into this Ottomanist narrative, I hope to achieve two things: first, I will continue with the approach that animates this entire project, which is to consider the Greeks as part of Ottoman society rather than somehow external to it; second, a consideration of the arguments about Islamization and social discipline from the point of view of the empire's most important Christian community will provide new perspectives on these selfsame arguments.

But first we must understand what Ottoman historians have in mind when they talk about these new developments in the sixteenth century.

An Islamic empire

The rise of a powerful Shi'a neighbor to the east, in the form of Shah Ismail, was profoundly threatening to the Ottoman sultans. Here was a ruler who not only represented a rival Islam; he also proved capable of attracting significant support from within Ottoman territories. Shah Ismail was wildly popular with the Türkmen tribes in eastern Anatolia. Selim I's defeat of his Shi'a rival at Çaldiran in 1514 eliminated the immediate military threat but the religious and ideological challenge remained, and it had long-lasting repurcussions for governance within the empire. The Safavids were criticized for their abandonment of the Friday prayers – due to the absence of a legitimate imam – and under Süleyman the performance of the congregational prayers came to be enforced throughout Ottoman territories. Gülrü Necipoğlu traces the rise of this emphasis on Friday prayers in the proliferation of mosques in the capital city. Whereas in the fifteenth century documents show that nearly half of Istanbul's neighborhoods bore non-religious names, by 1546 many neighborhoods were named after the person who had built a mosque there. Mosques in artisanal workplaces reflected the increasing importance of communal prayer in the life of the craft guilds. A petitioner in a *fetva* from the period asks whether a member of the guild who refuses to perform the prayers can be expelled. The answer is a resounding yes (Necipoğlu 2005: 48).

This new insistence on the performance of congregational prayers was not confined to Istanbul. In the late 1530s a *ferman* (sultanic decree) was sent out to every corner of the empire, commanding the construction of mosques in villages that did not have them. And the authorities in Istanbul followed up on this initiative; in 1546 the *kadi* of Vize in Thrace was commanded to investigate certain villages whose abandoned mosques had become dilapidated because their congregations stopped performing the prayers in them. The *kadi* was to warn these communities, order them to pray, and punish those who refused to do so. Further, he was to command the endowment administrators of ruined mosques to repair them and to replace incompetent imams, those unable to correctly recite the Koran, with capable ones, reporting the names of new appointees to the sultan (Necipoğlu 2005: 49). Necipoğlu shows how the very architecture of mosque complexes changed in the sixteenth century, as part of Süleyman's policy of a state-imposed religious orthodoxy. Guest houses were physically separated from mosques so that the whirling and chanting that took place in the former would not contaminate the prayers that were meant to be at the center of the latter (Necipoğlu 2005: 102).

Other measures to enforce religious orthodoxy were more forceful. In central and eastern Anatolia persecution of the *kızılbaş* – the "red-hat wearers," as the followers of Shah Ismail were known – was ongoing throughout the sixteenth century, even after the signing of the treaty of Amasya in 1555 brought hostilities between the Safavids and the Ottomans to an end, at least for the time being. Executions and deportations of real or suspected heretics – sometimes they were sent as far away as Hungary – were common (Imber 1979: 254). Across the empire tolerance for religious heterodoxy declined; it was in the middle of the sixteenth century that many of the more antinomian dervish orders were suppressed; those that remained were carefully monitored for signs of what the authorities now considered Shi'ism (Karamustafa 1994: 83–4).

Finally, with the conquests of Syria and Egypt in 1516 and 1517 respectively, the Ottoman Empire, for the first time, had a majority Muslim population. This, too, has been cited as a reason for the increasing emphasis on Islamic orthodoxy, but there has been less research in this area and the evidence is still rather thin. It is clear that Selim I gained enormous prestige from becoming the ruler of Mecca and Medina; a text written shortly after described him in millenarian terms such as "Master of the Conjunction" and "Shadow of God" (Subrahmanyam 2003: 137). But at the social level there are only a few hints as to what the addition of a large Arab population meant for the empire as a whole. Heath Lowry has shown that the terminology of the cadastral surveys produced after 1520 undergoes a dramatic change; the Turco-Persian of the earlier registers is replaced by Arabic (Lowry 1995: 193). On the other hand, in the *berats* given to church officials the earlier fifteenth-century term is the neutral *nasrani* (Nazarenes), but it changes to *kefere* (infidel) later in the century, that is, before the conquest of the Middle East (Konortas 1998: 301) We also know that in the sixteenth century *ulema* from Anatolia and from the Arab lands were sent to Bosnia to further its Islamization (Zhelyazkova 1994: 201). Beyond that the question remains an open one.[1]

If Süleyman had to watch the rise of a competitor in the east, things were equally fraught in the west, where Charles V came to the throne just one year before Süleyman himself. The simultaneous rise of several great powers, combined with the momentous events of the age such as the fall of Istanbul, the expulsion from Spain, the discovery of the new world, and, finally, the advent of the tenth century in the Muslim world, created a messianic fervor across Eurasia. In both Christendom and the world of Islam there was the conviction that one universal ruler, and thus one religion, was soon to emerge. Süleyman, with his vast empire and his triumphs in Hungary, was a serious candidate for the role of universal leader, and messianic expectations swirled around him during the first thirty years of his reign. Like Selim, Süleyman was also described as the *mujaddid* or "renewer of religion" and as the "Master of the Conjunction"; the chroniclers said that the sultan had been instructed by the Prophet and the saint, Hizir, and that the Prophet and all the saints had been seen at the battle of Mohacs, in

Hungary, where Süleyman had triumphed (Fleischer 1990: 169; Krstić 2011; Subrahmanyam 2003).

In the end, Süleyman has come down to us in history as the Lawgiver, not the Messiah, and this reflects the legacy of, primarily, his later years. Here, too, the project was defined in religious terms. Ebussuud, the famous jurisconsult of the sixteenth century, worked tirelessly together with Süleyman from the late 1530s onward to bring *kanun*, the secular or sultanic law, into harmony with the *şeriat*. Ebussuud's most monumental reforms were in the area of land tenure; the arrangements he put in place would last, mostly unchanged, until the land reforms of 1858 (Peirce 2003: 108). The vast majority of the land in the empire, the so-called *miri* land, belonged to the state, that is, to the sultan. Ebussuud gave such an arrangement a justification in Islamic law; he also redefined the ultimate owner of the lands as the Muslim community as a whole, thereby identifying the sultan's possessions with the good of the Muslim community. He also found a way, again through Islamic law, to allow the sultan to raise taxes on the land. The end result was to strengthen the power of the sultan, and a cynical observer might say that this was the only real goal all along. Nevertheless, the fact remains that the stature of the *şeriat* was increased as well, since the reforms were undertaken in its name. Again, the state had embraced Islam. In Colin Imber's words: "The interests of religion and the interests of the dynasty became one and the same" (Imber 1990: 183).

Ebussuud's efforts were not confined to the intricacies of land tenure. Alongside the specific focus on religious orthodoxy, discussed earlier, he presided over a more general effort to bring society within the purview of the law. In the beginning of the sixteenth century the chief *müfti* (jurisconsult) used a basket to haul up the questions that were posed to him every day. By the middle of the sixteenth century Ebussuud – now the chief *müfti* himself – could boast of issuing over a thousand *fetvas* per day, and he had a number of assistants to help him do so. At the same time, new colleges were being built at a furious pace to train future jurists. Leslie Peirce has shown how, in the city of Aintab in the middle of the sixteenth century, there was a concerted effort to encourage people to bring their disputes to court. The decree, in 1544, that no marriage contract was valid without the cognizance of a judge was typical of this drive to expand state power (Peirce 2003: 138–9).

Elite politics

If we add up all of these sixteenth-century developments – the monitoring of religious practice, the religious polemics of a millenarian age, a sultan who styles himself the *mahdi* (also a millenarian figure, the Imam of the Last Age) and the project to bring secular law into harmony with the *şeriat* – it might seem like a foregone conclusion that the sixteenth-century Ottoman Empire was a less hospitable place for Christians. This is indeed the argument that Heath Lowry makes. He is worth quoting at some length since he is one of the rare scholars who has asked what a more Islamic empire meant for the sultan's Christian subjects (although he focuses exclusively on the conquest of the Arab world). Lowry suggests

> that it was the addition of the Arab world to the Ottoman polity which on one hand meant that a state which theretofore had been overwhelmingly Christian in terms of population now became one in which numerically the Islamic element became preeminent (the immediate result being the influx of thousands of Arab bureaucrats to the Ottoman capital, who brought with them a system of ruling non-Muslims which had been developed throughout the preceding eight hundred years); and, on the other, it influenced the Ottoman rulers to begin thinking of themselves as the latest in a long line of great Islamic dynasties, rather than as a state whose earlier institutions had all been developed in the Christian milieu of the Balkans. It was this change which spelled an end to the policy of accommodation and the abandonment of the special rights and privileges which had previously been an essential factor in their being accepted by the Christian peoples they ruled. (Lowry 2002: 2)

Let us evaluate Lowry's general argument within the specific context of Greek elites and Greek institutions in the sixteenth century.[2] Here we shall see that the picture is more mixed, suggesting a certain divergence between an overall imperial orientation and particular experiences.

First, the Greek elite that I described in the previous chapter proved to be very enduring, lasting well into the sixteenth century.[3] Their importance is underlined by the fact that sources from the period referred to them collectively as "the archons" or notables (Zachariadou 1996: 67). They continued to be prominent in Ottoman finance right up through the 1570s, culminating in the remarkable career of Michael Kantakouzenos, also known as "Şeytanoğlu" or "son of the devil." Kantakouzenos, a descendant of Byzantine royalty, was for a time the highest Ottoman customs official, a revenue farmer, master of the salt and fish trade, as well as a protégé of many sultans and a friend of Sokollu, the Serbian-born grand vezir. Şeytanoğlu routinely spent his own money to supply the sultan with gallies for his fleet (Mauroeidi 1992: 136). He is by far the most famous (or infamous) member of the Greek elite in the second half of the sixteenth century, but research in the Ottoman archives has shown that there were many more in this period (Zachariadou 1996: 63). As late as 1581 a church official wrote to Martin Crusius about the Greeks that "they purchase the farm of royal taxes and, collecting the various annual taxes like tax collectors, some become rich while others don't do so well for themselves."[4] From the Venetian archives we learn that Antonios Koresse – from a dynasty that was active in both Venice and Istanbul – was close to Hayreddein Pasha, who conquered the Aegean islands for Süleyman. When we consider the fact that Hayreddin was himself a Greek convert to Islam, it seems that the fifteenth-century phenomenon of ties between Christian Greeks and Greeks who had converted to Islam had at least an echo in the sixteenth century, although this still awaits investigation. Konstantinos Kounoupis was a Venetian subject who supplied Ibrahim Pasha, the powerful grand vezir, with ships from Genoa, Ancona, and Naples (Mauroeidi 1992: 137). The families around the patriarchate also withstood all the changes of the sixteenth century; the Argyropoulos family was collecting taxes for the patriarch at the end of the fifteenth century and was still doing so a century later. When one combines the biographies – however slight – of these powerful Greeks with the much better-known lives of Ottoman Jews such as Joseph Nasi, it is clear that an increasing emphasis on Islamic governance and on Christian/Muslim polemics in no way constrained the sultan from surrounding himself with powerful non-Muslims if they could be of some use to him. Much of the usefulness of the Greeks came from their close ties to Venice at a time when the Ottoman–Venetian relationship was critical; we shall discuss this Italian connection in the next chapter.

With regard to the patriarchate, early in the sixteenth century we do see a small change that indicates a less accommodating stance on the part of the sultan. The *berat* that was issued in 1483 said that if the patriarch acts "against his own religious procedures, then the team of metropolitans" can investigate and even go so far as to ask the sultan to appoint someone else whom they have chosen (Konortas 1998: 124). The term "team of metropolitans" is a reference to the synod, which was, according to Byzantine canon law, the body responsible for electing a patriarch. The *berat*, then, was a nod to accepted Byzantine procedure and part of Fatih Mehmet's conciliatory policy. The next *berat* we possess was issued in 1525, five years after Süleyman came to the throne. There is no mention in it of the synod and, indeed, the synod would not be mentioned again until 1757 (Konortas 1998: 124–5).

Against this change, we must bear in mind the fact that from the very beginning it was the sultan who appointed the patriarch, and then the synod affirmed his decision, even if church chronicles preferred to elide this fact. The more conciliatory *berat* of 1483 only gave the synod the right to ask for the dismissal of a patriarch, not to elect one. An episode from the *Patriarchal History of Istanbul* the chronicle that is our most important source for the patriarchal church in the sixteenth century, provides an invaluable glimpse of how Ottoman officials, Orthodox clergy, and Greek notables came together in the selection of a patriarch. Patriarch Dionysios (1546–56) was elected patriarch despite the fact that he was opposed by most of the clergy and notables, as well as by the Grand Vezir Rüstem Pasha. He was then, apparently, chased out of his office, at which point his supporters – the notables of Galata – went into action. Learning that Süleyman would be going on a journey, they managed to meet up with him and to present their supplication that Dionysios be reinstated on the throne. After investigating the matter, the sultan said "May the will of my people come to be." He directed Rüstem to fetch the patriarch, and

> the pasha, not knowing what to do, for fear of the emperor, sent a sergeant and took the patriarch from Galata, where he was to be found after being chased there, and he brought him to the patriarchate and sat him on the patriarchal throne. (Shapiro 2011: 17)

What we see here is the intense involvement of Greek elites, but it is the sultan who is, in the end, the ultimate authority. The situation, in other words, is little different from what transpired with the election of Gennadios in 1454; admittedly, the case of Dionysios was a good deal more chaotic, but this was because he was an unpopular choice (Zachariadou 1996: 67).

At the same time it is true that the Greeks were not always able to prevail. Having lost the first patriarchal church, the Church of the Holy Apostles, to Fatih Mehmet so that he could build his own mosque complex – now part of the iconic skyline of Istanbul – they lost the second, Pammakaristos, in the 1580s. It was converted into the Fethiye mosque. Even more ominously, the "crisis of the monasteries," as it is known, between 1567 and 1571, threatened to destroy the entire institution of Christian monasticism, that is, the very backbone of Christian existence in the Ottoman Empire. Let us look at both of these issues and consider their relationship to the Islamic context of the sixteenth century that I described above.

The conversion of Pammakaristos seems to have been driven by two factors: the search for imperial prestige in an age of diminished opportunities and the increasing difficulty of building within Istanbul. Murat III seized Pammakaristos with the justification of his recent military victories in Georgia, although they amounted to very little. Having had no victories in Europe, Murat missed the opportunity to convert a cathedral church into a victory mosque, as his predecessors had done on so many occasions. Nor could he easily build a new mosque since mosques were only supposed to be built with the booty from war against the infidels.[5] Thus his gaze fell upon Pammakaristos and, going forward, the practice of converting churches in newly conquered territories gave way to the conversion of churches already within the imperial domains. In this way the shrinking horizons of the empire put extra pressure on Christian structures in urban areas (Necipoğlu 2005: 58–9).

But it was not only the Christians who were feeling the pressure. Gülrü Necipoğlu has meticulously detailed the fight over space in the capital city as the city's population swelled.[6] Many smaller mosques in areas of prime real estate were demolished to build Friday prayer mosques; this, by the way, was an additional justification for the seizure of Pammakaristos. Ebussuud wrote that the surrounding Muslim population was now large enough that it required a proper congregational mosque. Also in the sixteenth century the founder's privilege of building a mausoleum next to his mosque complex was restricted (excepting members of the Ottoman dynasty); this was the reason that Eyüp began to be used as a burial ground. The destruction of illegal buildings butting up against mosques became standard practice at this time as well (Necipoğlu 2005: 58–9, 111–13).

It seems to me, then, that pressures related to urban development probably drove the conversion of Pammakaristos more than any sort of Islamic agenda. This is not to say that the Christians were not more vulnerable to the seizure of their property, because they were. Also, the conversion of churches into mosques was extremely popular; even if their motivations had little to do with religion, the authorities certainly were not loath to frame such seizures as triumphs for Islam. When Murat III's grand vezir Koca Sinan Pasha bought the church of St. George in Thessaloniki and converted it into a Friday mosque, eyewitness accounts recorded the great enthusiasm evoked by converting such a sumptuous church into a mosque.[7] Similarly, Murat's conversion of Pammakaristos set off such enthusiasm across the empire that he had to send out a *fetva* forbidding the mass conversion of churches into mosques. But what this *fetva* also demonstrates is that the sultan insisted on being in control of the Islamist agenda. The Christians of the empire were his subjects, first and foremost, and he would decide how they were to be treated. In a very similar fashion, Süleyman's acceptance of a legal fiction in 1520 – that the city had surrendered in 1453 – allowed him to stop the seizure of the churches and thus to remain in control of the pace of Islamization (Necipoğlu 2005: 57).

In contrast to the amount of research on the seizure of Pammakaristos and, especially, the attempted confiscation of the churches in 1520, a good deal has been done on "the crisis of the monasteries." It began in 1569 when Selim II, through the device of a *fetva* issued by Ebussuud, declared that all monastic and ecclesiastical land was to be confiscated. The reasoning behind the *fetva* was as follows. The land in question was held as a trust, known in Islamic law as *vakıf*, whereas land in the empire was supposed to belong to the sultan, with certain limited exceptions. This conflict was not a new one – already in the fifteenth century sultans were battling the rising tide of land being converted into *vakıf* and thus beyond the reach of the state – but Ebussuud pursued the preservation, and extension, of state land with extraordinary fervor. In addition, and this extra twist was particular to the attack on property held by Christian institutions, Ebussuud ruled that a trust established for the benefit of monasteries and churches was by definition an illegal trust. Therefore, no revenues at all, from whatever property, could be devoted to a trust. This was very different from the treatment being meted out to Muslim trustees. Even if their land was seized for the state, on the grounds that it had been illegally converted, the trees, the vines, the mills, and whatever else existed on the land were always deemed legitimate in Islamic law for conversion into a trust. If Ebussuud had been able to follow through with what he originally threatened then the monastic institution in the Ottoman Empire would simply have crumbled. By definition, a monastery was a collective institution; the property that it owned belonged to the monastery, not to individual monks. But Islamic law, with its strong anti-corporate bias, makes only one provision for ownership by an institution rather than an individual, and that is a trust. Ebussuud had said the monasteries' trusts were invalid. What that meant was that only individual monks could own, say, a fruit tree, and a Christian who wanted to make the donation of a vineyard to a monastery could only donate it to an individual monk. The monastery would not own the property and, what with all the vagaries of inheritance, there would be no stable property basis for the monasteries' continued existence (Kermeli 2008: 194).

But the monasteries did survive and they survived because Ottoman officials – with Ebussuud at the top but including many others as well – decided to compromise. At Mount Athos and at other monasteries (the order for the confiscation seems to have been sent out to every monastery, at least in the Balkans) the monks were forced to relinquish their private control over the land; it was now registered as state land and integrated into the standard *timar* system. However, they were allowed to buy back all the property on the land – the vineyards, the windmills, the orchards, and so on and so forth – and to own it as a trust, as a *vakıf* – with the legal stratagem that the beneficiaries must be travelers and the poor, rather than churches and monasteries. In this way Islamic law was stretched to accommodate the collective nature of Christian monasticism. This accommodation, involving as it did complicated legal reasoning, was worked out at the very top, in Istanbul. In her study of how the monks of St. John's monastery on Patmos weathered this affair, Eugenia Kermeli has shown how compromises were also made at the local level. The judge on the nearby island of Kos (where all the documents were drawn up and signed) quietly inserted some rather glaring irregularities into the contracts. Most importantly, he allowed the properties in question to be made over to trusts fifteen days before the fisc actually put them up for sale, in blatant contravention of all Islamic law, which requires that only property that one owns absolutely can be endowed. The judge did this to make sure that other potential buyers would not be able to buy the property and thus disrupt the compromise required to keep the monasteries intact (Kermeli 2008: 197).

In their fight with the sultan and his agents, the monks had a major weapon that, in a pre-modern empire such as the Ottoman one, was bound to be effective. In the course of the negotiations the monks of Dionysiou Monastery on Mount Athos wrote the following:

> If you do not order an imperial document of confirmation, we will sell our possessions and pay back the gold we borrowed and we will scatter all around the world; it is certain that our monasteries will be deserted and our taxes, which we customarily pay in a lump sum (maktu') each year will be lost. (Kermeli 2008: 194)

So, a compromise was reached. At the same time, we must not underestimate both the traumatic experience itself, as the monasteries had to fight for their very survival, and the fact that they had to buy back their properties at a tremendous cost. In order to do so they had to borrow money and redouble their efforts at raising alms.

How should we think about the crisis of the monasteries? Colin Imber says emphatically that Ebussuud's intention was not to destroy monastic life in the empire but rather to "bring the legal status of their possessions into conformity with Ottoman feudal law and with the Hanafi law of trusts." He also suggests that the sultan was already planning the invasion of Cyprus and was motivated by the cash windfall that the crisis, in fact, produced for the state (Imber 1997: 160–1).

It is difficult to know what Ebussuud's intentions were. Although Imber says he was not interested in destroying the monasteries, his initial position – that monastic *vakıfs* could not be allowed – would have done just that. What actually happened, as Kermeli so carefully shows, was a mundane process of negotiation between center and periphery, resulting in the compromise described above. It would be helpful to know how other populations responded to Ebussuud's reforms; we know, for instance, that tax payers were unhappy about the legal argument he made that allowed for tithing rates higher than the customary 10 percent (Imber 1990: 183). Interestingly, it is historians of Ottoman Christians who have done the most work on resistance to Ebussuud's reforms, and the comparison between Muslim and Christian reactions has not yet been made. This broader perspective is necessary before we can decide whether we should think of the crisis of the monasteries as part of the withdrawal of special rights and privileges that had been granted to Christians in an earlier, less self-consciously Islamic age, or whether the episode was part of a broader assault by a newly powerful state on customary arrangements across the empire.

Whatever the intentions of the state it does seem that this confrontation with the monasteries – as with the conversion of Pammakaristos – was taken by at least some sectors of the Muslim population as giving permission to attack Christian populations. The monastery of St. John Prodromos, north of Serres, was pillaged by *medrese* students in 1570–1, that is, exactly when monasteries across the Balkan world were fighting for their survival. It is hard to believe that this was coincidental (Petmezas 1996a: 440).

In a later chapter we will see that in the middle of the next century Christians built several entirely new churches in the important city of Bursa, to the complete indifference of the local authorities. Yet in the wake of the fire of 1660, which destroyed two-thirds of Istanbul, the treatment of Christians who wanted to simply rebuild churches that had already been there was much harsher (Baer 2008: 96–101). In other words, just as Fatih Mehmet's appointment of Gennadios as patriarch in 1454 did not mean a steady and reliable relationship between the sultans and the church from that day forward, so too Ottoman policy toward churches and monasteries was contingent and must always be undersood within its particular context.

Sixteenth-century society

Having reviewed, now, the numerous and varied issues that pushed the empire in a more Islamic direction in this period, we can look at the developments discussed in the first chapter from a slightly different angle; namely, that the same century that saw a new and sweeping push to enforce (Muslim) religious orthodoxy and the rule of the *şeriat* also witnessed a burst of ecclesiastical construction. One eminent Byzantine historian has even called the sixteenth century a "Golden Age" for church architecture in the Balkans, particularly in Bosnia, Serbia, and mainland Greece (Ćurčić 2010: 792).

The confluence of these two trends suggests several important things about the empire and the place of Christians within it. First, in the Ottoman Balkans it was always in the cities that battles were fought over space, both real and symbolic. The large churches that were built were almost all monastic, that is, in the countryside. We can see the contrast if we recall Dousiko monastery, discussed in the first chapter. The impressive monastic church was erected in the sixteenth century without any impediment from the authorities. But just a few decades later, the Ottoman governor of nearby Trikala erected the impressive Kurşun (lead) mosque, based on a design by Sinan, even though the Muslim population of the city was quite modest. The intent was to mark the Ottoman presence in the city (Ćurčić 2010: 797).

As I said earlier, the fact that the monasteries were in the countryside does not mean in any way that they were somehow outside of Ottoman control or, more broadly, Ottoman society. There is the overwhelming documentary trail, which shows regular petitioning and negotiating with the Ottoman authorities, as well as artistic evidence that shows the influence of Ottoman aesthetic preferences. At the monastery dedicated to St. Nicholas at Ano Vathia in Euboea, built in 1570, the church exterior was covered with sculpted rosettes and cypresses, an Ottoman motif that is often found at tombs and fountains. Expensive Iznik tiles were placed in the masonry, showing not only wealth on the part of the monastery but an acute awareness of imperial aesthetic trends (Kiel 1990: 412) Similarly, the Church of the Panagia at the monastery of

St. Dimitrios, on the eastern slopes of Mount Ossa in Thessaly, can be dated to the sixteenth century precisely because its carved details show so many affinities with Ottoman architectural details from the same period (Ćurčić 2010: 793).

Second, not only was there a good deal of church construction in the sixteenth century, but it was of a uniformly high quality. This is a clear reflection of the relative peace, stability, and prosperity that characterized the period (Ćurčić 2010: 792). What this suggests is that the importance of overall economic conditions should not be underestimated; whatever the agenda emanating from the center, in a prosperous society there was room for the assertion of Christian identity.

When thinking about the coincidence of an Islamizing agenda and a golden age of Christian monasticism, the most fascinating question is also the most difficult one to answer: was there perhaps a relationship between the two? Let us remember that state initiatives vis-à-vis the empire's Muslims had a disciplining aspect to them; every village was to have a mosque and those refusing to perform the congregational prayers would be punished. In the same period we have a series of orders emanating from the patriarchate, commanding smaller monasteries to organize themselves internally along the lines of the monasteries on Mount Athos (Vogiatzis 1995: 35). Is it possible that the patriarch shared Ebussuud's concern for pious observance, perhaps was even encouraged by Ebussuud to take an interest in such matters out of the latter's concern for what we can call, roughly, law and order? Admittedly there is, at present anyway, no evidence for this but it is not as far-fetched as it might appear. The fact that the patriarch turned to the sultan for help in punishing clergy who married people outside the rules of the church shows that the patriarch was concerned with the behavior of ordinary Christians and that the sultan was willing to help him in this regard (Konortas 1998: 332). We can imagine that Ebussuud would be particularly sympathetic to the issue of tighter church supervision of marriage, given his own interest in bringing marriage under the control of the state. He gave explicit permission for the construction of new churches in *zimmi* villages without a *mektep* (elementary school) or mosque (Necipoğlu 2005: 523). More generally, Ebussuud was adamantly opposed to religious mixing. In one of his *fetva* responses that touched upon both Christian and Jewish life in the empire he said "The religious communities should be separate." In another he wrote that Muslims should not speak a language used by non-Muslims, lest the line between the two communities become blurred (Masters 2001: 26, 30). There is overwhelming evidence that the upper clergy of the Orthodox Church shared this point of view.[8]

It is also possible that the burst of church building was a response to the religious polemics of the age; at a time when Charles V and Süleyman were anticipating the imminent triumph of one world religion – Catholicism for the former, Islam for the latter – could it be that the Orthodox Church felt the need to make a statement? This is what Vogiatzis suggests in his 1995 study of church building and church architecture in the sixteenth-century Balkans.[9] Working against this hypothesis is the fact that Orthodox elites seem to have been relatively quiet during the millenarian age. This makes sense; given the end of the Byzantine Empire, and the many triumphs of both the Catholic Habsburgs and the Muslim Ottomans, one would not expect eastern Christians of any stripe to try and enter the race. A more activist church begins to emerge only toward the end of the sixteenth century, as evidenced by the appearance of neo-martyrologies and the rise of apocalyptic writings (Argyriou 1987). This is not to say that individual Christians were not swept up in the millenarian fervor of the age.[10] We shall consider this shortly when we turn to the topic of conversion in the sixteenth century. Nevertheless, when trying to explain the flourishing of Byzantine monasticism in the sixteenth century the most likely explanation remains the propitious conditions created by peace and prosperity. The emphasis on Islamic orthodoxy emanating from the center did not stand in the way of this.

Conversion to Islam

So far we have dwelled on the imperial capital and the great centers of Christian monasticism in the Balkan countryside. I have argued that the increasing emphasis on Islamic orthodoxy neither dislodged the Greek elite in Istanbul nor inhibited the flourishing of monastic life. It is a picture of continuity and accomplishment. But if we turn our gaze to the cities of the Balkan peninsula, a rather different picture emerges. The Muslim urban population grew throughout the sixteenth century and many of these Muslims were former Christians who had abandoned their faith to embrace the religion of the conqueror.

An older tradition of scholarship equated the Ottoman conquest of the Balkans in the fifteenth century with the forced conversion of the Christian population. The patient work of many scholars, for decades now, in the Ottoman archives has made it clear beyond the shadow of a doubt that conversion became a significant phenomenon only in the sixteenth century (Minkov 2004).

Let us first sketch out the map of conversion in this period. The detailed surveys (*tahrirs*) that the Ottomans kept show that, across the Balkans, no more than 2.5 percent of the population was Muslim by the end of the fifteenth century. But by the 1520s, when the next series of surveys was carried out, the number of tax-paying households that were Muslim had jumped to 22.2 percent, the vast majority of them in the cities (Minkov 2004: 40–1). Throughout the century, the Muslim urban population continued to climb. In a survey of twenty-nine Balkan cities in the second half of the sixteenth century Muslims account for an astonishing 60 percent of the urban population, while Christians are at 36 percent (Todorov 1983: 54). The important Macedonian town of Uskub (Skopje) had 623 Muslim and 268 Christian families around 1520; in 1546, Muslim households had risen to 1,004 while Christian hearths had declined to 216. There were also 32 new Jewish households (Lopasic 1994: 170). Also in Macedonia, Serres' Muslim population reached 67 percent by the end of the sixteenth century. Further north, the Muslim population of Sofia more than doubled in twenty-five years (Barkan 1957: 34–5). And in the Anatolian city of Trabzon, former capital of the Empire of Trabzon, the process began rather late but then proceeded swiftly; in 1523, only 15 percent of the population was Muslim, but just thirty years later that number had climbed to nearly half of the city's residents (Lowry 2009: 152).

How much of this changing religious profile can be explained through conversion? This is a difficult question to answer, as the population registers do not always identify converts. Working back from estimates of other Muslim populations in the Balkans at this time, Spyros Vryonis has estimated that 50 percent of the Muslims recorded in the 1520s registers (at which point they were 22 percent of the total Balkan population) were converts, and a more recent study puts the number even higher, at almost 70 percent (Vryonis 1972: 165; Minkov 2004: 47). We do have studies of several cities in the sixteenth century and these suggest that those numbers are a little high, given that in this period conversion was more prevalent in the urban areas than it was in the countryside. In 1500, which is admittedly quite early, 33 percent of the Muslims in Tarnovo were converts. In twenty-four Macedonian towns in 1569–80, converts accounted for, on average, 35 percent of the Muslim population, and in Bitola in the middle of the century one-quarter of the town's Muslims were apostates from Christianity (Dávid 1995: 76). Even if these numbers are lower than the estimates cited above, we are still talking about a very substantial population.

This process, however, was not uniform across the Balkans. As mentioned in the first chapter, Turkish colonization and then indigenous Muslim conversion concentrated in the eastern Balkans (Istanbul's hinterland) and, beyond that, Macedonia, Bosnia-Herzegovina, and Thessaly. So, too, cities in these areas were more heavily Muslim than cities elsewhere on the peninsula. Further west and south Ottoman cities continued to have very significant Christian populations. In the first half of the sixteenth century there were eleven Balkan cities whose population was over 90 percent Christian (Todorov 1983: 55).

To explain voluntary Christian conversion to Islam during the Ottoman centuries, a wide variety of factors – economic, social, and religious – must be taken into account. Moreover, their relative importance fluctuates over time. When it comes to the sixteenth-century conversions that I have been discussing, I believe that the most important explanation is also the one that has not yet received the attention that it deserves. Conversion in this period is inseparable from a more general process of urbanization, as overcrowded mountain hamlets emptied out into the cities.

Very little has been written about migration from the mountains to the lowlands in the sixteenth century. In fact, there is an enduring narrative that asserts that Christian populations fled into the mountains upon the Ottoman advance and did not start to come down until the eighteenth century.[11] But such a move toward the plains makes sense because we know there was rapid population growth in the sixteenth-century Ottoman Empire, as there was across the Mediterranean, and fifteenth-century Ottoman taxation registers show dense settlement in the mountains of the Balkan peninsula (Kiel 1996: 316). Braudel and others have shown that population saturation was a reoccurring phenomenon at higher altitudes, at which point some of the uplanders at least would leave to seek their fortunes in the coastal plains. Therefore, it seems more likely that an exodus from the lowlands happened not once, but twice; first in the fifteenth century and then again in the seventeenth century. In between there was a reverse movement and this is critical in understanding conversion to Islam, as well as other aspects of the sixteenth century.

The town of Sevlievo in today's northern Bulgaria shows these processes at work. Sevlievo was an entirely new settlement that emerged spontaneously in the early Ottoman period in the middle of a fertile plain where five roads met. Turkish colonists were the original settlers but over the course of the sixteenth century Christians from the surrounding villages moved in. In due course they converted to Islam (Kiel 1988: 126). Antonia Zhelyazkova, in her study of Vlachs in northeastern Bosnia, argues for a very clear connection: "As long as they stayed in the mountains, they kept their faith; it was their settlement in the plains that led to their Islamization" (Zhelyazkova 1994: 194).

Something very similar might well have happened in the Greek lands. Eleni Gara, who has worked for many years now with the voluminous court records from the town of Veroia in Macedonia, notes that sixteenth-century converts tended not to come from the town's rather substantial Christian population but rather from new arrivals, who came possibly with the idea of trying their luck (Gara 2007: 56). In the same century, the Christian population of Larissa (Yenişehir) began to rise, almost certainly because of the overcrowding of Thessaly's mountain settlements (Sdrolia 2008: 196). In Cappadocia in Anatolia it was the Christians who headed into town from the villages who became the converts (Vryonis 1971: 451).

The stories of the neo-martyrs support this theory. The neo-martyrs – whom we will discuss in some detail in a later chapter – were Christians who died for their faith, either because they refused to convert to Islam or because, having converted, they then insisted on returning to their original faith, an act that was punishable by death. Accounts of the neo-martyrs began to be written down in the late sixteenth century, although the first comprehensive compilation was not drawn up until the 1700s (Krstić 2011: 123). The salient point here is that stories almost all begin in an urban milieu, and just as often concern Christians who were working as artisans.[12] The martyrdom of George of Sofia is typical in this regard, and let us note as well that he was a migrant to the city. He was born in the small town of Kratovo, in today's Macedonia, which sits on the western slopes of Mount Osogovo. At some point his mother sent him to Sofia, to live in the home of a priest by the name of Father Peter. In Sofia, George worked as a goldsmith and it was conversations in his shop with a *müfti* that set in motion the fateful events that eventually led to his martyrdom (Vaporis 2000: 47).

In general we possess only glimpses of urban transformation, including conversion to Islam, in the sixteenth-century Balkans. But we are lucky enough to possess one case study, and that is Heath Lowry's 1981 study of the city of Trabzon (Lowry 2009). Trabzon, of course, is not a Balkan city but, location aside, it went through many of the same historical processes that I have been describing for the Balkans. As with the Balkan cities, it was a rapidly growing place; its population nearly doubled between 1553 and 1583, from 6,100 to 10,575 (Lowry 2009: 120). At the time of its conquest (in 1461) it was a Christian city that was overwhelmingly Greek Orthodox, and in the beginning conversion was minimal; it only became a significant phenomenon in the sixteenth century. By the end of that century Trabzon had become a majority Muslim city but a large Greek Orthodox community remained.[13] Therefore, Trabzon is eminently comparable to Balkan cities and is very well suited to shed light on developments that elsewhere remain in the shadows. And, as we shall see, a close study of one city suggests the questions that have yet to be resolved (or even raised) about the implications of an Islamizing agenda for the empire's Christians.

In 1486 a quarter of a century had passed since Fatih Mehmet had conquered Trabzon, but it remained very much a Greek Orthodox city. Sixty-five percent of the city's residents were Greek Orthodox while the Muslim community was under 20 percent. Because historians have frequently been stymied in their efforts to determine whether a new Muslim community is the result of immigration or conversion, it is particularly valuable that Lowry has been able to determine that the vast majority of Muslims in 1486 (nearly 80 percent) were settlers from other towns in Anatolia, and involuntary settlers at that. That is, they had been forcibly deported to Trabzon through the practice known as *sürgün*, a fact that suggests that Fatih Mehmet viewed the city as most important (Lowry 2009: 29). Only a very small percentage of the Christian population (less than 3 percent) had chosen to convert to Islam at this point (Lowry 2009: 152). In 1486, too, the Muslim and the Christian communities were physically separate for the most part; all Muslim neighborhoods were within the city walls while almost all Christians were in the suburbs that lay to the east and west of the city. This conforms to what we know about settlement patterns in the Balkan cities, where Turkish Muslim newcomers also chose to live in their own neighborhoods. There is a difference, however, which is that in Trabzon, at least initially, Muslims settled within the walled city in what were presumably the oldest neighborhoods. In the Balkans our limited evidence shows that the new arrivals preferred to build entirely new developments, leaving the Christians in place in the older quarters.[14]

The difference might be explained by the fact that the walled city in Trabzon was depopulated and thus available for settlement. And this, in turn, could reflect the fact that Trabzon had been, after all, an imperial city. The emperor, David Komnenos, was sent packing to Istanbul by Mehmet, along with all of his retinue, and they must have lived within the walls. Muslim settlement, then, was dictated by practicality, in Trabzon and elsewhere. Whatever the explanation, Trabzon does bear out the argument that separation was the norm. It also shows us something else. I had said that almost all of the city's Christians were in the suburbs. The exception was the Christian neighborhood of Orta Hisar (Middle Castle), which was within the walls (Lowry 2009: 38). This suggests that – absent a rebellious population – the preference for separate living was not absolute. The walled city, it seems, was largely available for new settlement but if there was an existing Christian neighborhood it was not going to be uprooted.

Finally, in 1486 Trabzon continued to be not just a Christian city, but a Greek one as well. The evidence for this is that in naming the neighborhoods the scribe continued to use their Greek names, such as *meso kastro* and *meso portis* (Lowry 2009: 56). Any study of the Greek world under the Ottomans, such as this one, must pause for a moment on this point. There is a strong tendency in the literature to assume that the religious divide between Muslims and Christians was also a linguistic one, such that anything Muslim cannot by definition be Greek as well. As this detail from Trabzon suggests – and there are other examples – this was not necessarily the case. Just as Islamization and Turkification are two distinct processes, the relationship between conversion to Islam and de-Hellenization was not a straightforward one and it deserves the attention that it has not yet received.[15]

The next survey was conducted in 1523 and it shows a city that remained solidly Christian; the Muslim population had actually dropped, from 19 percent to 14 percent of the city's residents. This distinguishes Trabzon from cities in the Balkans where, although the Muslim population at this time was still small, it was steadily climbing upward. The most likely explanation is that Muslims continued to find Trabzon unattractive; not only were new people not coming in, but it seems that some of those who had been deported to the city had managed to flee back to their home cities (Lowry 2009: 75).

Did the Ottomans see this as a problem? And, if so, how did they react? Our point of departure must be the astonishing turnaround by the time the next survey was taken in 1553. Muslims were now the largest group, constituting 47 percent of the population. The Greek Orthodox were next at 42 percent with the other Christians filling out the rest (Lowry 2009: 116). Was this the result of social engineering on the part of Istanbul, or rather the end result of processes bubbling up from below, similar to what I argued for Balkan cities? One of the essential mysteries concerns the fate of the Christian population between 1523 and 1553. In sharp contrast to the Balkans, the Christian population in Trabzon dropped sharply, with the Greek Orthodox suffering the most of all, a dramatic fall-off of 47 percent (Lowry 2009: 103). Although we cannot know for sure, Lowry makes a persuasive case that a large number of them were deported – again, the practice known as *sürgün* – to Istanbul sometime before 1540. In that year a survey of the capital city's population listed "the community of Trabzon" in a format that strongly suggests they had been deported. All were Christian. In the meantime, entire Christian neighborhoods had disappeared from Trabzon (Lowry 2009: 104–5).

Even if we are persuaded, as I am, that this is what happened, the question of motivation remains. At one point Lowry suggests that this was most likely a maritime community – they were settled next to the sea in Istanbul – and the sultan was looking to them to help keep the capital supplied with fish (Lowry 2009: 105). But elsewhere he offers a different opinion, that the sultan must have been alarmed at the continuing low numbers of Muslims in Trabzon and deported the Christians as a way of giving the Muslims a chance to prevail (Lowry 2009: 165). Through his examination of the 1553 survey Lowry has been able to demonstrate that over one-third of the Muslims were newcomers to Trabzon. How can we explain this? Again, Lowry seems to be in two minds. Trabzon was a staging area for the wars against the Safavids and, he argues, this must have created employment opportunities that finally made the city an attractive place for Muslims. But elsewhere he says that Muslim settlement was probably officially supported, with the deliberate goal of making the city more Muslim, even as he acknowledges that he has no proof of this (Lowry 2009: 107, 165).

In any event, the city's Muslim population continued to grow. By 1583, the date of the last survey that we possess, Muslims were the majority population. By this time immigration had slowed to a trickle so virtually all of this growth must be explained through conversion (Lowry 2009: 146).

Alongside the shifting demographics, other trends wound their way through the course of the sixteenth century. The physical separation between the Christian and Muslim populations broke down as Muslim neighborhoods, no longer confined to the walled city, appeared in the eastern and western suburbs. The reverse, however, did not happen and the Armenians and the Roman Catholics soon came to be identified with just one neighborhood each. The Greeks occupied a position somewhere in the middle. One can imagine that this must have had a certain psychological effect; possibly the Muslims came to be seen as the norm while the Christians, although still numerous, were increasingly viewed as the exception. Turkification slowly advanced – the place names in the surveys are increasingly Turkish ones – but even at the end of the century Greek must still have been the lingua franca. The number of Christian clergy, relative to the population, dwindled while the reverse happened with the Muslim community; at the time of the 1583 survey there was one imam for every 49 Muslims but just one priest for every 480 Christians (Lowry 2009: 143). Lowry asserts "a very active missionary spirit present in Trabzon at this time," based on the fact that *zaviyes* (dervish lodges) were built in predominantly Christian neighborhoods; similarly churches were converted and mosques built in areas that lacked a significant Muslim congregation (Lowry 2009: 166). Comparative studies of other cities (most logically, it would seem, in the Balkans) would help in understanding the significance of the location of *zaviyes* and mosques, as well as of converted churches.

A comparative approach would be helpful in answering all sorts of questions. Already we can compare some of what is known about Trabzon to other urban centers and see differences. One very important difference is the fact that, whereas in the Balkans converts tended to be new arrivals from the countryside, in Trabzon converts seem to have come from the existing urban community. Lowry discusses a convert named Haci Kasim who established a new Muslim quarter in the eastern suburbs sometime between 1486 and 1523 (Lowry 2009: 153). It would seem that in this case conversion also meant a break with one's neighborhood of birth. But we know that that was not always the case. Catholic converts in Bosnia, for example, continued to live with their Catholic relatives in the extended family arrangements known as the *zadruga*. Indeed, one of the most valuable aspects of Lowry's study is the way his close attention to detail makes us aware of the sheer variety of urban experience even within one city. In 1583 the neighborhood of Cami-i Atik (the old mosque) – in a desirable location right in the middle of the walled city with a settled Muslim population, very few immigrants, and no recent converts – must have felt entirely different from the eastern suburbs, still very heavily Christian, where converts could account for almost 40 percent of the fast-growing Muslim community (Lowry 2009: 162).

Let us return, now, to the larger imperial context. The transformation of Balkan cities into centers of Islam, with many converts in the mix, coincided with Istanbul's promotion of Islamic piety across the empire. It might seem logical that there was a link but I think the evidence for this is thin. Ebussuud's agenda did not include the conversion of Christians. Sixteenth-century conversions were more the end result of social processes that began with migration (although not in the case of Trabzon), rather than policies emanating from Istanbul. The limited but valuable evidence we have from the accounts of the neo-martyrs accords well with Tijana Krstić's argument in her 2007 study of religious conversion in the Ottoman Empire. The state, she writes, has been given too much importance in the literature on conversion; the most important people in an individual's decision to convert were not state bureaucrats but rather the Muslim friends, neighbors, and co-workers who already surrounded the potential convert (Krstić 2007: 89). Admittedly, we need to think more about where we locate the state. When Lowry writes of a missionary spirit in Trabzon, and cites the numerous *zaviyes* as proof, this begs the question as to where we should locate *zaviyes* within Ottoman society.

The fate of the cities is directly linked to the fate of the Greeks and Greek civilization. This is because across the Balkans the cities had traditionally been the preserve of Hellenism, even if the countryside was Slavic. Thus a traveler to the Macedonian town of Serres in the middle of the sixteenth century commented that the Christians in the town spoke "a vulgar Greek" while the villages around it had a mixed Greek and Slavic population (Petmezas 1996a: 444). It is interesting to see how the Vlachs can serve as a bellwether of the decline, and then the recovery, of urban Hellenism during the Ottoman period. When the Vlachs moved to urban centers in the sixteenth century their conversion to Islam quickly followed. But by the eighteenth century the cities had resumed their traditional role as centers of Hellenism (for Christians); some of the most famous figures of the Greek Enlightenment were Vlachs who, having left their villages behind, rapidly acquired Greek language and Greek culture.[16]

And yet there is little evidence to suggest that the church – that is, the patriarchate in Istanbul – had a strong reaction to the ever-rising number of conversions. The first neo-martyrologies, which functioned as a kind of "theological ecclesiastical propaganda" designed to prevent conversion, are not copied down until the end of the sixteenth century and the number of neo-martyrs in the seventeenth century was much greater than that of the century before.[17]

One explanation might be found in yet another paradox of the sixteenth century: yes, Muslim urban life was flourishing, but Christians in the cities were also doing quite well, although not to the same extent. In a period of rapid population growth, cities were growing even faster than the towns (Zachariadou 1996: 111; Todorov 1983: 66–7). Perhaps this was why the ever-increasing Muslim population of the town of Serres did not prevent the consolidation of a prosperous Christian community, as evidenced by the generous gifts that the community made to the nearby monastery of Prodromos. The metropolitan of Serres enjoyed a high rank in the ecclesiastical hierarchy, and church documents describe the sixteenth-century town as "honored, great, having many active and well-born leading members of the community" (Odorico 1996: 277). Church decoration in Veroia similarly testifies to Christian prosperity (Gara 2007: 55). Along these same lines let us remember from Chapter 1 that Zachariadou (1996: 106–7) speaks of "the flourishing of the metropolitans" in this period, by which she means their emergence as artistic patrons; Kiel adds that bishops were prominent as founders of a number of the largest churches in central Greece (Kiel 1990: 410). Bishoprics and metropolitanates, of course, were urban institutions.

Not all migrants, after all, converted to Islam; Synadinos, the priest of Serres whose chronicle of life in the town is an invaluable, and rare, source on Balkan urban life, was born in a nearby village in 1600 and sent to Serres to learn a trade in 1615 (Odorico 1996: 14). Further south in the Greek lands, where Muslims were few and far between, migration must have been a boon to the vitality of Christian urban life. In some cases we can even speak of Christian power vis-à-vis the Muslims. In sixteenth-century Trikala the wealth of the Greek community was such that they routinely appointed and dismissed Ottoman officials (Mantzana 2008: 206). Visiting Athens in the late seventeenth century the Ottoman traveler Evliya Çelebi said that the *reaya* (by which he meant the Christians) were dominant and had little respect for the Muslim population.[18] Christian power is presented in a more positive light in the obituary that Synadinos wrote for his father. He was on good terms with everybody, Muslim and Christian alike, and the *kadi* of the town used to say "Whatever the priest says, we accept it as reasonable" (Strauss 2002: 208).

The cities, then, were the site of many different social processes: in-migration, conversion, population growth, and physical transformation as new neighborhoods changed the shape of medieval settlements. Despite our being able to identify all these developments, the urban experience is not easily characterized and remains poorly understood. Balkan cities in the Ottoman period – particularly in the early centuries – are commonly described as bastions of Islamic culture, surrounded by an Orthodox countryside. This fails to account for the diversity of the urban experience. It also leaves unexplored the lived experience of the seeming contradiction raised by rapid Islamization and Christian prosperity in the very same place. Did Christians feel under siege watching their co-religionists convert or did the general prosperity of the time blunt the response? Perhaps the tendency of converts to be newcomers, migrants from the countryside, rendered their conversion a matter of little concern in the older Christian neighborhoods of the town? At this point we can only speculate but the following is certain: the cities were the sites of rapid social change and experimentation and the two populations, Muslim and Christian, were rubbing up against each other in ways they had not before. Heath Lowry speaks of "an atmosphere of continuous change and instability" and rightly concludes: "In short, the approximately 125 years covered by this study can only be characterized as 'a state of flux' for the city and its several generations of inhabitants" (Lowry 2009: 206–7). This must have been a dramatic period for Balkan cities as well, which makes it even more remarkable that we know so little.

Individual conversions were not the only source of contact. Evliya Çelebi saw a city divided by religion, but we know that as early as the sixteenth century some Athenian Christian women had contracted marriages with Muslim men (Faroqhi 2005: 388). Mixed marriages and, thus, mixed families were a phenomenon across the Balkans throughout the Ottoman period. And we now realize that converts often remained in contact with their original community, at least for a time, and thus conversion had the initial effect of increasing interaction across the religious line. We have already mentioned the example of converts continuing to live with their Catholic relatives in the *zadruga* in Bosnia, but even further south in relatively placid Veroia relatives stayed in close touch (Lopasic 1994: 168; Gara 2005/6: 165).[19] We must also bear in mind the difference between conversion to Islam and Turkification. Let us recall that in Trabzon at the turn of the seventeenth century, nearly a hundred and fifty years after the conquest, Greek was most likely still the lingua franca of the city (Lowry 2009: 164). For a time, then, the two religious communities would have shared a common language. Was this the case as well in the Balkans? Considering the high number of converts, as well as the preponderance of the Greek language in urban areas, it must have been the case that Greek had a more prominent place in Balkan cities in the sixteenth century than has been realized.[20] Moving beyond the question of language, the larger issue of convert culture remains. The "survival" of Christian practices in Balkan Islam has generated an extensive bibliography (and will be discussed in a later chapter), but cultural practices are not a matter of religion alone. Machiel Kiel has argued that artistic production was more conservative, thus more in line with Byzantine prototypes, in areas where Muslims were mostly local converts. "It is fascinating," he writes, "how much the ethnic composition of an area has determined the nature of its taste for Ottoman art" (Kiel 1979: 24).

Although the settlement of Turkish populations from Anatolia in the Balkans in the fifteenth century was an important step in the re-urbanization of the peninsula's cities, their contact with existing populations was minimal. Residential segregation was the norm and the new arrivals built their own neighborhoods, away from the historic center (Argo 2008: 268). Conversion, when it occurred, took place within the military milieu as Balkan nobles and their retinues joined the Ottoman armies. Ordinary Christians were far removed from these developments (Krstić 2004: 14). This social distance broke down in the sixteenth century; in urban centers across the Balkans Christians and Muslims (whether Turkish in origin or converts) began to live in much closer contact with each other. These developments were not part of any sort of state-directed effort, despite the heightened emphasis on Islamic piety in this period, but rather were a reflection of socio-economic pressures and opportunities bubbling up from below. In fact, as we shall see, by the seventeenth century both Muslim and Christian elites had become uneasy about what they saw as the collapsing of boundaries between the two communities. It is after 1500, then, that we see the beginning of a long experiment in co-existence in Balkan society. Ironically, it is in the same century that the intense Christian participation in the Ottoman military that was so characteristic of the fifteenth century begins to recede.

Christians in the service of the state

From 1400 through 1600 the *timar*-holding cavalry known as the *sipahis* and the famous (or infamous) infantry troops the janissaries were at the heart of the Ottoman army. We have seen that in the fifteenth century Christian *sipahis* were very numerous, in some areas even the majority. Given the centrality of the *sipahis* in both warfare and administration, it is not an exaggeration to say that Christian manpower was essential in the early days of the empire. Christian *sipahis* became a rarity in the course of the sixteenth century, not through any concerted move against them, but rather through their gradual conversion to Islam (İnalcık 1954: 116; Kiel 1985: 67). We do not know the state's attitude toward this change; probably it was seen as a natural progression; but a rare glimpse of popular attitudes, admittedly from late in the sixteenth century, suggests that at least in some places Christian *sipahis* were no longer acceptable. Faced with complaints that *zimmis* were serving in the fortress of Kütahya in Anatolia, the sultan felt it necessary to launch an inquiry into their origins (İnalcık 1953: 248).

Despite the tendency in the literature to write off Christian military forces after 1500, further down the ranks participation continued to be significant. We have seen already, in Chapter 1, Barkan's (1957) figures that in 1520 an impressive 90,000 Christians were serving the Ottomans in some, usually modest, military capacity. The Christian *voynuks*, who were used particularly along the frontier, maintained their military importance up until the establishment of a more permanent Ottoman presence in Hungary (1541), at which point more settled conditions rendered them less vital. They did continue to enjoy privileges in their role as caretakers of the horses belonging to the imperial stables (Murphey 2012). It is important, however, to consider the *voynuks* within the larger context of the sixteenth century, because then it becomes clear that their declining importance in the military cannot be solely attributed to their being Christian. Over the course of that century the Ottomans gradually discontinued their use of all auxiliary forces, whether they be the Christian *voynuks* or the Muslim *yayas* and *müsellems*, in both Anatolia and the Balkans (Imber 2002: 266–7; Faroqhi 2012). By 1600 a chronicler noted that all these groups were now registered among the ordinary tax-paying subjects of the empire, that is, they were henceforth *reaya* (Imber 2002: 267).

Let us recall Heath Lowry's narrative of the sixteenth century, which is that with the addition of the Arab lands to the empire the rights and privileges of the empire's Christian subjects were withdrawn. I think the more persuasive narrative is that there was a withdrawal of privileges and special status across the empire and across all population groups. This was part of the standardization (always relative in a premodern empire) of rule that was so characteristic of the reign of Sultan Süleyman. Its net result was a much sharper distinction between the *reaya* and the *askeri* class, but this distinction did not have a religious hue.

On the other hand, there is no denying the fact that the demise of Christian *sipahis* gave the Ottoman miltary a far more uniform character as a Muslim institution; in the sixteenth century Muslims shared *reaya* status with their Christian counterparts but it had become unusual, and was seen as such, for a Christian with *askeri* status to be in the army. The great melting pot of the fifteenth century, where elites across the Balkans could and did join the Ottoman enterprise, was over.

Outside of the military, the picture is more mixed. *Voynuk*, *derbendci*, and *celepkeşan* villages continued to dot the Balkan countryside in the sixteenth century as these groups provided important services to the state. The *martolos*, too, provided internal security right through the seventeenth century and paid no *cizye* (head tax) (Rossi and Griswold 2012). The *voynuk* and the *martolos* were exclusively Christian forces while the *derbendci* and the *celepkeşan* could be Muslim as well.

It is striking that the *voynuks* – who were most prominent in the northern Balkans, thus in the Bulgarian and, especially, the Serbian lands – were losing their *reaya* status just as Serbian influence in Istanbul was reaching its height. It was in 1557 that the Serbian patriarchate was re-established, and the same pattern that we saw earlier with the Greeks – whereby high-ranking clerics had close kinsmen, now Muslim, within the Ottoman elite – was now repeating itself with the Serbs.[21] Although individual *devşirme* could certainly exercise influence on behalf of their community – it was the Serbian *devşirme* Grand Vezir Sokollović, after all, who was responsible for the restoration of the patriarchate – they could not stand against powerful currents such as the reorganization of the army. Yet at the same time the fact that the Serbian experience so closely replicated that of the Greeks suggests that much had stayed the same at the level of elite politics in Istanbul. As the Ottomans expanded into Hungary, Serbs became even more vital in Ottoman defense – in 1545, there were 1,526 Serbian Christian soldiers serving at the fortress of Esztergom – and Serbian influence in the northern Balkans was underlined by the fact that Ottoman correspondence with Hungary, Wallachia, Venice, and Ragusa was written in Serbian (Hadrovics 1947: 48). All of this paid off in terms of influence in Istanbul, the nerve center of the empire.

As the Serbians were busy capitalizing on the empire's expansion into central Europe, the Greeks were not left empty handed. In the same remarkable period of conquests that began with Selim I (1512–20) the Ottomans expanded not only north but south, into the Aegean world that had been the stronghold of Latin Christendom ever since the Fourth Crusade in 1204. In the islands Catholic lords ruled over Greek-speaking Orthodox peasants, and thus the Ottoman conquests brought the Greek world front and center once again. In a century of Islamic piety, the sultans continued to hand the Greek Orthodox patriarch in Istanbul victories over Catholicism.

Notes

1. But see Pfeiffer (2014) for a groundbreaking argument, based on extensive research in both Arab and Ottoman sources, on the cultural effects, in both the Arab lands and the Ottoman capital, of the Ottoman conquest of the Arab lands. Also Casale (2010).
2. Although it is not directly related to our inquiry, it should be noted that Pfeiffer (2014) has shown definitively that no influx of Arab scholars occurred.
3. Matschke writes that "they created a very special kind of historical continuity in a period of enormous change" (Matschke 2002: 106).
4. Zachariadou (1996: 69). I thank Nikos Panou for helping me with the translation of this phrase.
5. Ahmet III went ahead and built the Blue Mosque anyway but he was severely criticized for doing so.
6. Necipoğlu puts the city's population at the end of the sixteenth century at 500,000. This is much higher than most estimates and she does not provide a source (Necipoğlu 2005: 57). A more likely figure is somewhere between 200,000 and 300,000. See Chapter 4, note 3.
7. Machiel Kiel ascribes this confiscation to enthusiasm related to the Muslim millennium, which was just two years away at the time of the event (Kiel 1985: 174).
8. There was, for instance, the attempt throughout the entire Ottoman period to stop Christians from using the Islamic courts.
9. He suggests, for example, that the fervor to build and organize monastic centers might have been related to the wave of conversions to Islam that occurred in the sixteenth century, while acknowledging that the research that could establish this connection has not yet been done (Vogiatzis 1995: 35–8).
10. After all, the portents and signs that flooded Istanbul in the sixteenth century were available for all to see. A Habsburg envoy to the city in 1533 wrote of the sighting of warriors in the sky above Istanbul, "two men-at-arms with lances in their hands, one speaking Latin and the other Turkish" (Finlay 1998: 19).
11. This is very pronounced in the Greek nationalist literature. But William McGrew (1992) assumes the same thing in his environmental study of Mediterranean mountain communities.
12. See the list of their vocations in Vaporis (2000: 5).
13. In 1583, Muslims were 54 percent of the population. Greek Orthodox were 38 percent, with the difference being made up by the Roman Catholics and the Armenians.
14. Here, of course, I am speaking of towns and cities that surrendered (as did Trabzon), rather than those that were taken by force.
15. On the other hand, the relationship between other Orthodox Christians

- such as the Bulgarians and the Albanians – and the Greek language has produced a voluminous literature.
16. The most famous being Iosipos Moisiodax (Kitromilides 2013: 158).
17. There were fifteen recorded cases in the sixteenth century and thirty-one in the seventeenth (Gara 2005/6; Minkov 2004: 83).
18. Strauss (1996: 328). I thank Helen Pfeiffer for translating the Strauss article.
19. According to Selim Deringil, converts kept in contact with the previous community right up until the nineteenth century, when the borders between the two tightened due to nationalism (Deringil 2000: 553).
20. And some convert communities never abandoned Greek, most notably in Ioannina and in Crete.
21. Hadrovics writes that "the Serbianization of the state" reached its height in the mid-sixteenth century (Hadrovics 1947: 48).

CHAPTER 4

The larger Greek world

The end of the Latin east

Ottoman victories in the fifteenth century came at the expense not only of the Byzantines, but of the Latins as well. The Latins were the various Catholic powers – the Venetians in Euboea (Negroponte), the Genoese in Chios, and noble families such as the Sommaripa in the Aegean – that had come in with the Fourth Crusade and were still hanging on as the Ottomans advanced into the Mediterranean world. In 1453 Fatih Mehmet brought an end to the Byzantine Empire but the defeat of Latin power was a much longer affair, with the conquests of Rhodes (1522), Cyprus (1570), and Crete (1669) being the most important milestones in this protracted battle.

Prior to 1453 the Byzantines were famously divided on the question of who was the greater enemy, the "Turks," as they called the Ottomans, or the Catholic west – the Franks, as they were called. For a hundred years the major political schism in Byzantine society was between those who were willing, very reluctantly, to accept union with Rome as the price to pay for western support and those who saw submission to Muslim rule as better than bowing down to the hated Latins. After 1453 that agonizing choice was no longer there and, having suffered the end of Byzantium, the Greeks were in a position to reap one of the benefits of Ottoman strength, which was the ongoing diminishment of Latin power. What had begun in the fifteenth century – the advance of Greek Orthodoxy at the expense of Catholicism – continued into the sixteenth. In the previous chapter I noted that the Ecumenical patriarch did not seem to have a strong reaction to the rising number of conversions after 1500; continued success against the Latins may have been a reason.

Ottoman advances to the north into Hungary favored the Serbs. But when the Ottomans went south they entered into the heartland of the long struggle between western and eastern Christendom. I have already mentioned the case of the island of Andros, where, in the wake of the Ottoman conquest, Orthodox monasteries were built for the first time since 1204. Let us look now more systematically at the conquest of the islands and what it meant for the Ottomans, the patriarch, and the islanders themselves.

The islands of the northeast Aegean – Thassos, Samothrace, Lesvos, and Lemnos – captured the attention of the Ottomans early on and they were all taken within a decade or so of the fall of Istanbul. This makes sense, given how close they were to the entrance to the Dardanelles. In the context of the long war with Venice (1463–79) Mehmet took the island of Euboea (Negroponte) just off the Greek mainland in 1470; it was the first serious defeat inflicted on Venice by the Ottomans. A lull ensued during the reign of Bayezit II, as it did across the empire, and then matters picked up steam again after the conquests of Selim I in the Middle East. His achievements united the southern and northern shores of the eastern Mediterranean under the rule of one sovereign for the first time since the seventh century. This new configuration meant that hostile powers now sat in the middle of the sea-lane that linked the new and vital province of Egypt to the imperial capital. The most fearsome of these were the Knights of St. John on the island of Rhodes, and Süleyman went after them in 1522. After a gratifyingly brief siege he drove out these symbols par excellence of the Crusades and took the rest of the Dodecannese islands while he was at it.

The "Thracian" islands – as Imbros, Thassos, Samothrace, and Lemnos were known – plus Lesvos were distinct from the better-known Cyclades, which were lost forever to the Latins after 1204. Soon after the recovery of Istanbul in 1261 the Byzantines managed to regain control of these islands so vital to the defense of the empire. Therefore, the Orthodox Church was never eclipsed as it was in places like Crete, which experienced nearly half a millennium of Latin rule. For example, the monasteries of Mount Athos and the monastery of St. John the Theologian on Patmos had many holdings on the island of Lemnos in the fourteenth and fifteenth centuries, and documents show the presence of seventy-five Christian sanctuaries prior to the Ottoman conquest in 1479 (Lowry 2002: 141–2). What they did lack was security, and the Byzantines held onto them only with great difficulty. The islands had to endure repeated assaults by both Latin and Turkish forces, as well as ongoing piracy. A Genoese corsair established himself on Lesvos in the middle of the fourteenth century and his descendants transformed themselves into the Gattilusio princes; they took over Lemnos shortly before the fall of Istanbul (Topping 1986).

The final establishment of Ottoman rule (there was some to-ing and fro-ing during the long Ottoman–Venetian war), and the extinction of the Latin threat in the northeastern Aegean, were most significant – for the islanders themselves and for the Ottomans – for the peaceful conditions that were established after a very long period of turbulence. In this it was very similar to the situation in Thessaly with which we began Chapter 1. Similar, too, was the fact that the treatment meted out to the various island populations depended upon whether they fought or surrendered. The Ottomans took Thassos and Samothrace by force and many of their inhabitants were then sent to Istanbul, where Mehmet's project to rebuild the city was in full swing (Topping 1986: 226). Lemnos, on the other hand, surrendered and then entered into a long period of recovery, much as happened in Thessaly (Lowry 2002).

Further south, in the southeastern Aegean, the misery was also long-standing. The Ottomans (and, prior to them, the emirates of Menteşe and Aydin) had been battling the Knights of St. John on Rhodes since the early fourteenth century, with predictably disastrous results for the Dodecannese islanders. The Knights withstood an unsuccessful Ottoman siege in 1480 and even during the sultanate of Bayezit II, a relatively peaceful period across the empire, fighting continued in this corner of the Aegean (Zachariadou 1966). So here, too, Süleyman's triumph over the Knights in 1522 ushered in a new era of peace.

The religious history of Rhodes under the Knights is an interesting one; the island sits in the middle of a continuum stretching from the Thracian islands, where the Latin Church was never able to establish a serious foothold, to places such as Crete, Cyprus, and the Cyclades, where the Orthodox Church was actively persecuted (Luttrell 1987). As soon as the Knights took the island, an agreement was made that gave the Master of the Hospital control over appointments and benefices of the Orthodox Church on the island. The Latin archbishop took over the palace of his Greek counterpart and half of the churches and ecclesiastical properties on Rhodes. The rest, however, were left in the hands of the Orthodox. There was a Greek metropolitan on the island, although it was the Master who made the ultimate decision on who it would be. The Orthodox were able to maintain their liturgical life and they energetically pursued the establishment of foundations and endowments throughout the Hospitaller period. Therefore, although they had to tolerate a good deal of interference, their position was better than in many parts of the Latin east. A final detail raises some fascinating questions: the Orthodox Church on Rhodes formally accepted papal supremacy, as did most members of the Orthodox community. Presumably this was reversed through some procedure once the Ottomans came in 1522 but the subject awaits investigation. In any event, the Ecumenical patriarch must have been pleased to see the last of the Knights in Rhodes. He would no longer have to suffer their slights, such as an incident in 1452 in which the patriarch appointed the metropolitan of Rhodes as archbishop of Kos but the Hospitallers refused to allow the appointment to go through (Luttrell 1987: 364). On the other hand, we must bear in mind that the Ottomans took the island by force, as was the case whenever they confronted Catholic power, and the population suffered accordingly.[1] Christians were banished from living within the walled city, and this must have been a real blow as the Greek urban population under the Knights was significant enough, and privileged enough, to play a role in municipal government (Luttrell 1987: 362–3). Their place was taken by Muslims from western Anatolia, sent to Rhodes under the policy of forced resettlement known as *sürgün* and, over time, the island came to have a substantial Muslim community, reaching nearly 40 percent by the beginning of the eighteenth century (Erdoğru 1996: 39).

The Ottomans showed no interest in the Cycladic islands, unlike the islands of the northern and eastern Aegean; after all, the Cyclades had neither strategic nor agricultural value. It was the admiral of the Ottoman navy, Hayreddin Barbarossa (himself a Greek convert to Islam), who took the initiative. Returning from his defeat at Corfu in 1537, he attacked the Cyclades in order, it seems, to recover his standing and to give his men an opportunity for looting. The operation was an enormous success and by the time of peace treaty with Venice in 1540 only the tiny island of Tinos remained in Venetian hands (Vatin and Veinstein 2004: 12).

As mentioned in an earlier chapter, when it comes to the Cycladic islands there was a great divergence between the Orthodox and the Ottoman response. The islands were of little interest to the latter and, in stark contrast to their actions in Rhodes and (a few decades later) Cyprus, they allowed the existing Latin aristocracy to stay on and run the islands for them, now as tributaries of the Ottoman state (Slot 1982: 78).

But the Latin rulers understood that times had changed. The duke of Naxos, Giovanni IV, now had to contend with the patriarch in Istanbul and to ensure that this powerful official did not move against him. This explains why, in 1558, the duke donated three wealthy monasteries on the island to the patriarchate. At about the same time Orthodox bishops began to be permitted (Slot 1982: 81). The same sorts of successes for the Orthodox Church were going on across the Cyclades, as emerging Christian Orthodox elites and a newly invigorated Orthodox clergy began to reverse the legacy of more than three hundred years of Latin rule. When we add to this the fact that the Muslim community on the islands, while not non-existent, always remained very small, Hayreddin Barbarossa's actions were an unambiguous victory for the Orthodox Church and for the Orthodox communities themselves.

The picture is more mixed when we come to Cyprus, that great prize that the Ottomans wrested from the Venetians in 1570. This was no accidental acquisition. In April of that year the Ottoman navy set sail from Istanbul with eighty galleys and thirty galliots (Hill 1972: 892). By September Nicosia and much of the island had fallen, but it took almost another year to gain Famagusta. After the city's surrender, the Ottoman commander told the population "that they may live as Christians, though not of the Latin Church, to whom neither church, home, nor anything will be conceded," thus making clear that Cyprus would be no exception to the rule that, as the Latin east came under Ottoman control, the fortunes of the Orthodox Church rose (Costantini 2008: 380–1). The extinction of the Latin aristocracy, too, whether in battle or through departure, created a power vacuum that the Orthodox clergy – the archbishop of Nicosia and other bishops, as well as the hegumens of the large monasteries – moved quickly to fill (Costantini 2008: 380, 382). As was the case with earlier Ottoman conquests in the Balkans, the clerical class in Cyprus showed itself to be very adept at learning how to pull the levers of power. Just a decade after the Ottoman arrival a group of monasteries sent a representative to Istanbul to protest what they said were tax-collecting abuses on the island. They managed to obtain a *ferman* from the sultan, instructing the local officials to make sure that everything was in order. The sultan also took the opportunity to admonish them, saying he hoped that similar problems would not arise in the future (Costantini 2008: 383).

The Ottoman arrival was certainly welcomed, too, by the Cypriot peasantry. Under the Franks and the Venetians the fertile island gained fame as a center of sugar and then cotton production, but the export economy meant harsh conditions for those who labored to produce the coveted products. Just as they had done in the Balkans, the Ottomans abolished the most hated aspects of the feudal regime.

But Cyprus, like Rhodes also a stronghold of Catholic power, had not surrendered peacefully and the islanders paid a heavy price for their resistance. The siege of Nicosia lasted three months and when the sultan's armies broke through there was widespread killing and enslavement; in the end 14,000 people were taken prisoner in the capital, fully one-quarter of the population that had sought refuge in the fortress during the fighting. And even though the residents of Famagusta, mindful of the fate of Nicosia, eventually surrendered, no Christians were allowed to live within the city walls in either place. Not surprisingly, the cities' Christian character collapsed as well. Of the thirty-two churches located within the walls of Famagusta, thirty were sold to private individuals, one was converted to a mosque, and the last was retained as a church to serve the small population of Orthodox artisans, the only group allowed to remain in the fortified city. In the aftermath of the war Famagusta was a city of soldiers, living among abandoned churches (Costantini 2008: 382). This was indeed a shocking development for a city that had been one of the great commercial emporia in the eastern Mediterranean.

Despite the short-term upheavals caused by the often brutal clashes between Ottoman and Catholic power – upheavals that the majority population, the Greek Orthodox, paid for dearly – the long-term trend of the sixteenth century was clearly visible. Everywhere in the insular world the Latin east was coming apart and, in the absence of both the Latin aristocracy (except in the case of the Cycladic islands) and the Catholic church, a new Orthodox elite began forming. This was true both in terms of the individuals who would make up the new privileged class and in terms of shifting property relations; on Andros the monasteries soon became the largest landowners on the island (Kolovos 2007: 72). On the islands closer to Istanbul, where the Orthodox hierarchy and land-holding had remained more or less intact, the peace established by the extension of the Pax Ottomanica to the Aegean and the Mediterranean nevertheless helped the fortunes of the church in a way that had not been possible during the turbulent fifteenth century.

Orthodox gains vis-à-vis Latin power in the sixteenth century were not limited to the physical liquidation of Catholic sovereignty as a result of Ottoman advances. As early as the tenth century the Byzantines granted a privileged commercial status to the Venetians in exchange for military assistance. Whereas most ships entering the Dardanelles, including those of Byzantine subjects, had to pay a tax of 30 *soldi*, the Venetians paid only 17 (Herrin 2007: 158). Over time these privileges grew and were extended to others; thus Italian merchants enjoyed a dominant position in Byzantine trade for many centuries. The Ottomans abolished these special arrangements, and the greatest beneficiaries of the changed circumstances were, once again, the Greeks. But before we turn to the fortunes of Greek commerce in the sixteenth century, let us look at one more Ottoman conquest that does not usually receive any attention when it comes to the history of the Greek world in this period.

In 1516 Selim I defeated the Mamluk emir Qansuh al-Ghuri at Marj Dabiq; the battle lasted only one hour, and the lands of Greater Syria – that is, today's Syria, Lebanon, Jordan, and Palestine/Israel – were joined to the empire (Hathaway with Barbir 2008: 39). As a result of his victories in the Middle East (he took Egypt one year later) the population of the Ottoman Empire became majority Muslim for the first time. But the conquest of Syria also brought in a substantial Greek Orthodox Christian population whose origins in the Byzantine world were evident in the fact that they continued to use Greek as their liturgical language. Although Arab Christians had suffered greatly as a result of the Crusades, their numbers were still substantial when compared to the much smaller populations of the islands we have been discussing.[2] And now, for the first time since the seventh century, they were to be ruled from Istanbul, that is, the city that was the seat of the Ecumenical Patriarchate of the Orthodox Church. This would seem to be a rather momentous event in the history of Greek Orthodoxy, so why is that we hear so little about it?

The answer is that Syria's transition from Mamluk to Ottoman rule, while very consequential in other ways, did not alter long-standing arrangements within the Orthodox Church. And this, in turn, reveals an essential truth about the historic viewpoint of Greek Orthodox elites, sandwiched as they were between Catholic Europe and the Muslim world. By the time the Ottomans took Syria, the Christians within the jurisdiction of the patriarchs of Antioch, Jerusalem, and Alexandria had been living under Muslim rule for a very long time, in the case of the latter two almost a thousand years. They had worked out their arrangements with the various Muslim sovereigns – the Umayyads, the Abbasids, the Mamluks, and so on – as well as with the Ecumenical patriarch in Istanbul. The move from one Muslim sultan to another did not disrupt this essential stability; through experience they had a good sense of how to fit in as Christians in a Muslim polity and the Ottomans did not disappoint. The Byzantines, for their part, had long ago all but written off active engagement with the Greek Orthodox of the Arab world, and the clerical elites in Istanbul continued this tradition into the Ottoman period. After the Arab conquests of the seventh century the Byzantines continued to appoint the patriarch of Antioch but he rarely took up his post, preferring to stay in Istanbul. In his absence the clergy and laity of Damascus (since at least the sixteenth century the residence of the patriarch) came to choose their own patriarch, invariably a local Arab cleric. In seventeenth-century Damascus the Christians were still, quite remarkably, electing and deposing patriarchs without any interference from the Ecumenical patriarch, the Holy Synod, or the sultan (Masters 2001: 48, 62).

The patriarch in Istanbul saw the lands recently delivered from Latin rule in a different light. One of the reasons was surely that Catholic domination, while long-standing in a place such as Cyprus, was still a far more recent event than the loss of Jerusalem to the Muslims. But probably more important was the potent combination of active Latin persecution of the Orthodox Church and Ottoman willingness to favor the Orthodox at the expense of the Catholics. Ottoman power gave the patriarch, and Orthodox clergy across the Greek world, the opportunity to gain back what they had lost to the Latins. For the Orthodox the Latins were the greater threat, and the proof of this would come early in the eighteenth century. In the early 1700s the Ecumenical patriarch woke from his slumber and suddenly became very alarmed at the situation of the patriarchate of Antioch. The reason was, once again, the Latins; by then Catholic missionaries had become active in Syria and were meeting with some success among the Arab Christians.

The conquering Greek Orthodox merchant

Histories of Greek commerce in the Ottoman period usually identify the middle of the eighteenth century as the moment when Greek merchants and shippers burst onto the international stage. The Seven Years War spilled out into the Mediterranean and the Greeks, as neutral shippers, were able to take over much of the trade that had formerly been controlled by the English and the French.

This chronology passes over in silence the sixteenth century, when a different, but equally vibrant, international order allowed for a Greek maritime world that stretched from the Italian peninsula to Istanbul and the northern shores of the Black Sea. Very much as is the case today, the history of the early modern Greeks cannot be contained within the borders of any one polity.

Let us start in the Ottoman Empire, which means starting in Istanbul. Nikolai Todorov's description of Ottoman Istanbul is worth quoting in full, as it conveys the tremendous wealth of the city as it rose from the ashes of the Byzantine Empire.

> The conquest of Istanbul realized the most treasured Muslim expectations. In its significance as the new seat of the caliph, Istanbul now became the premier Muslim city, a city as marvelous as the ancient capital of the Arab caliphs at Baghdad. To it flowed the enormous wealth provided by victorious wars, by contributions, by the continuous inflow of taxes and other imposts, by gifts, and by the income that resulted from a widespread commerce. Thanks to its key geographic position – at the crossroads of several major land and sea commercial thoroughfares – and to the privileges and facilities that it had enjoyed for several centuries, Istanbul was transformed into the largest city in Europe. (Todorov 1983: 55–6)

Population growth reflected the city's exalted status. In 1478, there were 16,000 households (around 64,000 individuals) in Istanbul and Galata. By the end of the sixteenth century the latter number had swelled to around 200,000 souls.[3]

Istanbul was certainly the premier Muslim city – in this period it became a showcase of Islamic architecture and the location of a generous imperial court that supported the poets, calligraphers, and scholars who flocked to this new center of patronage – but it was more than that as well. It was also a world city and – as world cities do today – it attracted people from all corners of the earth. This included the Greeks, from both humble and exalted backgrounds. Greek merchants from the Venetian colonies had many ties to the imperial capital and some even chose to settle there. The floating class of Greek maritime laborers in the eastern Mediterranean also found Istanbul an attractive destination in this period.

The Greeks of Ottoman Istanbul were closely associated with commerce, with shipping, and indeed with all the trades having to do with the sea. The neighborhood of Galata, across the Golden Horn to the north, quickly re-emerged after 1453 as the commercial center of the city, just as it had been under the Byzantines, and it was very much a Greek neighborhood. There were more Greek Orthodox than Muslims in Galata and the institutions associated with Christian life, from churches to taverns, lined the streets in ways that would have been considered scandalous within the walled city of Istanbul. The Greek elite – tax farmers, merchants, and shipowners – had their residences there (İnalcık 1991: 247; Mauroeide 1992: 70).

In addition to the tax farming that was discussed in an earlier chapter, the Greek merchants of Galata enjoyed an abundance of commercial opportunities due to the requirements of Istanbul, the largest city in Europe. The resource-rich Black Sea had always been vital in this regard and, now that the Ottomans controlled entrance to the sea, Greek merchants spread out along its shores, displacing or absorbing the formerly dominant Genoese. They brought timber, furs, dried fish, and caviar to Istanbul and carried the luxury goods of the Mediterranean, such as the sweet wine of Crete, back to the Black Sea. The Greeks took over the provisioning of the capital and by 1600 they were in control of much of the commerce of the eastern half of the Balkan peninsula.

This part of the story is well known, at least to Ottoman and Balkan historians. In this narrative Greek commerce benefitted from Ottoman strength, which ended Italian privilege and bolstered the fortunes of Ottoman subjects. This framing of the issue, while not incorrect, is incomplete and fails to capture the full extent of Greek commercial fortunes in the sixteenth century. It presents the upturn in Greek commerce and shipping as a purely internal Ottoman affair, one that is the result mainly of Ottoman policy. In fact the Greeks were operating on a much wider stage than this. In the sixteenth century Greek merchants benefitted not only from Ottoman strength, but also from the slow ebbing away of Venetian power. Venice was increasingly unable to restrict the lucrative Levantine trade between the metropole and Venetian colonial possessions – the most important being Cyprus, Crete, and the Ionian islands – to Venetian citizens alone. This allowed Venice's colonial subjects, who were overwhelmingly Greek Orthodox, to break into these exclusive circles. At the same time, faced with the relentless Ottoman advance, the Venetians also adopted a more conciliatory policy toward the subjects of the Ottoman sultan; thus Ottoman Greeks had new access to the city as well (Greene 2007).

The most important Greek overseas colony in the early modern Mediterranean was in Venice, and the founding of the Greek Fraternity of Venice in 1498 marked the community's coming of age. Up until that time the Greeks had chafed under the control of the Latin clergy. Now, with their own *confraternita* or *scuola*, they gained the right to draw up their own charter, to elect their own priests, and to take any decisions that they saw fit to make provided that they did not contravene the laws of the republic. Despite some difficulties with the authorities, both secular and religious, the confraternity slowly took root. The Church of St. George was finished in 1573; it would remain the nucleus of the community for centuries to come.

Although there is a tendency in the Greek-language literature to present the Greek Fraternity as the work of refugees fleeing Ottoman rule, its membership drew almost exclusively on those Greeks who were Venetian subjects, with the Ionian islands and Crete being particularly well represented. The most prominent members, including almost all those who held the position of president (*gastaldos*), were wealthy merchants (Greene 2010: 36).

Information on confraternity members shows that they moved easily between the metropole and the provincial capitals from which they had originally come. This was the case whether they chose to settle in Venice or to maintain their base in their city of origin. They pursued commerce at multiple levels, from the local – carrying goods between the Ionian islands and Venice – to the regional – between the eastern Mediterranean and Venice – and the international – carrying the wine of Crete or the currants of Corfu to England. The most important commodity they dealt in was grain, which they fetched from the ports of the Ottoman Empire and brought to grain-starved Italy (Mauroeidi 1976: 117).

These Greek merchants were intimately connected to the Ottoman world. Greek populations, after all, were spread out across the Venetian and Ottoman worlds and they were able to draw on family connections in their pursuit of commerce. Consider, for example, the Samarianis family. Originally from Methone in the western Morea, they moved to the Ionian island of Zakynthos when Methone fell to the Ottomans. Markos Samarianis, who was a shipowner, is listed as a member of the Fraternity from the early 1520s. Clearly a prominent member, he contributed generously to the construction of the church of St. George and served in many high positions. Samarianis brought grain from the Ottoman east, and he used his family connections – his sister was married and living in Patras – to secure it (Mauroeidi 1976: 124–5).

The connections were also encouraged by the new conditions of the sixteenth century, conditions that have received a good deal of attention when it comes to the Jewish diaspora in the Mediterranean but have not been considered with regard to the Greek experience. As the advantages they had enjoyed under the Byzantines came to an end, Italian merchants – and here we speaking principally of the Venetians and the Genoese – departed from the east and turned their attention elsewhere. In Venice the commercial class actually abandoned the maritime tradition and began to invest in agriculture and industry on the mainland. Trading opportunities between the east and west, however, were still tremendous; in addition to the demand for Ottoman grain in Venice, the Ottomans wanted the wool, fabrics, glassware, and paper of the west. Beyond strictly commercial endeavors, we know that in the early modern world traders and diplomats were often one and the same people; the complicated relationship between the Venetians and the Ottomans – sometimes at war, other times at peace, but always trading no matter what the conditions – created myriad opportunities for mediation. The Jews were ideally placed to offer such mediation, but so were the Greeks, since they were spread out across both Venetian and Ottoman territory.

Although no comprehensive study of this sixteenth-century Greek world has yet been undertaken, the scattered biographical details of certain prominent mercantile families point to a web of commercial, family, and religious ties between Istanbul and Venice.

The Marmaretos family were wealthy Greeks, leaders of the Istanbul community, who resided in Galata (Mauroeide 1992: 69–70). By the 1530s, one member of the family, Dimitrios Marmaretos, was established in Venice as part of the family business. He was a member of the Greek Fraternity and was trusted enough by the Venetian state that he was asked to give them a report on Ottoman war plans in 1537, on the eve of the war that would bring the Cycladic islands under the sultan's rule, which he did (Mauroeidi 1976: 130).

The Koresse were also residents of Galata, whose property, and family members, were spread out across the Aegean, the Black Sea, and the Balkans. The Koresse probably had their origins in Chios, but by the sixteenth century they were landowners in Crete; they traded with Italy, Moldavia, the ports of the Black Sea, and many points in the east. Their ties to Venice ran very deep. The family enjoyed the status of *cittadinanza Veneta originaria* for services they had rendered to the Republic. These included spying and the management of the public debt vis-à-vis the sultan. One Antonios Koresse was established in Venice at mid-century, where he was one of the most active members of the Greek Fraternity. At the same time, he had a close relationship with the famed Ottoman naval commander Hayreddin Pasha (Mauroeidi 1976: 131).

The pattern of establishing family members in both Istanbul and Venice occurs often enough to suggest that service to both the Venetians and the Ottomans was considered an effective way to augment and preserve the wealth of the family. A court case before a Venetian official in Istanbul shows how the advantages could work. Manoles Kantakouzenos, a relation of the notorious Ottoman tax collector Michael Kantakouzenos, established himself in Venice, where he was a member of the Greek Fraternity. His brother, Antonios, remained in Istanbul to handle that branch of the family's business. When the Venetian official ruled against Antonios in a commercial dispute the latter took advantage of his status as a *haraci* or Ottoman subject to dodge the judgment (Mauroeidi 1992: 135).

Finally, Greek gains were not limited to the route connecting Venice to Istanbul. The policy of Venice in its colonial possessions had long been to exclude non-Venetians from the lofty summits of international trade, and to make sure that products from the *stato da mar* were directed toward the metropole. But by the sixteenth century this had broken down and local merchants were charting their own separate course, a course that was oriented toward the Ottoman world that surrounded the island. The best example of this is Crete, the crown jewel of Venice's overseas possessions.

As they set sail, Cretan merchants certainly went to Venice but the pull of Ottoman ports is very obvious as well. Already at the beginning of the sixteenth century, 150 years before the Ottoman armies would arrive, a Venetian merchant noted that the Cretans brought their wine, honey, cheese, silk, and cotton to the ports of the eastern Mediterranean, as well as to North Africa, Puglia, and Naples (Alexiou 1985: 65). In 1589 an administrator on the island wrote: "The Cretans sail with their boats in times of peace to Syria, to Alexandria, to Istanbul to the archipelago and to other places in Turkey in every sort of boat and skiff; they are skillful and daring men" (Spanakes 1940: 23). Istanbul itself was full of Cretans, so much so that "Cretans of the Venetian nation," Mario Sanudo tells us, were in charge of defense in Galata (Mauroeidi 1992: 85).

The Cretans surely benefitted from the fact that they came from the island that produced one of the most sought-after products of the early modern Mediterranean: the sweet wine known as *malvasia*. They sold it throughout the Mediterranean – they drink no other wine in Alexandria, a Venetian official wrote – and as far away as London (Pashley 1989: 426). A story of love gone awry in sixteenth-century Istanbul begins with the unlucky fiancé returning to Crete to fetch good wine for the wedding (Mauroeidi 1992: 74).

The story of Constantine Corniactus shows how far afield the islanders ventured and how high they could rise, thanks to *malvasia*. Corniactus, who was born in Crete in 1517, made his money selling Cretan wine in Lwów. He was settled in nearby Moldavia, by then an Ottoman vassal state. After 1563, when his brother was murdered by the Moldavian princes, he moved to Lwów, where he prospered once again. He became a money-lender to the prince of Poland and restored an Orthodox church in his adopted city. Born a subject of Venice, he died a member of the Polish nobility.

Nor was Corniactus the only Cretan merchant in Lwów; between 1560 and 1603 we have records of forty others who were selling wine there as well. Writing in 1578, a Venetian official estimated that between 1,200 and 1,500 bottles of *malvasia* arrived in Istanbul every year, heading for Poland (Patrinelis 1973: 252).

The business of the Greek Orthodox Church was also an international affair; a shared religious faith brought together Greeks from across the Ottoman and Venetian worlds. This was particularly true at the level of church elites, and in that way the hierarchy of the Orthodox Church resembled the Greek mercantile elite. We can see the connections in the ordination (in the 1570s) of Gabriel Severos as metropolitan of Philadelphia. Prior to this post, Severos had been a priest at the Church of St. George in Venice. His ordination in Istanbul, which involved a considerable outlay of money, was sponsored by one Leonino Servo, a rich merchant from Crete, who was now settled in the Ottoman capital. The most famous patriarch of the seventeenth century – and possibly of the entire Ottoman period – was Kyrillos Loukaris, who was born a Venetian subject in Crete. His education was sponsored by his uncle, who was the patriarch of Alexandria in Ottoman Egypt (Greene 2010: 71–2).

The rise of Ottoman power also meant opportunities in Istanbul for sailors and other workers of the maritime world. A Venetian report from 1558 noted that both Cretans and Ionian islanders were settled in Istanbul, working for the navy, and another report written just a few years later explained that the Greeks preferred to work for the Turks because they could earn in four months what it took a year to earn in Venice (Sfyroeras 1968: 26).

Writing from Crete in 1589 Zuanne Mocenigo informed the senate that few boats were being built in Candia's arsenal, and he went on to explain why:

> The necessary workers are not to be found in this Kingdom, due to the tremendous expense involved as well as the dearth of these past years. [There is also] a lack of commercial traffic and therefore profits are low. As a result of this, few boats are being built. These workers, seeing that they won't be able to exercise their profession here because of the difficult situation, turn to other professions in order to earn their living, or they go to other countries, principally Istanbul, where workers are paid well and money circulates easily. (Spanakes 1940: 171)

Greek maritime labor, both free and slave, was in fact prominent in Istanbul from the very beginning of the Ottoman period. As early as

1474 Greek rowers and shipbuilders each had their own guild at the imperial arsenal (Sfyroeras 1968: 21) And we can go back much, much earlier; just two decades after the battle of Manzikert (1071), when the Byzantine defeat opened the door of Anatolia to Turkish migration, a Turkish maritime principality formed at Smyrna. The leader's ships were built by the local Christians (Vryonis 1971: 481). As different Turkish emirates reached the shores of the Aegean in successive waves between the twelfth and the fifteenth centuries, the demand for maritime labor – from sailors and rowers to caulkers and pilots – continued apace. It was the Greeks, with their long experience of maritime life, who had the necessary talents.

The state's appetite for this specialized workforce reached its zenith in the sixteenth century. Partly this was the result of the conquest of Egypt, as a result of which new and vital maritime routes had to be protected. Even more consequential, however, were the epic and ongoing clashes with the Spanish Habsburgs in the Mediterranean; this was the century when galley warfare reached its height, before crumbling under the weight of its own requirements. As the warships became bigger and bigger, the Ottomans of course needed ever greater numbers of rowers (this was often slave labor), sailors, and shipbuilders.[4] In 1521 a Venetian official in Istanbul wrote home that he had never seen such a large fleet in the works. One hundred large galleys and ninety-two smaller ones had already been built and were in the arsenals at Gallipoli and Istanbul, and still the work continued (Sfyroeras 1968: 28). Süleyman was preparing of course for the attack on Rhodes that would come the following year. But this was just one of many large-scale sea battles over the course of the century. At Algiers, at Gerba, at Malta, the Ottomans and the Habsburgs fought each other for control of the Mediterranean, all the way through to the epic battle of Lepanto in 1570.

From every direction, then, Greeks poured into Istanbul, adding to the population that was already there. They came as captives, they came as merchants, they came as skilled laborers seeking their fortune, and they came as miserable galley slaves. Thus, even as the empire became a majority Muslim empire with the addition of the populations of the Near East, Istanbul re-emerged as the capital of the Greek world. This is not to suggest in any way that the Greeks, however defined, were once again ruling in the ancient city, because of course they were not; they were a legally subordinated population that did not share the religion of the governing class. But it is to say that, as more and more competitors to Ottoman power fell by the wayside, no other city, not even Venice, was its equal as a center of Greek life, in terms of sheer numbers, opportunity, and the far-flung networks that all radiated outwards from the Bosphorus.

The objection can be raised, indeed should be raised, that in the sixteenth century the city's Greek population was in decline. Despite the city's rapid growth, the number of the sultan's Greek Orthodox subjects had actually dipped from, roughly, 12,000 in 1478 to 8,500 in the middle of the sixteenth century. Part of the decline was probably due to conversion, which suggests that even in the former Byzantine capital the new religion was attractive to many, just as it was in the cities of the Balkans (Yerasimos 2005: 394). But the Greek community of sixteenth-century Istanbul looks different if we widen the lens and include those who were not the sultan's subjects. As is so often the case with the Greeks, there is an international as well as a local dimension to the story, and it is very clear that, in this period, Istanbul was a city of opportunity for Greek Orthodox across the Mediterranean world, even if they did not settle there permanently.[5]

The dominant position of Istanbul in the Greek world in the sixteenth century is probably best illustrated by comparing it to the very different landscape that prevailed in the middle of the fifteenth century, as Byzantine Istanbul entered its final days. Not only was the city much smaller then but in a fragmented political situation there were other Greek centers, places such as Trabzon and Mistra, and even Famagusta in Cyprus and Candia in Crete, which rivaled the Byzantine capital in importance. By the end of the sixteenth century all of these places except Candia had fallen to the Ottomans and some part of their populations – whether by force or of their own free will – followed the conquerors back to Istanbul, where a revitalized city was rising at the crossroads of Europe and Asia.

We can think, too, of the fragmentation of the clerical leadership of the Orthodox Church in the wake of the Fourth Crusade. Sitting in Istanbul the patriarch found it hard to prevail against distant Catholic authorities who routinely obstructed his efforts to control appointments in Orthodox lands. Recall the Hospitaller refusal, in 1452, of the patriarch's choice for the archbishop of Kos. Now, in the middle of the sixteenth century, a new political authority, the Ottoman sultan, still had to be contended with when it came to clerical appointments, but all of the action was in Istanbul, making the city the uncontested center of Greek Orthodoxy.

It is well known that as the Ottoman sultans extinguished other centers of Muslim power – the various contenders in Anatolia and, most importantly, the Mamluks in Egypt – Istanbul rose in the sixteenth century to become the capital of the Islamic world. It is ironic that Ottoman victories also helped to restore the place of Istanbul within the Orthodox world, particularly in the eastern Mediterranean, where the Latins had been dominant since the Fourth Crusade.

At the edges of the Greek world

To round out our tour of the Greek world we must pause, briefly, at opposite ends of the empire, first in the far north and then in Anatolia. In the sixteenth century neither area was a center of Greek life, but both would become so. Their incipient quality illustrates a characteristic that, among the Christian communities of the empire, was unique to the Greeks.

In both the Byzantine and the Ottoman Empires the Hellenizing mission – or, if one wishes, Hellenic imperialism – was always an option. Because the Byzantine state was the representative of both Orthodox Christianity and Hellenic culture, the expansion of one ideally meant the expansion of the other as well.[6] For example, in the ninth and tenth centuries, a determined effort by the center helped to bring southern Greece – which had been overrun by Slavic settlers – back into the fold of the Hellenic world. Sitting once again at the very center of the empire, in the Ottoman period the Ecumenical Patriarchate and the elites surrounding it still had the ability to draw Christians from all different backgrounds into the orbit of Hellenism. In the absence of the emperor the mechanisms for such a project were quite different, but they were real and they were effective. As we shall see, this Istanbul-based Hellenizing mission is most pronounced in the eighteenth century. In the nineteenth century it was the Greek state that took over this project, launching a grand effort to Hellenize the Christian Orthodox of Anatolia. Despite the newness of the regime in Athens, the venture was a familiar one.

Because of this historic tendency, Greek elites possessed the ability to rebound from setbacks, to expand, and to claim large parts of the Orthodox world for Hellenism. This distinguished the Greeks from the Serbs and, even more so, the Bulgarians, both of whom were confined to a more regional identity. The geographical boundaries of Hellenism, then, were always fluid.

The provinces of Wallachia and Moldavia, at the northern extremity of the empire, would emerge as critical locations in the history of the Greeks during the Ottoman period. So here let us describe how they came to be part of the Ottoman Empire.

Squeezed in between the behemoths of Poland, Hungary, and the Ottoman Empire, Wallachia and Moldavia enjoyed no more than a fragile independence. In fact, Vlach settlement in the area, followed by the establishment of kingdoms, was only a century old by the time Fatih Mehmet invaded in the middle of the fifteenth century. Prior to roughly 1350 the fertile plains, which were wide open to the steppe lands in the east, suffered repeated invasions and consequent devastation. In the middle of the fourteenth century a joint Hungarian–Polish army pushed out the Tartars and a measure of stability was achieved.

Therefore, Mehmet was concerned about either a Polish (through Moldavia) or a Hungarian (through Wallachia) attack on Ottoman territory, and for that reason the two princes of the provinces were already bound by ties of vassalage to the Ottomans. When the Wallachian prince Vlad IV refused to pay the customary tribute in 1456, Fatih invaded and installed a prince who would be more obedient. Stephen the Great of Moldavia, which was by now also a vassal state, brought the wrath of the Ottomans down upon him when he invaded Wallachia in 1471. The resistance was a long one (and included a victory over the Ottomans in 1475 at the battle of Vaslui) and it took until the early sixteenth century for Ottoman control to be established once more. It would last into the nineteenth century.

Moldavia and Wallachia were solidly Orthodox territories. The creation of Vlachs who were fleeing from persecution in Catholic Hungary, their connection to the larger world of Orthodox Christianity was strong. Roughly 20 percent of the land in Wallachia was owned by monasteries – some of them in Wallachia itself – and Stephen the Great was a benefactor of Mount Athos (Sedlar 1994: 168). In this far northern area the Ottomans were disinclined to undertake the financial and logistical challenge of full incorporation into the empire. Therefore, they gave the nobility – known as the boyars – the right to elect their own princes.

These two facts – the Orthodox character of the land and the existence of a Christian aristocracy established with Ottoman consent – rendered Moldavia and Wallachia potentially fertile ground for the extension of Greek influence. This is, in fact, what came to pass in the seventeenth century (Camariano-Cioran 1974).

Turning to Asia Minor, we are confronted by the magnitude of the Greek loss, documented many years ago by Speros Vryonis in his magisterial study. The Ottoman tax registers compiled between 1520 and 1530 show that the Christian population of Anatolia had dropped to a staggeringly low 7.9 percent, and that included Armenians as well as Greeks (Vyronis 1971: 445). The Greeks were not evenly spread out, however, and significant pockets of Greek population remained. In the province of Rum in north central Anatolia 30 percent of the population was still Christian, and the percentage was even higher in the principal cities; Sivas was majority Christian (74 percent) and Tokat was nearly evenly divided between Christians and Muslims. Neither of these populations survived into the seventeenth century. In Cappadocia there were about twenty Grecophone villages; they maintained their Orthodox faith throughout the Ottoman centuries but quickly became Turcophone.[7]

But the most important communities by far, in terms both of numbers and of survival, were those of the Pontos, as the southeast corner of the Black Sea littoral is known. Essentially coterminous with the Empire of Trabzon, the Pontos and the people who live in it have a fascinating and complicated history that has attracted the attention of many.[8] In the early sixteenth century the province – which stretched from Giresun in the west to Rize in the east – was almost entirely Christian; the Muslim population amounted to less than 10 percent (Bryer 1980: 38–9; Lowry 2009: 69). In the capital city, Trabzon, the Christian population (mostly Greek) was 85 percent of the total.

What can account for these astonishing numbers, in an Asia Minor that had become overwhelmingly Muslim? Three factors are paramount. First, in the Empire of Trabzon the church had a powerful protector and so remained strong all the way up until the Ottoman conquest in 1461, whereas in the rest of Anatolia the church was in disarray if not total collapse. Second, the conquest was both chronologically late and swift, sparing the population the upheavals of prolonged warfare that had plagued the rest of Anatolia for centuries (Vryonis 1971: 451). Finally, the towering Pontic mountain range ensured the remoteness of the region, while also creating a climate along the coast that was unattractive to Türkmen and the pastoral economy (Bryer 1980: 42).

As discussed at some length in the previous chapter, conversion to Islam in the city proceeded swiftly after 1525; by the middle of the century, half of the population was Muslim. At mid-century Muslims were gaining on the Christians in the countryside as well; in the district of Of, Muslim households now accounted for 15 percent of the total, up from just 2 percent in 1515 (Bryer 1980: 45).

Conversion would continue apace in the Pontos, in both the cities and the villages, but unlike almost everywhere else in the Greek world, where conversion also led to the loss of the Greek language,

Greek-speaking Muslims were a prominent feature of the region until very recently. Michael Meeker's study of the district of Of, which lies to the east of Trabzon, reveals a complex situation. The district is dominated by two valley systems that run from the coast, along their respective rivers, up into the highlands, which stretch away to the south. The population of the eastern valley was almost exclusively Turkish speaking while in the western valley – also Muslim – Greek speakers predominated. Meeker suggests a more insular western valley due to a different topography that did not encourage movement out of or into the area, while cautioning against the conclusion that all of the Greek speakers in the western valley shared a common Greek origin. The eastern valley was more open to immigration from the highlands of Erzurum (Meeker 2002: 155–6). In Tonya district, just slightly west of Trabzon, there were also Greek-speaking Muslim villages as recently as 1970. And yet there is no record of Greek settlement there in the medieval period. Therefore, in Tonya too, the presence of Greek as a language does not necessarily indicate the presence of people we would conventionally identify as Greek (Bryer 1980: 45).

Smyrna, a city that of course figures so prominently in the history of the Greeks in the late Ottoman period, was still an insignificant port. Fewer than 5,000 souls were living there as late as 1600, and the Greeks were a small minority within that. The massive growth of the Greek population later on was the result of in-migration, from the nearby Aegean islands as well as from other areas of Anatolia, and was not continuous with the pre-Ottoman past (Goffman 1990: 11).

The two bookends of the Danubian Principalities and the Pontos are testimony not only to the geographical capaciousness of Greek culture during the Ottoman period, but also to the diversity of its manifestations. In the former we see the adoption of Greek high culture by an indigenous elite whereas in the latter the Greek language remained while Greek Orthodoxy did not. Neither one is captured by conventional references to the Greek community.

Notes

1. Vera Costantini nicely sums up the Catholic attitude, although she is speaking here specifically about the Venetians: "Throughout the course of the centuries-long history of the conflicts between the Empire and the Republic, episodes of surrender were extremely rare. The neutral vocation of Venice in the modern age did not stop its governors from expecting their generals to defend their positions to the death" (Costantini 2008: 379).

2. There were probably between one million and one million and a half Christians in Greater Syria in 1516 (Masters 2001: 49).
3. İnalcık thinks the number may have reached as high as 300,000. The census of 1478 was the last general count until the nineteenth century, and this makes population estimates difficult. So, too, does the fact that travelers' estimates do not always make it clear if they are referring to Istanbul *intra muros* or greater Istanbul. However, the physical expansion of the city, as well as ongoing building activity, are well recorded and these make it clear that the city was growing fast during the sixteenth century (İnalcık 2012; Yerasimos 2005).
4. And not only the Ottomans but the Venetians as well. See Greene (2007) for a discussion of the demand for Greek maritime labor across the Mediterranean.
5. By the seventeenth century the Greek Orthodox population of the city was climbing again and it reached an astonishing 40 percent of the total population. Yerasimos comments that, given the robust figures of both the fifteenth and the seventeenth centuries, the drop in the sixteenth century is a problem that needs investigation (Yerasimos 2005: 394).
6. I say "ideally" because sometimes the Byzantines, faced with a powerful opponent such as the Bulgarian khans, had to content themselves with a Christianizing mission that allowed for the use of the Bulgarian language. Unlike the western church, which insisted on the use of Latin in every instance, the Byzantines were more flexible about the imposition of Greek (Herrin 2007).
7. Chatziiosiff provides an overview, and a critique, of the historiography of Ottoman Anatolia, which has concentrated on the Muslim cities to the neglect of the Christian countryside (Chatziiosiff 2005).
8. Among them the filmmaker Yeşim Ustaoğlu, whose 2003 film *Bulutları Beklerken* (*Waiting for the Clouds*) is set in the Pontos in the 1970s. The protagonist is an elderly Muslim villager who has hidden her Greek Orthodox past for fifty years. It is based on the novel *Tamama* by Georgios Andreadis.

Figure 1 The palace of the hospodar of the Danubian Principalities in Bucharest. Plate 13 in Luigi Mayer's Views in the Ottoman Dominions, vol. 1 (London: 1810). Photo courtesy of Vassar College Libraries.

Figure 2 Saints (Basil, Athanasius, and Cyril of Alexandria) with decorated vestments drawing on Ottoman motifs. 1652, Driovouno monastery, Macedonia, Greece. Photo courtesy of Theocharis Tsampouras.

Figure 3 Decorative pattern drawn from Ottoman motifs. 1641, Catholicon (main church), Monastery of the Dormition of the Virgin, Spelaio, Macedonia, Greece. Photo courtesy of Theoharis Tsampouras.

Figure 4 Vase with carnations. 1671, Stegopole Monastery, southern Albania. Photo courtesy of Theocharis Tsampouras.

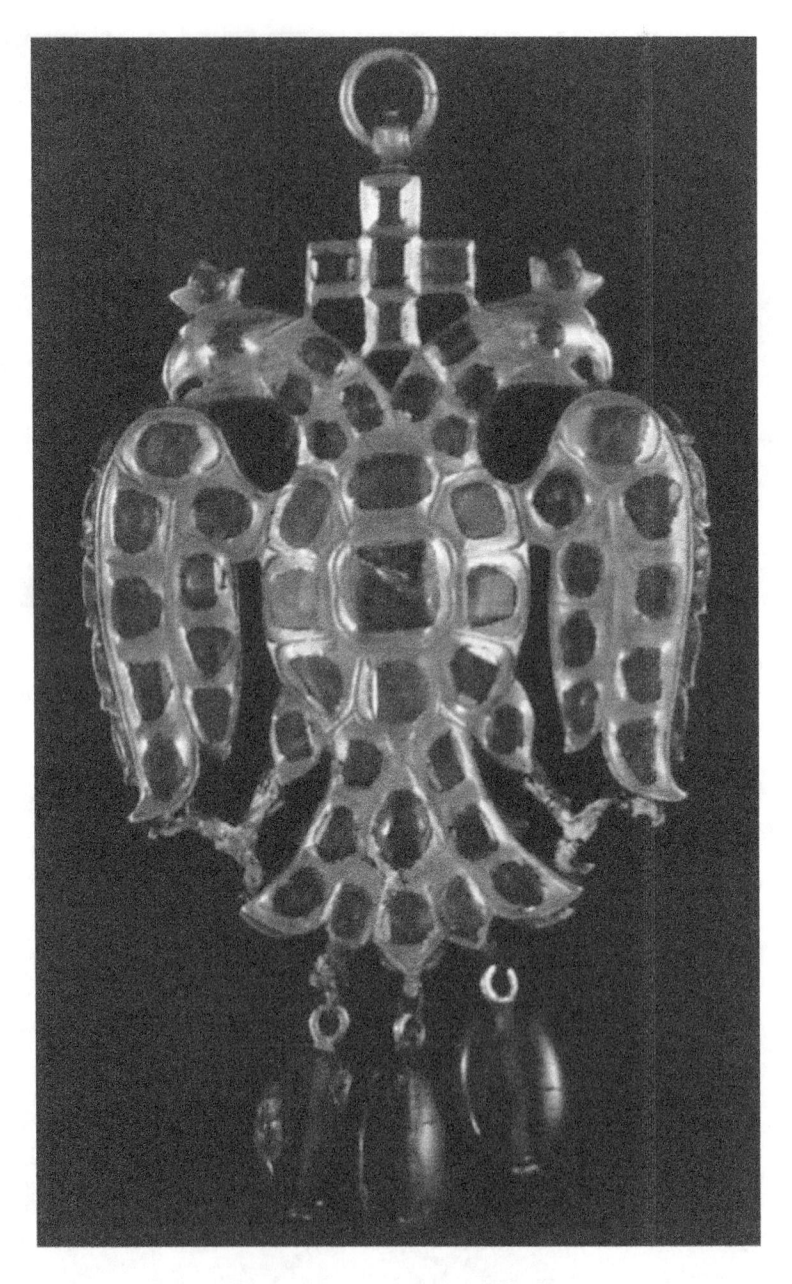

Figure 5 A prelate's pectoral, obverse side. Istanbul, late seventeenth century. "Greek goldsmiths of Constantinople were renowned for their skill. In 1647 the Turkish traveler Evliya Çelebi reported that the best enameler in the city was the Greek Michael Simicioğlu, who made watchcases and knife handles that were sent as official gifts to the shah of Iran" (Ballian 2005: 79). Photo courtesy of the Benaki Museum, Athens.

Figure 6 Myrrh flask. 1670, from Trabzon. "*The flask contained the holy myrrh with which the believer was anointed in the mystery of the chrism, after baptism. Its shape is Islamic. The typical Ottoman style of the decoration brings to mind Bursa opulent silks or Iznik ceramic panels. Of different character is the engraved floral ornament on the rim, which reflects the new trends taking shape in the capital of the empire at this time, under the influence of European art*" (Ballian 2005: 84).

CHAPTER 5

The Greeks and the seventeenth-century crisis

Over the course of the sixteenth century twenty monasteries were built in continental Greece, but only three of these date to after 1568. The same holds true for the iconographic programs that decorated the interiors of the monastic churches (Patrinelis 1991–2: 36). The sharp drop-off in the last quarter of the century started with the shock occasioned by the crisis of the monasteries and the significant debt that was taken on in order to allow for the purchase of ecclesiastical property. The testimony of the monks in a small monastery in southern Albania shows just how long the burden of the debt lingered for some monasteries. The inscription runs,

> In 1650, we, the monks and priors of this monastery, finally paid off our debt of thousands of *akçes*. He who indebts our monastery again shall be cursed by the Father, the Son and the Holy Spirit and the Virgin Mary shall be his fierce enemy.[1]

The quality of artistic production in the cities, too, where metropolitans and other urban elites had patronized renowned artists in the sixteenth century, declined sharply in the opening decades of the seventeenth century. When work was commissioned, it took many years and often the small contributions of many ordinary people, rather than the benefaction of a wealthy patron, to finally complete, for example, the iconic program in a church.[2]

The drop-off in construction and artistic creation, after such a long period of intense activity, was part of an empire-wide crisis that affected everyone, not just the Christian community and monastic building programs. Gülrü Necipoğlu describes changing patterns of Muslim architectural patronage, which can provide insight into the less explored Christian situation. During the reign of Murat III (1574–95) the grand vezirate changed hands far more often and, as a result of this instability, the grand vezirs were no longer patrons of great architectural projects, and neither were the sultans. The new patrons were sultanas, ordinary vezirs, and ascendant dignitaries, all of whom were striving for higher status through architectural visibility in the capital (Necipoğlu 2005: 506).

The type of building changed as well. In the seventeenth century we see a surge in *medrese* complexes – as opposed to the splendid Friday mosques that had been favored earlier – and they are more modest affairs, due to the reduced availability of building sites and the limited wealth of non-royal patrons. The two great mosque complexes that were built in this period – the Blue Mosque and the Yeni Cami – were both highly controversial, as times were difficult and there had been no victories in Christian lands (Necipoğlu 2005: 509).

The crisis of the elites that Necipoğlu demonstrates was true for the Christian community as well. Just as the grand vezirs moved in and out of office more quickly than they had in the past, the patriarchate became more unstable in the seventeenth century. Between 1580 and 1600 alone patriarchs were removed from the throne sixteen times, often in violent circumstances; during the same period the price of securing the office from the sultan soared upward by 1,000 percent (Tsampouras 2013b: 45; Konortas 1998: 53–60). The instability continued into the following century. Between 1500 and 1600, thirty-two patriarchs had served in office; over the next one hundred years that number almost doubled (Krstić 2011: 206). And a short tenure in office was not the worst fate awaiting a seventeenth-century patriarch. Three sitting patriarchs and an ex-patriarch were executed in the short space of time between 1638 and 1657 and for a while the grand vezirs prevented the patriarchs from even presenting themselves to the sultan (Hypsilantis 1870: 158).

The destabilization of the late sixteenth century, long a well-known turning point, had multiple causes. I shall refer only to those that had a broad impact across the entire empire. Externally, the influx of Spanish silver brought serious inflation into Ottoman society, and the government's response was to devalue the coinage. The troops, who were paid in silver coin, responded with a series of revolts and thus began a problem that would be with the empire – with greater and lesser intensity – for the next two centuries. Changing methods of warfare were another source of external pressure and they led to fundamental restructuring within the empire. Faced with the increased use of infantry forces and firearms, the state began to retreat from its reliance on the *sipahis*, or provincial cavalry, as the backbone of its fighting force, while the number of janissaries soared.[3] This fundamental restructuring of the military – which also included the recruitment of peasant mercenaries equipped with firearms – compelled a change a change in taxation as well. In the past, 30–40 percent of military expenses had been met by the revenues that the *sipahis* drew from their fiefs in the countryside (İnalcık 1980: 311). Now, with the increasing obsolescence of the cavalry army and the urgent need for cash to pay the janissaries and the mercenaries, Istanbul turned sharply toward tax farming. *Timars* were converted into tax farms of various sizes and auctioned off.

The new tax farmers, the *mültezims*, were a mixed lot but shared a common origin in the Ottoman elite. Pashas, beys and governors, on the one hand, and palace folk on the other – the women of the harem and scribes among others – all figured prominently as the beneficiaries of the new order (İnalcık 1980: 331). Harem women and governors, of course, had no intention of dwelling in the villages where they had their revenue assignments, as the provincial cavalry had done, so a class of lesser officials spread out across the empire and acted as their agents. The need for intermediaries was built into the system and thus was a step along the way to the rise of a local elite to assist in the collection of taxes, but this group, known as the *ayan*, would not come into their own until the eighteenth century.[4] In the meantime, with the demise of the *sipahi* class, which had provided not only military service but also administration in the countryside, provincial life became far more insecure. I shall return to this issue shortly.

The crisis of the elites, then, was empire-wide. Both at the center and in the provinces old sources of revenue declined while new ones rose. While the tax farmers who snatched up the contracts were not "new men" (and women) – they already enjoyed high positions in Ottoman society – their prominence in finance and in linking the provinces to the imperial capital was a real departure from older arrangements.

Before leaving Istanbul and turning to the provinces, there remains one more group to be considered in the light of this tumultuous period. The great difficulties of the patriarch have been fairly well documented, but what about the "archons," the Greek notables who figure so prominently in the history of the Ottoman capital between 1453 and the end of the sixteenth century?

Given the larger context of crisis and change, it is tempting to see the arrest and execution of Michael Kantakouzenos – the infamous notable who made and unmade patriarchs and who supplied the sultan with precious furs from Russia – as the end of an aristocracy with its roots in the late Byzantine era. Arrested in 1576, Kantakouzenoss was executed two years later, in his palace on the shore of the Black Sea (Iorga 1935: 120). The wealth that was on display at the auction to dispose of his fortune was so immense that the saying "it looks as if you bought it at Şeitanoğlu's auction" remained.[5]

Was it the end of an era? Scholars have divided on this point, which means, too, that they differ in their assessment of the Phanariots, the far better-known Greek elite that emerged in the second half of the seventeenth century. Some argue for a link between the Byzantine aristocracy and the Phanariots – this was, not surprisingly, the position taken by the Phanariots themselves – while others see a break between the late sixteenth century and the new Phanariot elite that emerged around 1650 (Janos 2005/6: 179).

Part of the difficulty is that the early seventeenth-century history of this community is obscure. The sixteenth century produced its share of chroniclers but around 1600 the practice appears to have come to a halt, at least temporarily.[6] Still, we can catch some glimpses of the Istanbul Greeks at this time, most of them thanks to the tensions produced by a growing Catholic presence in the region.

While one may remain agnostic on the question of actual familial continuity, it is clear that early seventeenth-century Greek elites continued to provide the same sorts of services to the palace that they always had.[7] These services clustered around trade and foreign relations, particularly with Russia, the sultan's increasingly powerful neighbor to the north. Both before and after 1600, it was the Istanbul Greeks who brought Russian furs – that coveted mark of status for Ottoman officialdom – to the empire. Prior to his execution Kantakouzenos received 60,000 ducats a year from the sultan to import furs from Russia and in the first half of the seventeenth century we know that another Kantakouzenos – Thomas – was trading with Russia on a regular basis. Greeks were still bringing back furs from Russia in the eighteenth century (Iorga 1935: 121; Hering 1992: 64; Stoianovich 1960: 262). Trade and diplomacy, of course, went hand in hand and in 1621 we see Thomas Kantakouzenos heading up an Ottoman embassy to Moscow. The embassy originated in an overture that the powerful patriarch, Kyrillos Loukaris, made to Sultan Osman II. Loukaris proposed asking the Muscovites to move against Poland, an intervention that would take pressure off the empire. This was not a disinterested suggestion. The patriarch had his own reasons for wishing to put Poland on the defensive and the coincidence of Ottoman and church interests in the early seventeenth century must have rendered the Istanbul Greeks as useful as ever.[8]

In the late 1580s Patriarch Jeremiah traveled to Muscovy, the first trip ever by an Ecumenical patriarch to the eastern Slavic lands.

His extraordinary move was occasioned by the church's alarm over Catholic overtures in Russian and eastern Europe, overtures that would culminate, just a few years later, in the Union of Brest. By the terms of the Union the Polish–Lithuanian Commonwealth broke with Istanbul and Moscow and put itself under the authority of Rome. After Jeremiah, Loukaris himself had been intimately involved in Orthodox efforts to prevent this, traveling to Poland in 1596 (Ware 1964: 24). A quarter of a century later, now Patriarch Loukaris was hoping to convince the sultan to ask Orthodox Russia to move against Catholic Poland, and the 1621 embassy shows that Osman was willing to consider this proposal. The flurry of activity occasioned by the Union of Brest – as early as 1611 the Habsburg ambassador in Istanbul observed that the "Greek notables" of the city were pushing the Turk toward war with Poland – allows us a glimpse of the Greek elite of Istanbul at a transitional moment when they have been less visible to the historian, sandwiched in between the wealthy tax farmers of the sixteenth century and the Phanariots who rose to prominence later on.[9] That glimpse suggests that the expertise that they could provide to the palace – in trade, in diplomacy, and in the linguistic skills that both required – differed little from century to century.

Having said this, however, there was something genuinely novel about the elite that emerged in the second half of the seventeenth century. Their relationship to the state was far more stable than what their antecedents had enjoyed and the Phanariots, as they came to be known, functioned more as bureaucrats than as personal servants of the sultan. This transformation did not belong to them alone but was part of a larger trend in Ottoman governance toward bureaucratization, which, in turn, owed much to greater stability in the second half of the seventeenth century.

To the mountains

If in seventeenth-century Istanbul Greek elites continued to serve the sultans as diplomats, traders, and translators, far from the imperial capital radical change was afoot in the provinces. From Bosnia to Palestine, rising levels of insecurity and changing methods of provincial administration combined to make life harder for the Ottoman peasantry. In response, peasant communities transformed themselves and in some cases these transformations created new opportunities for enterprising provincial actors. The Balkan sheep market is a good perch from which to view these transformations.

"In 1579 the voyvoda of Moldavia reported that 180,000 sheep had crossed the Danube at Ishakci on the way to Istanbul" (Greenwood 1988: 22; see also Lyberatos 2009). These sheep were participants in a system that had been set up to ensure Istanbul's provisioning in all sorts of goods, of which grain and meat were the most important. Rural producers, located in an arc around Istanbul that ran from the southern shores of the Danube in the northwest to Thessaly in the southeast, were obligated to provide a certain quota of sheep to Istanbul on an annual basis. Sheep breeding was the province of the hills and the mountains where it would not compete with intensive agriculture; very few sheep were demanded from the plains of Thrace, for example, since livestock would interfere with the intensive agriculture of the lowlands (Greenwood 1988: 116). The peasants had to sell their sheep at an artificially low price, set by the state, and local Ottoman officials kept registers of the number of sheep purchased, the date when the sheep were dispatched to the capital, and the name of the person into whose care they had been entrusted.

This system changed quite abruptly at the end of the sixteenth century, in the space of about fifteen years. The peasants' obligation to provide sheep was converted into a tax and a separate position was created for the task of ensuring that sufficient numbers of sheep were brought to the city (Lyberatos 2009: 168–9). This was the solution that the Ottomans devised to confront the increasing inability of the system to supply the required number of sheep.[10] There had always been corruption in the system – the drovers might, for example, sell off some sheep along the way – but the new problem of inflation, and, possibly, decreasing security, made the issue much worse. The state responded by contracting out the problem. Although we are speaking here about sheep, it is vital to bear in mind that the turn to contractors was a general one, affecting the collection of taxes and provisioning of goods across the entire empire. The motivations were several. As outlined earlier, changes in military organization drove the turn to tax farming, while the declining ability of the state to intervene effectively in the provincial economy was behind the decision to change how sheep would be brought to Istanbul. Regardless of the reason, the end result was the same: in the capital and in the provinces a wider pool of enterprising individuals was able to grab a share of the state's business for themselves. This was true for both Muslims and Christians.[11]

In the sheep-herding villages of the Balkans, then, the Christian contractor emerged as an important force in society. Often combining the collection of the sheep tax with the provision of sheep to the capital, by the second half of the seventeenth century these *celeps*, as the sheep merchants were known, controlled herds numbering in the thousands and vast areas of pasturage. Andreas Lyberatos' study of nineteenth-century elites in Plovdiv in today's southern Bulgaria demonstrates the intimate link between social status and the sheep economy.

The Tsalikov family was a powerful clan in nineteenth-century Plovdiv with its roots in the mountain village of Koprivštiča. In Plovdiv they were members of the *çorbacı* class, a title that, by this time, had come to denote the local Christian nobility.[12] Chatzi Voulkos (1730–1810), the founder of the clan, was a *celep* as well as the collector for the tax that the villagers had to pay in lieu of the former tax in kind, and all of his descendants followed in the same path. The *çorbacıs* of Edirne, too, were all from the mountains and all were in the sheep business (Lyberatos 2009: 170). Although the *çorbacı* class would not come into its own until the eighteenth century – the century when all provincial power holders in the empire realized their greatest strength – its origins lay in the transformations of the early seventeenth century. These Christian elites proved to be remarkably enduring; the Tsalikov family, as we have seen, can be traced back to 1730. Consider, too, that the village of Kotel in today's eastern Bulgaria, the birthplace of the future Phanariot prince Stephanos Vogorides, not only was a center of prominent sheep merchants but also enjoyed the status of a *derbend* village, those favored settlements granted tax exemptions by the Ottomans in exchange for the guarding of mountain passes. This raises the possibility that the geography of the sheep economy can be traced back even earlier than the seventeenth century.

It is not a coincidence that this Christian elite-in-the-making began to form in the mountain villages of the Balkans. Their rise was part of a shift of Christian society, away from the plains and into higher altitudes, in the seventeenth century (Tsampouras 2013b: 38). The desertion of the plains was, in fact, an empire-wide phenomenon but its causes and its consequences were not identical across the area.

The series of revolts that rocked Anatolia in the early seventeenth century are known most commonly as the *celali* revolts, but the term *Büyük Kaçgun*, or Great Flight, is also used because so many peasants fled their villages. The traditional explanation has been that, as with the shift to tax farming, changes in military organization were the key factor in creating the disturbances.[13] By the end of the sixteenth century Ottoman military leaders – from the sultan to provincial governors and on down the line – were looking for people who knew how to use firearms, and that meant the recruitment of mercenaries, referred to in the sources as *sekban* or *sarıca*. The pressure on the governors was especially acute as the central state attempted to offload military costs onto them. They came to understand that the recruitment of a mercenary army, the larger the better, was the key to political power. Anatolia was their recruiting ground and the arming of the Anatolian peasantry led to the militarization of the countryside (Barkey 1994: 155). If the first *celalis* were those cavalrymen dismissed from the Ottoman frontlines in Hungary, the subsequent scramble on all sides for adequate manpower ensured that the phenomenon would take on much larger proportions. The mercenaries did not in any way enjoy the stability of the janissaries, who, as *kuls* or slaves of the sultan, were official members of the *askeri* or ruling class. İnalcık's description of state recruitment of mercenaries vividly conveys the risks of such a system. The sultan would send out standards equal to the number of companies that were to be formed, and an appointed commissioner was tasked with recruiting the required number of men. Under each standard a *bülük*, or company, of fifty or one hundred *sekban* under a *bülük-başı* would be assembled. The moment a standard was taken back the *bülük* was considered legally dissolved and any further military activity was illegal (İnalcık 1975: 200–1).

Unsurprisingly, things went otherwise in practice and soon the Anatolian countryside was full of peasants-turned-militiamen who did everything from robbing and looting the peasantry, to collecting illegal taxes, to serving in the retinues of ex-governors who had gone into full-scale revolt. For those peasants who did not take up arms the response was flight, to the mountains and to the cities. Refugees from eastern Anatolia showed up in places as far away as Varna, Istanbul, and even Crimea (Faroqhi 1994a: 437). Armenian migration to Aleppo was extensive enough that at mid-century the government came up with a new kind of head tax, the *yave cizye* (the "*cizye* on those who had strayed"), in recognition of the changed conditions (Masters 1988: 85). Across Anatolia villages in the plains simply disappeared, while those in hilly country survived much better (Faroqhi 1994a: 442–3).

When we turn to the Balkans we see a similar retreat from the plains, along with a dwindling number of villages. The well-preserved records from the town of Veroia in today's northern Greece, for example, show this very clearly, as does documentation from central Greece (Gara 2007: 56; Hütteroth 2008). But there were no *celali* revolts in the European areas of empire.[14] There was little recruitment of *sekban* or other mercenary troops among the Balkan populations, whether Christian or Muslim (Faroqhi 1994a: 437; İnalcık 1975: 200). Flight from the plains and village collapse seem to have been driven by more mundane, although equally consequential, developments, namely a rise in taxation as well as extra-legal exactions from the peasantry.[15] In addition to the hunt for new revenue as the *timar* system fell into disuse, the seventeenth century saw a sharp rise in the amount demanded as head tax (the *cizye*) from the non-Muslims (Kiel 1996: 332). This was of course extremely consequential in the mostly Christian Balkans. As the villagers fled (or were pushed out) profit seekers rushed in and took over the fertile plains. In most cases, they converted the land from agriculture to pastoralism, as the latter required less labor. Although we do not yet know whether environmental degradation contributed to the flight to the mountains, it is clear that the rise in pastoralism did have deleterious effects. The land could support grazing even without upkeep and thus drainage was neglected. The land turned swampy and malaria became widespread. This, in turn, increased the attractiveness of the mountains, which were poor but healthier and safer (Hütteroth 2008: 29–35).

Cultural dynamism followed the Christians into the mountains. Early in the seventeenth century small monasteries – mimicking the trend in Islamic architecture away from ornate Friday mosques toward modest *medreses* – appear in out-of-the-way areas that had no previous tradition of monastic life. This development was extremely widespread, and has been documented for southern and continental Greece, for Macedonia and Epirus, and for Bulgaria and southern Albania (Tsampouras 2013a: 19). It is, at first glance, a rather puzzling phenomenon, given the well-known stress at the established monastic centers due to both the confiscation crisis of 1568 and the overall economic situation. In fact the growth of monastic life in the mountains of the Balkans appears to be a direct response to the insecurity of the early seventeenth century, and deserves to be included in any discussion of the Ottoman peasantry's reaction to the unsettled conditions of the times. All of these monasteries acquired a significant amount of property in a short period of time, and the reasons seemed to be tax relief and protection. Monasteries continued to enjoy a lower tax rate than that paid by ordinary peasants laboring on their plot and thus there was an incentive for a peasant to donate his property to a monastery. He would continue to cultivate the land, just as he had before, but the tax burden would be less. More generally, there was a sense that property that now belonged to a monastery was more secure at a time when the land regime was in upheaval, for the reasons explained above. In short, monasteries offered at least the hope of protection in a turbulent age and thus even those without land tended to cluster around them, hoping for employment as well (Tsampouras 2013a: 19–20).

Despite the rapid acquisition of land by the monasteries, the new mountain communities were not (yet) places of wealth. The difficult conditions of artistic production mentioned earlier – long delays in the completion of the interior decorations of churches, the assembling of large groups of small donors in order to fund projects – were on full display in the mountains. But the willingness of ordinary villagers to fund such projects shows an ability to respond creatively to new conditions, as did the appearance of a new kind of artisan.

This was the traveling painter, usually a villager, who traveled constantly and far and wide in order to find commissions. The most prolific and well established, as documented in research published in 2013, all hailed from the extremely remote area in and around Mount Grammos, the massif that towers almost 5,000 feet above today's Greek–Albanian border. In the beginning the "Mount Grammos painters" were neither well trained nor artistically talented; oftentimes they painted iconic programs in the incorrect sequence and it is clear that that worked in a rush.[16] The impression is of a group of entrepreneurs who had found something that they could sell. They clearly enjoyed great success, since samples of their work have been found as far away as Bulgaria. Their ability to win commissions must have been helped by the fact that, although Greek was probably the mother tongue of most of them, they were also able to work in the Cyrillic alphabet.

These peripatetic adventurers traveled along already established routes that were used by nomadic herders, who moved between the mountains of Pindos in the summertime to the plains of Epirus, Macedonia, and Thessaly in the winter, and small-scale itinerant traders. Their business model, in fact, was very similar to that of the traders; both had to travel constantly, and often very far, in order to find customers (Murphey 1996: 188).

In time, these herders and traders would become the well-known merchants of the upland communities, carrying the products of Balkan animal husbandry – wool, milk, butter, cheese, and hides – all the way to Vienna. In the first half of the seventeenth century, however, neither the traders nor the painters had yet come into their own. It is only later that a new level of cultural confidence becomes very apparent, as does a symbiotic relationship between the producers of art and the movers of goods. Artistic quality improves markedly and the painters of these later decades develop a new visual style, one that combines elements of a number of different traditions, including Islamic decorative patterns (Tsampouras 2013a: 8). At the same time, inscriptions show that merchants begin to appear as patrons. Earlier icons were painted and churches were decorated solely through the efforts of the monks themselves, often supported by the laity as mentioned before. But now a rising commercial class begins to take over, following a time-honored social tradition in which Christian elites signaled their status by sponsoring artistic production (Tsampouras 2013b: 398).

The formation of commercial elites in the period after 1650 coincides with numerous signs of stabilization across the empire, although the connection between the disparate developments is still unclear. We shall return to the question of stabilization later on, but, before leaving the mountains, the fact of parallel trends deserves to be underlined. This is because the migration to the mountains is often presented as a flight from the empire itself, there to live in splendid isolation. When trade is discussed, it is often the eighteenth-century commerce with central Europe that is emphasized. Such an argument is misguided on several counts. First, there is the evidence of chronology. The crisis in artistic production reached its height between the first and third decade of the seventeenth century, precisely when conditions in the empire were at their most turbulent (Tsampouras 2013b: 10). Similarly, prosperous merchants and gifted painters emerged as the situation improved. Second, as the example of the Tsalikov family suggests, the upland economy was always connected to the world of the plains. Traveling through Macedonia, Evliya Çelebi commented on the opulence of the fair of Dolyan, held once a year in a broad plain near the city of Stromnica, in today's Republic of Macedonia. In addition to the slaves, the cherries (the fair was held at the time of the cherry harvest), and the fabrics of silk and velvet for sale, there was also the sheep market, where "hundreds of thousands of lambs and goats are bought and sold" (Asdrachas 2007: 94). Finally, the Mount Grammos painters included Ottoman motifs in their work, of the sort "easily found in any Ottoman city" (Tsampouras 2013a: 6). Most commonly the saints were depicted wearing the silken garments characteristic of the Ottoman elite (Tsampouras 2013b: 409).

Urban centers

If it is certain that, across the empire, peasants were fleeing the plains in the seventeenth century, it is not so clear that they all headed for remote locales. Anatolians in particular migrated to cities in their quest for security.[17] Although some cities suffered terribly as a result of *celali* attacks – they laid siege to Ankara and even briefly occupied Bursa – other cities actually grew during this period (Aleppo and Izmir) or seem to have managed to recover quite quickly (Sivas). Thus the fate of the cities in this period is more mixed than the clear downward trends in the countryside (Faroqhi 1994a: 442).

Cities in the Balkan peninsula present a picture of stability in the seventeenth century; they were neither the destination of refugees (although we know that some of those fleeing the violence in Anatolia did end up there) nor did they suffer the population losses occasioned by the *celalis* in Anatolia. This is important to note not just because of the contrast between the two areas of the empire – to equate the seventeenth century with the *celali* revolts is to fail to take into account the rather different history of the Balkans – but also because the undoubted growth of Christian settlement in the mountains should not be allowed to sweep up all of Christian life in its wake. Balkan cities continued to have important Christian populations and the historical record indicates that life for these urban dwellers was relatively calm. The dramatic changes that we have been describing in the rural areas seem not to have left much of a mark.

For instance, consider Veroia, where Eleni Gara's work has done so much to illuminate the life of this Macedonian city. A Byzantine scholar's assessment of the history of Byzantine Veroia, Gara tells us, is broadly true for the Ottoman period as well.

> The city happened to be located in the hinterland of a mighty empire, an empire which brought serenity and peacefulness to those within its embrace. It makes sense that the historical record will have little to say about a city in such a privileged place, as is the case for all those in a similar geographical situation. (Gara 2007: 53)

This relative stability is apparent in the number and ratio of the city's neighborhoods: at the beginning of the sixteenth century there were twelve Muslim and seventeen Christian neighborhoods; fifty years later there were eighteen Muslim neighborhoods while the Christians held steady at seventeen. One hundred years later, in the middle of a very difficult century, the numbers were sixteen and fifteen respectively (Gara 2007: 57). Kyrillos Kontares was the metropolitan of Veroia prior to becoming the Ecumenical patriarch (in the 1630s) and Metrofanes Kritopoulos, an intellectual figure of the seventeenth century who studied at Oxford and became patriarch of Alexandria, was born in Veroia in 1589.[18]

Moving further east, to Serres, we are fortunate to have the exceptional manuscript penned by Synadinos, a local priest in 1642. In his commentary on the text, Socrates Petmezas notes that Synadinos does not give us the impression that the city is suffering from population decline, much less anything that could be called catastrophic, and Evliya Çelebi, the indefatigable traveler who passed through there roughly twenty-five years later on his way to Crete, described it as a flourishing town, with impressive houses belonging to wealthy merchants (Petmezas 1996a: 463–4).[19] Armenians in eastern Anatolia suffered the full brunt of the *celali* attacks, and their chroniclers described scenes such as the following:

> They resorted to inhuman torture, hanging the peasants by their feet to force them to reveal where they had hidden the remainder of their victuals. An old sick monk in the Cloister Hovhannanvank was tortured to death in an effort to make him disclose the hiding place of the church-treasures and vestments. (Barkey 1994: 183)

Although he is writing in the same period (the chronicle covers the period 1598–1642), there is nothing like this in Synadinos' account. He records instead seemingly endless rivalries with other priests for positions in local church administration, rivalries that included frequent trips to Istanbul to denounce the other side and thus gain an advantage. There are, of course, more serious problems. Famine struck in the early 1620s and in 1630 all of the shops were destroyed by a huge fire, which was followed by looting. Many people, he noted, never recovered (Odorico 1996: 84, 109). And the residents of Serres added to the misery by pursuing violence against each other; Synadinos relates the story of one Alexander Tartarhane, who, together with the *voyvode* (an Ottoman official) of Serres took a stroll into the neighborhood where the hash-smokers resided. A fight broke out and a "Turk" was severely beaten. After a series of investigations and accusations, all of the blame was settled on Alexander and he was hanged for the crime (Odorico 1996: 106).

Such events, although certainly distressing for the residents of the town, are in no way comparable to the upheavals caused by the *celalis* in Anatolia and were not enough in and of themselves to disturb the essential stability of life in seventeenth-century Serres.[20]

Perhaps the most powerful image of social peace is found in the obituary that Synadinos penned for his father in 1635. His father, he wrote, made between four and six trips to Istanbul in his lifetime in order to negotiate lower taxes, which he did successfully. He was also able to obtain permission to build a new church, for no better reason than the fact that the existing one was too far from the village. Synadinos praised his father for the hospitality that he extended on a daily basis to "Christians and Turks, Koïnari and gypsies." When he died, Synadinos continued, he was mourned by all (Strauss 2002: 207–8).

As we saw in the case of Veroia, stability has a way of being overlooked in the historical record. But Christian urban culture in the Balkans was overwhelmingly Greek, no matter the character of the rural population. In the case of Serres, for example, a sixteenth-century French traveler noted that the Christians in the town "parlant un grec vulgaire" while the countryside was Greek and Slavic (Petmezas 1996a: 444). Therefore these overlooked urban dwellers in the Balkans should lead us to question both the mistaken assumption that the cities were exclusively Muslim and the habitual focus on a few well-known centers, namely Istanbul, the Danubian Principalities, and, to a lesser extent, Chios. Scholars do recognize that in the eighteenth century Christian populations in the urban centers began to grow by leaps and bounds, and as a result we know quite a bit more about the eighteenth century. What I am suggesting here is that Christian communities, and hence Greek culture, had a longer, and more continuous, history in the cities than has conventionally been recognized.

Changing cities

If Balkan urban centers in the seventeenth century managed a relatively stable demographic profile, in other respects significant change was underway. It is in this century that we see the emergence of communal structures as the result of the changing fiscal practices mentioned earlier, particularly the appearance of new taxes, paid in cash, which were levied on communities, rather than individuals, and collected by tax farmers rather than *sipahis*. A much older generation of Greek scholarship explained the growth of communities as the result of a developing national spirit, but new scholarship has very clearly established that it was new fiscal demands that led to the greater articulation of communities (Petmezas 2005). Decisions had to be made about who would pay and how much, and community leaders appeared who set about doing just that.

Documents from the *kadi* court of Veroia show the beginning of this process, in the seventeenth century when information is still fairly scarce (Gara 1998). Collectivities such as "the Christians of the town" and "the Christian town neighborhood" appear much more frequently starting in the middle of the century. So, too, do references to community representatives, although they are designated in a rather random fashion that suggests that their positions had not yet stabilized. These collectivities appear in court most frequently with regard to tax matters, whether they are appointing a representative (*kethüda*) to undertake the actual tax collecting or chasing down a recalcitrant tax payer. But they have other roles too. In Veroia the community is farming the *monopolye* tax, which is a tax on spirits imported into the town. It also possesses a common fund that it lends out and uses to pay taxes, as well as to buy and sell real estate (Gara 1998: 152, 160).

In all of these activities the Christians of Veroia exactly resemble their Muslim counterparts elsewhere in the empire. This is not surprising, given that the new cash taxes were imposed on Muslims and Christians (and Jews) alike. But their parallel paths, and certain aspects of Christian collective activity, do raise important questions in light of more recent historiography.

When discussing the Balkan sheep contractors who arose as a result of the rise of tax farming earlier in the chapter, I had framed them as entrepreneurs who were able to profit from the services that they provided to the state. Such a framework is deliberate and endorses the new historiography on the seventeenth and eighteenth centuries. Ottoman commentators at the time, as well as many Ottoman historians of earlier generations, bemoaned the entry of outsiders (*ecnebis*, literally "foreigners") into Ottoman state administration in this period as a sign of Ottoman decline. These would be the new tax farmers. These commentators and historians also saw the decay of the feudal system as a corruption of the empire and the proper order of things. Now a new paradigm is being argued, which sees not corruption but the expansion of market relations, and not decline but rather growth in the number of individuals who had a stake in the system (Tezcan 2010).

However, this revisionist vision of a society transformed by market relations and an increasing number of stakeholders is very much confined to the Muslim community. In the opening pages of Tezcan's book, it is a group of soldiers who hope to use their profits from tax farming to purchase even more lucrative government positions. And the widespread use of the cash endowment (*vakıf*) in which people basically lent money at interest – a key component in Tezcan's argument about the growth of market society – has so far only been considered in relations to Muslims.

We know that there were Christian tax farmers, in Veroia and elsewhere (Darling 1994: 128). The question of Christian cash endowments is far murkier. The common fund of the Christians of Veroia and the uses to which it was put, sound similar to the cash endowments that were being set up all over the empire at this time. Muslim neighborhoods also used the interest generated by the endowed cash to pay the taxes owed (Tezcan 2010: 33; Behar 2003: 67; Canbakal 2004: 131–8). However, the cash endowment was a very specific, and rather peculiar, institution that generated enormous controversy and was subject to regulations, such as limits on how much interest could be charged, as part of making it more acceptable (Çizakça 1995: 332). Given the limited research on this question, any statement must be tentative, but at this point it seems more likely that Christian common funds were not held as cash endowments. An entry from the registers of Veroia speaks simply of "the money of the neighborhood of Ayo Yani" (Gara 1998: 151). George Salakidis has published one court register from Larissa in the middle of the seventeenth century in its entirety; cash endowments are ubiquitous in the Muslim community but not one appears for either the Christians or the Jews (Salakidis 2004: 78).

Salakidis comments that in Larissa the cash endowments were a significant source of credit, accounting for about 50 percent of the lending recorded in the register. Both Muslims and Christians were borrowers. Christians, however, never appear as lenders. The important role of the cash endowments in the credit market in Larissa brings us to a final point about this institution; these funds were not expended only on the tax obligations of neighborhoods and villages. They provided credit for consumption and for entrepreneurial activities as well. It is this latter role that makes them so important to Tezcan's argument about an emerging market society (Tezcan 2010: 33).

The seeming minutia of tax-farming contracts and the legal status of cash reserves are directly relevant to an evaluation of Tezcan's arguments from the point of view of the sultan's Christian subjects. Can it be argued that changing fiscal practices created Christian, as well as Muslim, stakeholders? Did Christians, too, participate in emerging market relations?

In the seventeenth century Christian elites begin to emerge in the urban centers as a direct result of new ways of collecting taxes that rely on greater community involvement. These elites are still in their infancy in this period but assuming (as I think we must) that prominent individuals valued their new role in urban administration, then we must conclude that Christians, as well as Muslims, found something valuable in "the second Ottoman Empire," to use Tezcan's title. In addition, Muslim and Christian urban elites emerged from the same processes. As we shall see in the next chapter, this view of the seventeenth century differs from the conventional narrative, which argues that, with the end of the *devşirme*, Christian participation in Ottoman governance declined

Having made this argument, however, the following difference must be underlined. While Christian elites found that they were able to enhance their position through the domination of communal instutions – and this would become even more true in the eighteenth century – these selfsame institutions were also the only opportunity that Christians had within Ottoman state structures, with the important exception of the Phanariots and the church (Petmezas 2005: 72). This would explain why Christian funds, too, seem to have been much more closely connected to communal needs, whereas the cash endowment was used by Muslims for a wider range of purposes. In other words, trends in Ottoman governance created opportunities for new elites but Muslim horizons were wider than those of their Christian counterparts.

When it comes to the growth of market society, of course no one would protest the inclusion of Christians. This is because of the very strong association – for good reason – of Christians with commerce, particularly external commerce with the rising powers of Europe, in this period. The corollary of this, in the conventional narrative at least, has been the decay or decline of something conceived as Muslim or Ottoman society. Put most crudely, it is the stereotype of the Greek as trader and the Turk as soldier. An appreciation of a general move toward market, as opposed to feudal, relations in Ottoman society in the seventeenth century undercuts this binary and suggests several things. First, the fortunes of Christians and Muslims were not moving in radically opposed directions. Second, Christian merchants – among whom the Greeks were the most prominent – were part of a changing society. It is a mistake to think of them as the dynamic exception in an otherwise declining empire. Having said this, it does seem that, in the seventeenth century, there was more room for Christian entrepreneurship in the mountains than there was in the plains and the cities. However, possible links between the emerging Christian communal institutions in the cities and a nascent merchant class have yet to be explored. For example, litigation from Veroia in the first half of the seventeenth century shows that the community lent money to two salt merchants named Kiryazi and Dimo and thus obviously Christian (Gara 1998: 151).

Smyrna

As the upland communities of the Balkan peninsula were beginning their slow ascent into centers of overland trade, a new kind of maritime settlement was developing on the shores of western Anatolia. This city – Smyrna to the Greeks, Izmir to the Turks – would turn out to be very consequential, both in the history of the empire more broadly and in the history of the Greek Christian subjects of the sultan more particularly.

Writing in 1923, in the immediate aftermath of the dramatic events of 1922 when the nationalist forces of Mustafa Kemal Atatürk expelled the Greek army, and the civilian Christian population, from Smyrna, the Red Cross officer Winthrop Lane said the following:

> Three thousand years ago tiny, daring ships pushed out from the Peloponnesus, the southern part of the Greek peninsula, crossed the Aegean Sea and landed on the shores of Asia Minor. From them debarked thousands of adventurous spirits who, seizing the central section of the 750 miles of coast line, founded city after city ... From that day to this Greeks have shared the western part of what we now call Anatolia with Persians, Turks and whoever happened to be there. (Lane 1923: 18)

Probably under the spell of Greek irredentist myths, Lane wrongly assumed that the Greek presence in western Anatolia had been continuous for three thousand years. As we have seen, the Turkish (first Seljuk, then Ottoman) conquest of Anatolia had reduced areas of significant Greek population to just two, both of them far from Smyrna – the area around Trabzon and a scattering of villages in Cappadocia. Although Ottoman records show a small community in Smyrna in the sixteenth century, significant Greek settlement did not begin until the following century. As with the flight to the mountains, Greek migration to Smyrna was the result of developments that were specific to the period.

In the third decade of the sixteenth century Smyrna was a small town of 207 households, of which only 14 percent were Christian (Goffman 1990: 11). The town grew steadily throughout the sixteenth century, but in this it was no different than towns and cities across the empire. Throughout this period Smyrna was just one port among many along the western Anatolian coast, all charged with supplying Istanbul with foodstuffs at fixed low prices and thus leaving little room for economic expansion (Goffman 1990: 14).

Then the town began to take off. Between 1589 and 1626 the customs tax farm for the area doubled and European consuls – French, English, Dutch, and Venetian – set up shop in the burgeoning port. The explanation was increased European interest in Ottoman primary products, in this case cotton, and a willingness, or even eagerness, on the part of local Ottoman actors to sell to them, rather than to government agents coming from Istanbul, and thus benefit from the higher prices that the Europeans were willing to pay. This is, of course, in line with the general trend toward market society that Tezcan has identified as an essential aspect of the "Second Empire."[21]

Attracted by the new opportunities, non-Muslims began to migrate to Smyrna. Their migration was visible enough that in 1640–1 the government took a census of the non-Muslims resident in the district of Izmir, precisely because it felt the need to stay on top of the dramatic changes in western Anatolia. The census revealed that the recent arrivals (in the previous twenty to thirty years) among the Armenians, Jews, and Greeks "outnumbered by four to one the entire non-Muslim population of the town in 1575" (Goffman 1990: 85). Greeks constituted 65 percent of this new group.

Many of the Greek residents of the city had migrated from Chios, which in this period lost its status as the entrepôt for international trade (Goffman 1990: 59–64). Nevertheless, in this period the Greeks were not yet the high-profile merchants they would become. It was the Armenians who were the traders, bringing in luxury goods from the east, while the Greeks were the shopkeepers, selling rather mundane items such as straw, lime, and homespun woolens. They were also highly visible in all of the professions – sailors, caulkers, and so forth – having to do with the sea. The Jewish community in Smyrna also had its distinct profile; the Jews were the tax collectors, the middlemen, the money-lenders, and the translators (Goffman 1990: 85–6).

What made Smyrna different, besides its rapid growth, was the unusual visibility of the European community. Already by the 1620s the Europeans held most of the shoreline properties in the city, and they proceeded to build secure homes and warehouses for themselves. This was the area that became known, famously, as "Franks Street." The French traveler Tournefort observed it thus in 1700:

> the Turks are seldom seen in the *Franks* Street, which is the whole Length of the City. When we are in this street we appear to be in *Christendom*; they speak nothing but Italian, French, English or Dutch there . . . They sing publickly in the Churches; they sing Psalms, preach

and perform Divine Service there without any trouble; but then they have not sufficient Regard to the *Mahometans*, for the Taverns are open all Hours, Day and Night. (Goffman 1990: 137)

If part of Smyrna's later notoriety came from the great fortunes that Greek merchants made there, the other part was due to the unease created by European encroachment. Smyrna came to be known as *gavur* Izmir, or "infidel Izmir." Also due to a constellation of forces that developed later, the Greeks came to be associated with the Europeans. But the Greeks must not be lumped in with the European community in the seventeenth century. They still had a rather humble profile and, as we shall see in the next chapter, relations with Catholic powers in particular – the Venetians and the French – were far from smooth.

In some ways, in fact, non-Muslim migration to Smyrna can be seen as just another variant on the many migrations that were so characteristic of this turbulent period, in this case movement from one city to another. Both Jewish and Greek newcomers to Smyrna came from older, established urban centers and it could be the case that the tax burden in a relatively new center such as Smyrna was less than what was being levied in places such as Thessaloniki. For the Jews the collapse of the textile industry in the latter city was key in their migration to Smyrna (Goffman 1990: 84).

In the long run, however, the growth of the Greek Orthodox population of Smyrna, and of western Anatolia more generally, would be extremely significant, which is why it merits a separate discussion. If the Ottoman conquests had, more or less, ended the Greek presence in Anatolia (with the notable exception of the eastern Black Sea), the seventeenth century witnessed the revival of Greek life there. Much later, in the nineteenth century, cultural missionaries would head out from Smyrna into the interior, with the professed goal of Hellenizing the Anatolian Orthodox populations. From now on, the heavy weight of the Balkans in Greek history under the Ottomans would be somewhat tempered by the rising fortunes of western Anatolia.

Stabilization

In 1666 Panayiotes Nikousios – a native of Chios who had already served as an Ottoman advisor during the Cretan War – was appointed the first chief dragoman (*baş tercüman*) of the Ottoman Empire. Earlier in the chapter I presented evidence for the durability of Greek elites in the capital, even during the difficult years of the early seventeenth century. Nevertheless, Nikousios' appointment was a novel departure and it is correct to see it as a turning point. Prior to 1669, Greeks such as Thomas Kantakouzenos had worked for the sultan in an informal capacity or, to be more faithful to the spirit of the times, as a personal servant to the Ottoman ruler. But in 1669 Nikousios was appointed to an actual office, the office of the chief dragoman, which enjoyed a fully official status within the chancery (Janos 2005/6: 182). From this position of relative security, prominent Greeks in Istanbul were able to acquire other offices as well – the dragoman of the fleet and, a little bit later on, the governorships (*hospodar*) of the vassal states of Moldavia and Wallachia. These office-holding Greeks came to be known as the Phanariots, after the neighborhood in Istanbul in which they lived, and the very fact that they came to have a name is an indication of the stability and permanence of their position.

It has often been argued that, as high-ranking Christian functionaries in a Muslim empire, the Phanariots were a strange anomaly, and it is true that their religious identity gives them the appearance of rather odd ducks. But the tendency to write them off as a fringe phenomenon is wrong.[22] The Phanariots are emblematic of a larger trend in Ottoman governance toward bureaucratization (Faroqhi 1994b; Findley 1980). From the scribal service to palace officials, servants of the state in the seventeenth century were marked less and less by their personal service to the sultan and more and more by their administrative responsibilities. Although some sultans were more activist than others, the bureaucracy took over much of the governance that had formerly belonged to the sultan alone. The Phanariots were able not only to acquire these offices, but to establish a monopoly as well; Armenians and Jews were forbidden from holding them and office-holders came exclusively from Phanar (Janos 2005/6: 184) In this way they were a precocious example of eighteenth-century trends. In the 1700s imperial elites managed to secure their positions against both the sultan and competitors further down the social hierarchy (Zilfi 1988).

In the mountains, too, a new elite emerged and cultural production came to rest on a firmer, as well as a more traditional, base. To judge from their appearance in inscriptions, merchants took over from monks and the laity as patrons of art. As we have already seen, earlier in the century in the village of Poratzonas (near today's Greek–Albanian border) forty-six villagers, offering 100 *akçe* each, had gathered together in order to begin the decoration of the interior of the small church of Agios Nikolaos. In 1684 just one patron, described as "the notable Balanos from Ioannina," successfully undertook the renovation of the entire church (Tsampouras 2013b: 10). The centers of patronage tended to be the developing trading towns, places such as Zagora in central Greece and Moschopolis in southeastern Albania (Tsampouras 2013b: 399–400).

It is also in the second half of the seventeenth century that the quality of artistic production improved, and the conservative tendencies of an earlier generation gave way to a new visual style. The appearance of elements from the Cretan school was facilitated by the ever-increasing geographic mobility of the Grammos painters, the rising fortunes of the Orthodox merchant class, and the arrival of Cretan refugees in the nearby Ionian islands (Tsampouras 2013b: 412). In the same period the use of Islamic motifs became much more widespread as wealthy patrons showcased their knowledge of contemporary decorative style (Tsampouras 2013b: 407–8).

Not everything, however, marched in lockstep. The office of patriarch continued to be insecure and major changes in the status of that office would not come about until early in the eighteenth century. This time lag, if we can call it that, raises the question of the relationship between different aspects of the rising fortunes of the Christian community, as well as the relationship between the Christian ascent and the Ottoman state.

With regard to the latter, the changing face of elite Greek education and the advent of the Köprülü vezirs were both key developments. In the seventeenth century Greeks began studying medicine at the renowned University of Padua. The careers of Nikousios and the second chief dragoman, Alexander Mavrokordatos (1641–1709), illustrate the intimate connection between medical knowledge and political power. Nikousios received his early education in Chios from the Jesuits and then went on to study at the Patriarchal Academy in Istanbul. He followed this up with several years study in Padua and then returned to Istanbul, at which point he became the personal doctor to Fazil Ahmet Pasha, the second of the Köprülü dynasty of vezirs who dominated the second half of the seventeenth century. It was after he took up this position that the pasha appointed him the first chief dragoman. Mavrokordatos, too, studied in Padua, as well as Bologna, and then succeeded Nikousios as Fazil Ahmet Pasha's doctor. In due course he became the second chief dragoman. In the literature on the Phanariots their western contacts are usually invoked to explain why they became such valuable diplomats. This was certainly true but it was the medical knowledge they gained abroad that gave them their entry into the highest levels of Ottoman governance (Janos 2005/6: 193–4).

Being the protégés of the Köprülüs, as Nikousios and Mavrokordatos certainly were, undoubtedly helped these early Phanariots stabilize their positions. Famously, the Köprülüs ruled with an iron fist and brought the factionalism and instability that had plagued the ruling elite for many decades under control, albeit at the price of massive repression.[23]

Up until the appointment of Panayiotis Nikousios as palace doctor, that position had been dominated by Ottoman Jews. From now on, most palace doctors would be Greeks. This change was part of a larger shift in which the sultan's Jewish subjects suffered a loss of privilege, while the Orthodox Christians saw their fortunes steadily rising. The reasons for this reversal have received some attention, with most concentrating on superior Christian education (Baer 2004). Marc Baer, however, has underlined dissatisfaction with the Jews; the messianic movement of Shabbatai Tzevi rendered the Jews unreliable in Ottoman eyes. We see this very clearly in the history of the palace doctors in the 1660s, when the Shabbatean movement was in full swing. Shortly before Nikousios' appointment the powerful Hatice Turhan, mother of Mehmet IV (1648–87), forced Moses Raphael Abravanel, the sultan's senior doctor, to convert or lose his position (Baer 2004: 180). It seems, then, that a combination of Greek usefulness and suspicion of the Jews brought about the change in the relative position of the two groups in the empire.

If the changing circumstances of the Greeks and the Jews in the second half of the seventeenth century have been fairly well documented, future research should take up the larger questions generated by these events. First, and this is a perennial question, what is the relationship between the power of elites and other members of the community? It is striking that the 1660s saw both the rise of Panayiotes Nikousios and tremendous hardship for the Greeks of Istanbul. Having told these Greeks in 1661 that they could rebuild on the properties that had been devastated by the great fire of 1660, the authorities changed their mind in 1662 and seized most of the rebuilt properties. Permission had only been given to build houses, not churches, and the Christians were charged with having built churches in the guise of houses. The man at the head of the reversal in policy was Fazil Ahmet Pasha, the very same man who was so instrumental in Nikousios' career (Baer 2004: 171). It was also Fazil Ahmet Pasha who decided to lend his support to Vani Mehmet Efendi, the leader of the Islamic reform movement known as the *kadizadeli*. Fazil Ahmet brought him into the palace, from where Vani Efendi launched various campaigns against the Christians and the Jews. For example, he convinced Fazil Ahmet to destroy the city's taverns and to end the legal trade in alcohol, a decision whose effects of course landed squarely on the non-Muslims (Baer 2004: 164).

The narrative of the second half of the seventeenth century takes it for granted that the rise of one group necessitates the fall of another. This makes intuitive sense but it remains to be investigated. Should it be considered as a principle of Ottoman governance? We know that in the same period Syrian Christians and Armenians took over the control of customs in Syria and Egypt, a position that had previously been dominated by Jews (Arbel 1995: 193). How is this development related, if at all, to the Istanbul story? Among Muslim elites in these later centuries, when clientelism and patronage were the fundamental building blocks of political life, the fall of a patron at the center meant the collapse of many individual careers all across the empire. Should we think of these ethnic groups as chains of patronage and clientelism as well?

This last question leads us into the murky waters of the relationship between the new prominence of Greek elites in the capital and evidence of a rising merchant class in the mountains. Particularly when compared to the clear links between the Köprülüs and the first Phanariots, we know next to nothing about this latter topic. Based on very little evidence, admittedly, I think links between the capital and the trading centers in the mountains begin to be established at some point late in the seventeenth century. I say this for several reasons. Tsampouras' work shows that artistic patronage moves out of the community itself and begins to attract the resources of merchants, such as Balonas of Ioannina. Research into Phanariot artistic patronage, outside of Moldavia and Wallachia, could help solve this puzzle. In addition, the evolving logic of Ottoman governance would seem to all but mandate such ties.

Here I am referring to the household, an institution that became a prominent part of Ottoman political culture in the seventeenth and eighteenth centuries (Hathaway 1995). In a reflection of the increasing dispersal of power, Muslim elites – both in the capital and in the provinces – gathered around themselves a following of slaves, servants, bodyguards, and assorted clients. Chronicles from Egypt referred to such formations as a *bayt* or house. Never a formally recognized legal status, membership in a household was nevertheless highly significant. Evidence from Egypt suggests that being a client of a household (*tābi'*) was a more important determinant of status than the slave/non-slave divide (Hathaway 1995: 43). These households were not local affairs; they drew together a diverse group of people, both ethnically and linguistically, from across the empire.

The household was not confined to Muslim elites. By the end of the eighteenth century, too, the Phanariots were consciously styling themselves as Ottoman households, albeit with some differences due to their status as non-Muslims. But certainly they had been building up their retinues for much longer than that and we know of several migrations in the seventeenth century. The founding member of the Ghika family – in the top echelon of Phanariot society in the eighteenth century – had come to Istanbul from Albania in the middle of the previous century. The Kallimaki family had done the same, coming from the Romanian principalities as had the Aristarchis, whose origins lay in the Black Sea area (Philliou 2011: 16, 28).

In the eighteenth century these processes became much more visible. It is likely, however, that they began in the latter half of the seventeenth century. One of the significant results of the rise of the Phanariot households was the Hellenization of those who joined them, just as provincial Muslims became Turkish in their orientation (Philliou 2011: 16). We shall return to this topic in the discussion of the eighteenth century. For now let us simply note that the Hellenizing aspect of Phanariot patronage, along with the Phanariots themselves and the success of the merchants of the upland communities, all served to prepare the way for the efflorescence of Greek culture and society in the eighteenth century.

Notes

1. Athenagoras (1929: 13–14). I thank Theocharis Tsampouras for the translation of this passage.
2. An inscription from 1612 tells us that forty-six donors contributed to the painting of the narthex of a church in a village in Epirus (Tsampouras 2013b: 8).
3. But see Baki Tezcan, who, in a sharply revisionist treatment, rejects what he sees as the technological determinism of the conventional narrative and attributes the changing nature of the military to "an intra-elite power struggle that encouraged each vizier to place as many of his clients as possible in the payroll of the sultan" (Tezcan 2010: 181).
4. İnalcık, in an article written in 1980, sees the *ayan* as directly following upon the changes of the late sixteenth century, but the prevailing view now is that in the seventeenth century Ottoman officials still dominated the tax-farming system.

5. Iorga (1935: 211). "Şeitanoğlu," or "son of the devil," was his nickname, as we have seen.
6. I thank Henry Shapiro for this information.
7. On the question of family continuity, however, it is worth pointing out that, after a brief stint in the galleys, Michael Kantakouzenos' son Andronicus was rescued by the grand vezir and was able to buy back his father's house (Iorga 1935: 121). In addition, Panayiotes Nikousios (to be discussed later on in the chapter) was the first Greek to hold the office of imperial dragoman, thus beginning the Phanariot period in the empire's history. Nikousios was appointed in 1666; his father had been a fur trader in the early seventeenth century (Bayraktar Tellan 2011: 102).
8. Gudziak (1998: 100). On one of his trips to Moscow, Thomas Kantekouzenos told a Muscovite that Sultan Murat, whose mental state was clearly poor, fed gold from his imperial treasury to fish in the Bosphorus (Hering 1992: 75).
9. See Hering (1992: 47) for the observations of the Habsburg ambassador. In his detailed study of Osman's reign, Baki Tezcan notes that many around the sultan did not feel that the Polish threat was important enough to warrant the sultan's personal participation but Osman II insisted on it anyway. Tezcan suggests he might have wanted to enhance his own position by leading a campaign. Could enthusiastic Christian support also have counted for something (Tezcan 2010: 136–7)?
10. Research by Sam White has made it clear just how desperate the situation was with regard to the meat supply for the capital. Mehmet III (1595–1603) "turned to the poor semi-arid province of Karaman in south-central Anatolia with a stunning demand for 200,000 head – probably more than twice as much as the region had ever provided in a single year" (White 2013: 76–7).
11. In my framing of this issue I am drawing on more recent Ottoman historiography, which emphasizes increasing participation in the imperial project in the seventeenth and eighteenth centuries. See the works of Tezcan (2010) and Yaycioğlu (2008).
12. The equivalent Greek term is *kocabaşı*.
13. But see White (2013), where he offers an important revisionist argument, namely that an environmental crisis lies at the origins of the *celali* revolts.
14. In his long article on the *armatole* system and the world of the mountains from the sixteenth century through 1821, Petros Pizanias does refer to two uprisings in the western Balkans at the end of the sixteenth century and beginning of the seventeenth. But it is not at all clear what the relationship is, if any, between these events and the much better-researched *celali* revolts in Anatolia (Pizanias 2013: 60–1).
15. Hütteroth (2008: 32). The abandonment of agriculture in the plains, even in the absence of *celali* rebellions, does lend support to White's argument for empire-wide environmental stresses. Nevertheless, almost all

references to environmental change in this period discuss only Anatolia. The Balkans remain to be investigated.
16. The phrase "Mount Grammos painters" was coined by Theocharis Tsampouras. To date he has been able to identify twenty-four painters from the villages around Mount Grammos (Tsampouras 2013a: 10).
17. As mentioned earlier, Armenians migrated to Aleppo at this time.
18. As was Ioannes Kottounios (1572–1657), who ended up as a professor of philosophy and Greek at the University of Bologna (Gara 2007: 58).
19. The Balkan cities produced many Muslim intellectuals but their work, by and large, does not shed light on local conditions because the cultural model was to write in a high Ottoman-Turkish style that was uniform across the empire. Thus there was little difference between a poet from Larissa and one from Baghdad. See Strauss (1996). In addition, the hundreds of thousands of Muslim emigrants and refugees from Thessaly, Epirus, and Macedonia have been silent about their origins and cultural heritage, in sharp contrast to the Orthodox Christian refugees from Asia Minor. For a rare study of Muslim émigrés from today's Greece, including a fascinating discussion of their history in the Balkans, see Tselatka (2011).
20. And see Doxiadis (2011: ix), who makes the same point about the relative tranquility of the area around Athens throughout most of the seventeenth century.
21. This is the term that Tezcan has coined for the period 1580 to 1826.
22. Here I am drawing on the arguments so well developed in Philliou (2011).
23. Finkel notes that it was at this time that the grand vezir's office was moved out of the palace, in the hope that by maintaining a distance from palace intrigues the office could recover some of the power it had lost (Finkel 2007: 253–5).

CHAPTER 6

Living with others

In 1616 the Orthodox patriarch of Alexandria Kyrillos Loukaris – who in just a few short years would become the Ecumenical patriarch in Istanbul – wrote the following words:

> For as long as we have been under the Turks our beliefs and our orthodoxy have remained inviolate. Now (we are confronted with) the recent arrival of the so-called Jesuits who, with great cunning and hypocrisy, are scheming to overturn and to ruin everything for us. (Hering 1992: 58–9)

One year later a Greek Orthodox refugee from the Ottoman Empire who had found safe haven in Oxford, England, published his account of the trials and tribulations he had suffered a decade earlier. Arriving at a moment of tension in Athens from one of the Greek islands, he was arrested as a possible spy for the Spanish. He was offered the chance to convert to Islam to escape from his difficulties but refused. Despite being scourged with rods dipped in salt water he remained steadfast in his faith. Happily it turned out his captors were willing to accept bribes and he was able to escape from Athens. Eventually he made his way to England (Krstić 2004: 121).[1]

These first-person texts give us an Orthodox perspective on two major challenges to Ottoman Christian society in the seventeenth century. The first was the arrival of the Catholic Reformation in the empire, most prominently in the form of the Jesuits although other groups were significant as well. The second was the specter of conversion to Islam. I have deliberately chosen the word "challenges" and avoided the use of the word "threats" because to use the latter is to uncritically adopt the perspective of religious elites, who, of course, did see both of these developments as profoundly threatening to the survival of the Orthodox in the empire. And they were threatening, but they were other things as well. The Latin missionaries also brought new opportunities and spurred educational and cultural initiatives in the Orthodox world. Changes in Ottoman society, some of which we have touched upon in the previous chapter, made conversion more attractive for certain Orthodox Christians, even as other Christians – such as Panayiotes Nikousios – found that they could thrive, as Christians, at the very pinnacle of Ottoman society. There is a paradox, actually, in the fact that even as the Phanariots carved out new positions of security, a major wave of conversions can be dated to the second half of the seventeenth century.

To begin, let us consider the Catholic presence in the empire. The first Catholic missionaries – three Jesuits and two Dominicans – arrived in Istanbul in 1583, riding on the coattails of the Ottoman–French alliance. Just three years later two of the three had died of the plague and the mission ground to a halt. But the Jesuits returned a decade or so later and this time they stayed. Other missions were soon established, in Chios, Smyrna, and Jerusalem. Although the various Catholic protagonists did not always agree on whether the missionaries should be pursuing the conversion of the Orthodox Christians (and the Armenians), the missions did consistently function as centers of education. At St. Benedict's in Istanbul, according to a missionary account, "there were people of diverse religious backgrounds in the classes. There were Greek monks and deacons and more than fifty children, Greeks as well as Franks. Some they taught how to read while others studied Greek and Latin grammar" (Belin 1872: 44–5). It was at just such a Jesuit school that Panayiotes Nikousios received his first education (Janos 2005/6: 192).

And there were other ways of making an impression. An anecdote from Smyrna in 1625 conveys how the reputation of the missionaries spread through society. Some relics in the possession of the Jesuits had acquired a reputation among the Greeks for helping barren women (Legrand 1869: 13).[2] A Turkish woman learned of their healing powers from a Greek woman and begged her to bring the relics to her. No sooner was the relic in the Turkish woman's house than she was cured. However, it took the Jesuits more than two months – and many entreatries – to retrieve the relics because the woman was afraid that, once she returned them, her maladies would return (Legrand 1869: 13–14).

Although we must allow for the tendency of missionaries to exaggerate their successes, the response of Loukaris and others makes it clear that the Orthodox leadership felt threatened by the Catholic presence in their midst. We have already seen, above, that Loukaris accused the Jesuits of cunning and hypocrisy. Speaking of a missionary school he wrote, according to Belin: "Ce collége était destiné à l'enseignement gratuit, *sous prétexte de charité*, de la grammaire, des langues et des arts libéraux" (1872: 45).

But it was not only that the Orthodox feared the new zeal of the Catholics; the Catholics, too, feared the Orthodox, particularly the brilliant Kyrillos Loukaris and his friendly relations with the Protestants. The brief, but dramatic, history of the Greek printing press in Istanbul illustrates the depths and the bitterness of their rivalry. Loukaris had been thinking about the printed book as a weapon against Catholic propaganda since at least 1614; it was in 1627 that he got his chance. A Greek monk from Kefalonia went on an extended trip to London and brought back not only printed books in Greek, but the complete apparatus of a printing press. With the help of the English ambassador, permission was quickly secured from the grand vezir and the printing press went into action. The titles chosen for publication were all polemical texts against Catholicism.

The French ambassador was deeply alarmed, as was the papacy, and went into action. He went to Ottoman officials and told them that the supporters of the printing press were printing books that contained anti-Islamic material, that they were also secretly printing counterfeit money, and so on and so forth. The calumnies had their effect; in early 1628 the janissaries were sent to destroy the press. Subsequent to the destruction the Ottoman authorities learned more about the role of Catholic interests in destroying the press and severe action was taken against the French and the Jesuits. Nevertheless, the Jesuits were allowed to stay and the press was not reconstituted (Hering 1992: 205–12).

The fracas over the printing press – which drew in the Orthodox leadership and the ambassadors of all the major European powers, as well as a number of Ottoman officials – was just one of the many highly visible clashes between Orthodox and Catholic interests in the seventeenth century. Control over the Church of the Holy Sepulchre in Jerusalem was another frequently contested battlefield (Frazee 1983: 79). As events that deeply concerned European elites, they have received a good deal of attention in the literature. But there is another story beyond the one of high politics, and this is the struggle within Ottoman society between those who wanted to establish clear religious boundaries and those who resisted such an attempt.

In setting up shop in the port cities of the Ottoman Empire, the Jesuits were not only coming into contact with Orthodox and Muslim populations. There was also an established Catholic community and this community already had its own way of getting along with the

Orthodox. Tensions between local Catholics and the missions were quick to surface as the latter tried to pull apart existing social arrangements. The patriarchal vicar, for example, tried to ban marriages between Catholic and Orthodox. He was disturbed by the practice in which wealthy Catholic families purchased a Greek bride, often sent from the islands expressly for that purpose. The marriage might well last only as long as the Catholic husband was resident in Istanbul (Frazee 1983: 80). The Vatican went after the practice of Jesuits and Capuchins offering mass in Orthodox churches and tried to forbid new converts from attending the services of their co-religionists (Frazee 1983: 91). These attempts to change social conventions failed utterly. Missionaries continued to say mass in Orthodox churches and the Orthodox gladly crowded into Latin houses of worship for instruction and for religious celebration. As late as the beginning of the nineteenth century the two Orthodox churches on the Aegean island of Syros still had Latin altars for the use of the Catholic clergy (Ware 1964: 20). And it was not only the Orthodox laity that welcomed the Jesuit presence; many clerics were enthusiastic as well. A letter written by Iakovos, metropolitan of Smyrna in 1632, to the king of France, no less, is entirely characteristic.

> From the time that [the Jesuits] arrived in our holy metropolis of Smyrna, they have never rested but instead have devoted themselves to helping any and all Christians [by providing] a good example and by proclaiming the word of the Lord in our churches and by teaching our children every kind of science and the fear of God and good ethics. (Gregoriou 1958: 190–1)

And this even as Catholic circles in Istanbul were continuing their battle to depose Kyrillos Loukaris from the patriarchal throne.

As for the missionaries, of course they had been sent out to bring the Orthodox into communion with Rome. Although we do not yet have a study on the evolving attitudes of the Jesuits and Capuchins who served in the Ottoman Empire, what seems to have happened is that, with residence in the empire, they came to take a far more lenient attitude toward the local population than that held by the Congregation de Propaganda Fide, which continued to see the Orthodox as the enemy (Frazee 1983: 91). A Capuchin missionary wrote the following in response to Rome's decree that converts not be allowed to continue to frequent Orthodox churches.

> It seems to me that one should leave the decision in this matter to the missionaries, who for a long time have held the opinion that converts

should not be forbidden to attend common services. The opposite opinion destroys every possibility and hope of doing any good in this mission and will lead to disastrous consequences. (Frazee 1983: 91)

In the words of one scholar of the subject, 'On the local level the fact of schism was in practice quietly ignored' (Ware 1964: 23).[3] This world of social practice co-existed with the brutal politics surrounding control of the patriarchate. In other words, there was not just one Catholic–Orthodox encounter; there were many.

The kind of pragmatism that the missionaries ended up adopting gave the Greeks the upper hand when it came to the Catholics, despite the sense of alarm that the Catholic presence created among the higher clergy of the Orthodox Church. They had the advantage because they could benefit from the educational opportunities that came with the Catholic missions, while deftly avoiding the conversion that the missionaries hoped would come with a Catholic education. This was true from the bottom to the very top of society. Panayiotes Nikousios went all the way to the Greek College of Rome to continue his education and even so, having attended a college created specifically to create an educated elite of converts to Catholicism, he returned home as an impassioned defender of Orthodoxy. The bitterness, and wonderment, this caused are evident in a report written for the *Propaganda Fide*: "Panionotto, a Schismatical Bishop (and heretofore the Grand Vizier's Interpreter), who was educated in our Greek College, has proved to be the greatest persecutor of the Catholicks, and contrived false writings to deprive them of the Holy Sepulchre" (Steele 1715: 51).

In addition, given the fluid situation in the Ottoman Empire, as well as the conflicting agendas of the many parties and the physical distance between Rome and mission stations further east, it was next to impossible to assess the sincerity of those who presented themselves as converts. Throughout the seventeenth century a string of petitioners came to Rome with requests for assistance, based on their supposed new Catholic identity (Greene 2010: 160–1). The Vatican, unsurprisingly, was very frustrated by this unwelcome result of their efforts, and the visitors from the east may well have contributed to its hardline attitudes relative to the missionaries. We shall see below that the archbishops of Ohrid made a series of overtures toward Rome; for now let us just consider Pope Urban VIII's response to the archbishop's request for help in the 1620s. The pope chose to read the prelate's vague words about submission as an acknowledgment of the primary of Rome, but even so, he clearly had his doubts. He wrote that the archbishop and his clergy could guide thousands of souls to the Catholic Church and he hoped that God would lift the yoke of slavery from them, as long as submission to the pontiff was being "made with an honest heart and not with false faith" (*si corde sincere et fide non ficta*) (Varnalidis 1979: 151).

Although Orthodox clergy were understandably anxious about contact between their flock and the Catholic missionaries, they actually had little to fear from what proved to be the small trickle of individual conversions. The real danger came from elsewhere, and that was the inability of the Ecumenical Patriarchate to control its own hierarchy. In the seventeenth century the Orthodox Church was buffeted by the threatening combination of weakness vis-à-vis the Ottoman authorities, discussed in the previous chapter, and Catholic overtures toward certain hierarchs. In Poland it was the Kievan bishops, after all, who had led their flock out of the Orthodox world and into union with Rome, a fact of which Loukaris was painfully aware, having been sent to Poland in 1596 to spearhead the Orthodox opposition to what became known as the Union of Brest (Greene 2010: 204).

The fractiousness of the Orthodox Church in this period was manifest at the very highest level. The instability of the patriarchal throne itself was not only due to changes within the empire – discussed in the previous chapter – but was also the result of incessant struggles between pro-Orthodox and pro-Catholic factions. Loukaris himself was deposed more than once by an alliance of Catholic powers in the capital (including the French ambassador) and sympathetic Orthodox clergy (Varnalidis 1979: 137–42).

Sitting in Istanbul, seventeenth-century patriarchs had to worry, too, about possible breakaway dioceses. Extensive research on the archbishopric of Ohrid, in today's Republic of Macedonia, allows us to see how these processes worked.

The medieval ecclesiastical history of Ohrid was a tortured one, the city sitting as it did on the border between Byzantine and Bulgarian zones of influence. The Byzantines watched as Tsar Samuel, setting up his empire, established a patriarchate at Ohrid. Later on, as Bulgarian strength declined, the Byzantines settled for an autocephalic metropolis in the city, and Bayezit maintained this compromise (Kiel 1985: 284). This wound in the Orthodox hierarchy began to fester again toward the end of the sixteenth century. The archbishops began to style themselves a "patriarch" and during the reign of Jeremiah II (1589–95) the archbishop, one Prochoros, bribed the Ottoman authorities in an attempt to gain control over the bishopric of Veroia (Tsampouras 2013b: 17).

Renewed Catholic interest in the Orthodox gave local actors more options and the clergy at Ohrid seem to have been particularly attracted by the new opportunities, perhaps because of their history, perhaps because of their location in the western Balkans on the outskirts of the Catholic world. Leo Allatius, a Chiot who rose to become a professor of Greek at the Vatican and the most prominent Greek Catholic intellectual of his day, listed four archbishops of Ohrid who pursued policies friendly to Rome, routinely initiating direct contact without going through the Ecumenical patriarch (Tsampouras 2013b: 16; Varnalidis 1979: 125). The letter that Archbishop (or Patriarch, as he called himself) Porfyrios wrote to Pope Urban VIII in 1624 is typical. He said that he and the metropolitan of Durres had been tasked by the local clergy to write to the pope and ask for help. The situation of the patriarchate of Ohrid, he explained, was terrible, as they were weighed down by massive amounts of debt. He concluded with vague promises of obedience if the pope would help, in both word and deed (Varnalidis 1979: 127–8).

How should we think about Porfyrios and other clerics like him? We can start with the interpretations that are not persuasive. However worrisome his activities must have seemed to the patriarch in Istanbul, it is highly unlikely that he ever intended to lead his flock out of the Orthodox world and into submission to Rome, as had the hierarchs in Kiev. Nor was he a proto-nationalist leader looking for liberation from Ottoman rule.[4] Here we are aided by the voluminous literature on the various personalities of the late eighteenth and early nineteenth centuries, when centrifugal tendencies in the empire were at their height. An older generation of historians argued that men such as Ali Pasha of Ioannina, Mehmet Ali of Egypt, and the Serbian revolutionaries of 1804 were intent on leaving the empire, motivated either by nationalism or simply by the desire for independence. Ottoman historians today are far more persuaded that what they and others like them were after was local control and local autonomy. Indeed one could argue that this agenda was so widespread, and appears so often in the history of the empire, that it should be seen as a perennial, if not always manifest, aspiration.

The archbishops of Ohrid, too, aspired not to leave the empire but to increase their stature within it. Thus we saw, above, Prochoros trying to expand his jurisdiction at the expense of the patriarch in Istanbul, and bribing the Ottomans in order to do so. The search for funds was also part of the attempt to raise the status of the ecclesiastical seat at Ohrid, as was the revival of the title "patriarch of Ohrid." Catholic overtures were attractive precisely because they were seen as an opportunity to dilute the power of Istanbul. In the first half of the seventeenth century the archbishops embarked on an ambitious program of artistic patronage, despite the straitened economic circumstances. It was because of their support that we can see today an extraordinary number of wall paintings in very remote places that, in that period, fell within the boundaries of the archbishopric. Saints with a local significance, such as Klemes and Acheillios, were heavily favored. The sponsorship of a local artistic style was inseparable from the quest for local autonomy and authority (Tsampouras 2013a: 17–18).

The boldness of the archbishops of Ohrid was inseparable from the weakness of the Ecumenical Patriarchate in the seventeenth century. As such, it must be understood within the general context of the Ottoman crisis, although it is likely that the pre-Ottoman history of the ecclesiastical see contributed to rebellious tendencies.

It turned out that Ohrid's fate, like that of the patriarchate of Peć, was most closely linked not to either the Catholic or the Orthodox Church, but to Ottoman fortunes in the northern Balkans and central Europe. We shall return to this question at the end of the chapter.

Neo-martyrs and Ottoman society

The neo-martyrs were the other face of Orthodox anxiety, in this case directed toward the Muslims in whose midst they lived. The neo-martyrs (so called to distinguish them from the martyrs of early Christianity) were those Christians who were put to death either because they refused to convert to Islam or, having converted, came to regret it and publicly returned to Christianity. The punishment was death.[5] Incidents of neo-martyrdom began to enter the historical record in the fourteenth century, as the Ottomans expanded in Anatolia and the Balkans, but the number of recorded cases made a major leap in the seventeenth century. Some of the accounts were written by people at the very pinnacle of Orthodox Christian society, such as Ioannes Karyofylles (d. 1692), who was a high official (*megas logothetes*) at the Ecumenical Patriarchate (Minkov 2004: 83; Sariyannis 2005/6: 250). In addition, the dramatis personae in the stories began to change in the late sixteenth century; spiritual advisors assumed a prominent role whereas they had been absent in earlier stories (Krstić 2011: 126).

In the words of one scholar of the phenomenon, the lives of the neo-martyrs were meant to function as a kind of "theological ecclesiastical propaganda" (Zachariadou 1990–1: 55). But propaganda with what goal in mind? It makes sense that part of it must have been to strengthen the faith of ordinary Christians, given ongoing conversions to Islam, and indeed this is the reason cited most often by historians. In this telling, the heightened attention that the church gave to heroic individuals who refused to abandon their faith was directly related to the rising numbers of converts. But the historical reality of conversion in the seventeenth century, while an important topic, is only part of the story. Across the board the age is one of heightened religious anxiety in the Ottoman Empire and the challenge is to understand what, if any, connection this anxiety had to the spectacle of non-Muslims embracing Islam.

There is an emerging consensus that conversion reached its height in the seventeenth century, which is in direct contrast to an older view that the phenomenon dropped off after the sixteenth century (Krstić 2011: 133–4; Terzioğlu 2013: 84; Minkov 2004: 4). This rests on arguments about demographic trends.[6] These are much more difficult to track in the seventeenth century than in the previous two hundred years because the Ottomans, due to changing fiscal practices as well as new realities on the ground, stopped producing the surveys that have provided historians with such a wealth of information for the period 1400–1600 (Darling 1994: 118–31). Scholars are forced to rely on the *cizye* (head-tax) surveys, which did continue to be drawn up. Thus systematic population information is being gathered only for the non-Muslims, and the problems this presents for studying conversion are immediately apparent. The argument, in a nutshell, is that Christians must have been converting to Islam because their numbers were dropping so dramatically. A study of a large swath of the eastern Balkans, based on the *cizye* records, shows that the non-Muslim population dropped by a third over the course of the century. In some areas in the second half of the century it fell by an astonishing 70 percent (Minkov 2004: 54–5).

The problem is that there is another consensus about the seventeenth century, and that is that overall population was dropping, as part of the general crisis that was affecting all of Europe as well. The distress was greatest in the countryside, which is where conversion had moved to by this period. This would mean that those missing Christians were not becoming Muslims; they were simply dying, alongside the equally unfortunate Muslim population (Faroqhi 1994a: 442).

I would submit that, although we cannot know the extent of conversion in this period, when the documents record a 70 percent drop in the Christian population, conversion must be at least part of the explanation and it is clear that the Christian population was not thriving. Gradeva, in her careful study of the city of Sofia in the seventeenth century, makes a similar point.

> I could not find relevant data about the number of Muslims and it is impossible to judge whether there was a general drop of the number of Sofians, or whether this only applied to non-Muslims in general or even only to Christians, but the very high number of people bearing Abdullah as a patronym and other details suggest widespread conversion to Islam among the Christians in Sofia at the time. (Gradeva 2005: 157)

Fortunately, there are narrative sources that can supplement the quantitative data, and these do suggest an atmosphere of crisis that could account for the new prominence of neo-martyrologies.

The dramatic reign of Sultan Mehmet IV (1648–87) is central to the story; among other reasons, the spectacular increase in the number of neo-martyrs came in the second half of the seventeenth century (Sariyannis 2005/6: 250). He broke with recent convention in numerous ways, several of which were very consequential for his Christian subjects, particularly those in the Balkans. First, by preferring Edirne as his capital and by launching campaigns in eastern and central Europe, he brought the Ottoman war machine to the Balkans. Second, these wars had a very special quality to them. He went personally on campaign in Poland because he wanted to revive the image of the sultan as *gazi* or warrior for the faith. The wars, in fact, were an extension of the ongoing religious revival known as the *kadizadeli* movement. Vani Mehmet, the fiery preacher who stood at the head of the movement in this period, went with Mehmet to war and played a direct role in battle (Baer 2008: ch. 8) Finally, in a real break with tradition, Mehmet IV was an active convertor of souls. Whether on campaign or on a hunting expedition, he made it his business to personally convert his non-Muslim subjects, which he did: "Hundreds of men and women changed religion at his feet during conversion ceremonies in which the sultan displayed his magnanimity by re-dressing the converts head to toe" (Baer 2008: 179). These were dramatic ceremonies, as were the ones that took place in at the palace, either in Edirne or in Istanbul. The sultan hosted a banquet for tens of thousands of people at the circumcision festivities of his sons in 1675. Among the guests were thousands of Muslim children who were circumcised as well; each received a set of clothes and some coins, thus making the sultan their symbolic father (Baer 2008: 190). But that was not all: the chaplain to the English ambassador attended the festivities and he noted, with regret, that there were several hundred Christian converts to Islam in the group. "There were at least 200 proselytes made in those 13 days. It is our shame, for I believe all Europe have not gained so many Turkes to us these 200 years" (Baer 2008: 190). In the 1660s and 1670s conversions before the sultan became so frequent that the grand vezir ordered the codification of the procedure (Baer 2008: 191).

These conversions were, quite literally, spectacles. They were also part of an attempt on the part of the dynasty to assert its importance at a time when other centers of power were attempting to rein in the sultan (Baer 2008: 201). In other words, making Muslims out of Christians was central to Mehmet's vision of the empire and this may have alarmed the leadership of the Orthodox Church. I must emphasize that this suggestion is purely speculative; no one has yet taken up the challenge of researching the response of Christian elites to Mehmet's reign.

For Mehmet – and the pious circles that surrounded him – campaigning and conversion were intimately bound up with each other. For the peasants of the Balkans the presence of troops often translated into misery, and this was the other way that war probably led to conversion. The group of converts known today as Pomaks – Muslim Bulgarians living in the Rhodope mountains – converted in the seventeenth century. A number of contemporary Bulgarian sources directly link troop movements through the area with acts of violence perpetrated against Christians (Hupchick 1983: 308). Some sense of the religious fervor of Mehmet's reign is conveyed by an account of his return to Edirne after having taken the fortress of Kamaniça in Poland. Commoners waited along the route in front of the palace and kissed the ground that the sultan's horse would soon tread; when they finally saw him they understood that he was "the powerful sultan of Islam who causes fear and dread, the deliverer of conquest and ghaza, Sultan Mehmed Khan" (Baer 2008: 169).

And the events in the Balkans were not the only source of pressure. The office of the patriarchate was very insecure throughout the seventeenth century, as mentioned earlier, and – on top of everything else – two great fires swept through Istanbul in the space of just a few months in 1660, the first devastating the Christian district of Galata, the second leveling Eminönü, which was the center of Jewish life in the city (Baer 2004: 159).[7] In yet another break with past practice, Islamic laws prohibiting reconstruction were strictly applied, and the construction of mosques in Eminönü and Galata "symbolized the Islamization of the two districts" (Baer 2004: 160).

In the midst of these discouraging developments, and in response to the constant drumbeat of piety coming from the highest circles of Ottoman society, it makes intuitive sense that neo-martyrs would assume a new prominence, as the church tried to fortify the Christians of the empire. But is it possible that the genre, and the spiritual advisors who urged the neo-martyrs to commit apostasy in the most spectacular way, were responding to something rather different?

It seems logical that the dramatic events of the second half of the seventeenth century would trickle down into society at large in theform of increased tension between Muslims and Christians. A recent study, however, suggests that it was precisely in this period that the boundaries between the two communities were becoming more and more blurred, and cites the increasing use of the *kadi* courts by Christian women as a particularly strong indication of this "acculturation" (Krstić 2011: 133). The neo-martyrologies, then, would function as a way of trying to sunder these bonds, much as the Catholic missionaries hoped to separate Catholic and Orthodox Christians (Krstić 2011: 137).

This is a difficult claim to substantiate. If we consider Christian recourse to the *kadi* courts, there is overwhelming evidence that it went on throughout the entire Ottoman period, including the nineteenth century (Gradeva 1997: 45–57; 1995: 182–4). A quantitative study of the phenomenon might reveal some interesting trends – both synchronically and diachronically – but this task, which would be enormous, has not yet been attempted. Beyond the legal system, ordinary Muslims and Christians were connected to each other through a wide array of practices and institutions, from marriage and blood brotherhood and godparentage to ordinary friendship (Gradeva 1995: 181; Greene 2000: 106). Then there is the additional layer of relations between converts to Islam and their original community; again, the evidence shows that they continued to celebrate Easter, to speak their native tongue, and to dance and drink wine with the Christians (Gradeva 1995: 183; Deringil 2000: 553).[8] The propaganda and the prohibitions against these practices, from both the Muslim and the Christian side, went on throughout the centuries, proof that the practices themselves were impossible to root out (Gradeva 1995: 182–3).

Given the current state of research, then, it is unlikely that the uptick in the production of texts about neo-martyrs had anything to do with the blurring of communal boundaries. This is not to say that the boundaries were always clear cut; they were not. Nor is it to say that the church was not concerned; it certainly was. It is to say that the seventeenth century was no different in this regard than the century before or the century to come (Gradeva 1997: 69).

Finally, when thinking about pressure on the Christian Orthodox in the seventeenth century it is very difficult to separate the influence of the Catholic presence from the influence exerted by successive waves of Muslim piety during that period, culminating in Sultan Mehmet's zeal for conversion. Historically, the two were always linked. Christian Orthodox were sensitive to the Catholic charge that Christians living under Muslim rule could not be good Christians. As far back as 1367 John Kantakouzenos responded with spirit to a papal legate who spoke disdainfully about the daily blasphemies that were the lot of the Orthodox under Turkish rule. Kantakouzenos replied that these Christians "were more honorable and better than those living under Christian rule because, although subjugated by the infidel, they persisted in their faith" (Zachariadou 1990–1: 62–3).

The age of confessionalization?

Whether writing about Catholics, Orthodox, or Muslims, I have emphasized the inability of religious elites to pry apart communities and to stamp out social practices that did not meet with their approval. When it comes to the Orthodox and the Muslims, at least, this runs against an emerging argument in Ottoman historiography. There is a new scholarly interest in Muslim piety in the Ottoman era; part of the argument is that in the seventeenth century many critics of society were concerned to improve the quality and strength of belief within the Muslim community, possibly under the influence of new methods of religious surveillance in Catholic and Protestant Europe (Terzioğlu 2013: 103). This, in turn, was part of a broader project of social discipline, described here by Terzioğlu:

> This belief in religious instruction as a key to social discipline also signaled a broader shift in Ottoman understandings of piety. Whereas piety had been defined in earlier Ottoman texts mostly as an otherworldly quality that manifested itself through extraordinary acts, from the turn of the 17th century onwards it came to be defined increasingly as a virtue that manifested itself through constant adherence to the shariah.[9]

Yet at the same time, Terzioğlu acknowledges the limits of this agenda, and they are spatial ones. The "sheer scale" of the empire, she writes, meant that the "state's Sunnitization measures worked best with the already nominally Sunni population in urban milieux in the central lands of the Empire" (Terzioğlu 2013: 113). Outside of these select cities, the authorities settled for obedience.

Limited evidence suggests that the Orthodox Church, too, was more aggressive in the cities than in the countryside. It could be, because the parish network was tighter there and the clergy had more sustained contact with their parishioners. In the villages the elders of the community put themselves in charge of dispute resolution and they often took decisions, based on customary law, which violated canon law. For example, canon law accepted that a husband's physical violence was grounds for divorce, but customary law considered such violence to be a normal state of affairs (Gradeva 1997: 41, 57). This bifurcation in legal regimes mirrors the patterns of Muslim communities in the empire (Peirce 2003: 123).

There are several conundrums here that at this point can only be posed, not solved. The first is the long-standing argument that Balkan Christianity was stronger in the countryside than it was in the cities. An attempt at resolution could begin by considering what is meant by an assertion of religious strength; this conceptual work has not yet been done. In addition, one would have to differentiate between villages far from monasteries and those that were in the vicinity of the great monastic centers. The relationship between the monasteries and the surrounding peasant communities is still very much underexplored. Nevertheless, in an article based on archival documents from a number of monasteries – both insular and in the mountains – Sophia Laiou argues that the relationship was primarily an economic one. Christian villagers confronted the monasteries as peasants, and the monasteries did not hesitate to expand their holdings at the expense of the peasantry (Laiou 2011: 207). It is not obvious, then, that the urban relationship of clergy and parishioners finds its reflection in the countryside.

It is curious, too, that the tracts on proper Islamic piety in the seventeenth century paid little attention to recent converts, in sharp distinction to earlier centuries. Instead the emphasis was on stamping out "error and heresy" within the established Muslim community (Terzioğlu 2013: 84).[10] Again, the distinction between urban and rural may be the key. Christian conversion to Islam in this period was largely a rural phenomenon, and therefore might well have not caught the attention of reformers, whose interests lay in the urban areas (Minkov 2004: 52, 55).

The religious history of the countryside remains largely unexplored.

Although we know that across the centuries Muslim and Christian authorities railed against what they deemed to be improper relations between the two communities, this constant background noise, as it were, has yet to be studied in the context of particular historical periods. Given that converts remained in contact with their former co-religionists and given that new Muslims continued with habits that were associated with Christianity, significant conversion in the seventeenth century must have led to more, not less, mixing. Do we see a corresponding increase in attempts at social discipline on the part of both Muslim and Christian authorities? In other words, when we read of a synodal decision in the seventeenth century threatening all Christian priests who continued to baptize the children of Muslims with defrocking, was this the consequence of particular developments or did it reflect more timeless concerns (Vryonis 1972: 174)?

After *devşirme*

The question of conversion in the seventeenth century is also germane to an important, although underdeveloped, argument in the field, namely the consequences of the end of the *devşirme*. Around the middle of the seventeenth century, regular levies for the janissary corps ceased, and then died out all together by the beginning of the eighteenth century (Minkov 2004: 74; Tezcan 2010: 44–5). The reason for this was that the corps had become so swollen that the challenge was no longer how to staff it but rather how to limit its numbers.

Years ago, in a volume that has become a classic in the field, Metin Kunt wrote that, although the *devşirme* was stopped for institutional, not religious, reasons, "the result was that the main avenue for *zimmis* to Ottoman leadership was cut off, adding to the sense of alienation increasingly felt by Ottoman non-Muslims towards the state" (Kunt 1982: 64). Almost thirty years later Baki Tezcan made a very similar claim, linking the end of the *devşirme* and other changes in the period to the demotion of non-Muslims within Ottoman society (Tezcan 2010: 17).

The classical system of recruitment – whereby young Christian peasant boys were chosen by palace officials to become janissaries – certainly did come to an end but more decentralized patterns of recruitment into state service rose up to take their place. A far more ad hoc process of soldier recruitment could create openings in unexpected places. More recent research allows us to see this process unfolding in two places: the island of Crete and the hinterlands of Trabzon. In both cases, the combination of war and conversion gave rural Christians opportunities for social advancement.

The district of Of sits midway between the cities of Trabzon and Rize. An overwhelmingly Christian area when the Ottomans conquered it at the end of the fifteenth century, its Muslim population grew slowly but steadily over the course of the sixteenth century, due to both immigration and conversion (Meeker 2002: 158). The process picked up in the next one hundred years and by the end of the seventeenth century the Oflus were almost all Muslim (Meeker 2002: 163). It is only at this time that the Oflus emerge into the historical record as participants in imperial institutions.

In 1695, during the long war of 1683–99 in the Balkans, Istanbul ordered 7,700 soldiers from the entire length of the southern Black Sea coast to report for an imperial campaign in Hungary (Meeker 2002: 162–76). The vast majority (5,500 out of the 7,700) were called up from the eastern districts, that is, from the very places that had had large Christian populations within living memory. Meeker concludes that the state expected new Muslims to be more responsive to the call-up than those communities further west that had been Muslim for centuries. Further, he argues that what was emerging in Of in the closing decades of the seventeenth century was not simply a majority Muslim community but a "state-oriented society." By this he means that conversion was intimately linked with an eagerness to penetrate imperial institutions and a willingness to remake oneself in order to so. The Oflus were very successful in their endeavor both as soldiers and as scholars; famously, Of quickly developed into a center of religious learning and many Oflus served as irregular soldiers.

Meeker distinguishes this from earlier periods when conversion had a more instrumental character. Those who were willing to register as Muslims in order to enjoy certain benefits nevertheless continued with their old religious practices – whether Christian or Shi'a inflected – when they were in the village and away from the gaze of the state.[11] They also continued to live alongside their Christian neighbors, whereas the late seventeenth-century conversions resulted in a dramatic shift in intercommunal relations. It was at this time that a significant number of Christians, both Armenian and Greek speaking, left the area and settled in places that had not been part of the Byzantine Empire of Trabzon (Meeker 2002: 166).

Mass conversions to Islam occurred during the same time period on the island of Crete, under similar, although admittedly more dramatic, circumstances. The long war for the island (1645–69) gave those islanders who were willing to do so the opportunity to join the fight, as long as they converted to Islam. Just as new Muslims from Trabzon went to fight in Hungary, new converts on Crete fought on the Ottoman side and in so doing found social advancement (Greene 2000: 39–44). Court records from the island preserve the Christian origins of many soldiers, including janissaries, a fact that they were unconcerned to hide. In 1672, for example, one Hassan Bey b. Abdullah from a volunteer regiment (*gönüllü*) came to court in order to claim his share of his cousin's inheritance. His cousin, also a soldier and a convert, had died and his property had been seized, on the assumption that there were no heirs. Hassan Bey testified that Ahmet beşe b. Abdullah (the deceased) was his cousin since their fathers – Manoles and Georges – were brothers. Two other Muslims from the same regiment, and no doubt converts themselves, backed up his testimony and he won his case (Greene 2000: 38). Another inheritance case makes it clear just how high some converts at least could rise in the military hierarchy. It was also an inheritance problem that brought Ali Bey b. Abdullah into court. He testified against Ioannes, a Christian from Ali Bey's village, who was illegally occupying a vineyard that the latter should have inherited from his father, Modatsos. Ali Bey was careful to tell the court that he had converted to Islam after his father's death, as otherwise the inheritance would not have been legal. In the course of the testimony we learn that this one-time Christian villager became the assistant (*kethüda*) to Kapudan Mustafa Pasha, the commander of the Ottoman fleet during the final year of the seige (Greene 2000: 42).

As in the eastern Black Sea, it seems that in Crete, too, we are witnessing the emergence of Meeker's "state-oriented society." And there is another similiarity; in both cases the converts remained Grecophone. According to a source published in 1888, lessons in the Muslim religious academies of Of were sometimes given in Greek, although most of the population spoke Turkish by that point. Many women, however, did not, and religious sermons and instruction were still given in Greek in the 1960s (Meeker 2002: 165). The Greek language was even more prominent in Crete, in the sense that very few of the islanders ever learned Turkish. A traveler in the 1830s referred to Greek as "the common language of the island" and many other observers made similar remarks (Greene 2000: 39).

The question of intercommunal relations remains. Here there appears to be a divergence. As mentioned earlier, the seventeenth-century conversions in the hinterlands of Trabzon seem to have led to an exodus of the remaining Christians. Crete remained a majority

Christian island, although one with a sizable Muslim population. A traveler who came to the island about a decade after the end of the war estimated a nearly one-to-one ratio of Muslims to Christians. An early eighteenth-century traveler suggested a more realistic Muslim–Christian ratio of one to two. Either way, the Muslim population was clearly substantial (Greene 2000: 53). But the two are perhaps not commensurable; Crete, after all, is a much bigger place than the district of Of. A document from the latter dated 1631 refers to just 441 Christian households, and forty years later an estimate put them at only 90 (Meeker 2002: 161). In Crete, by contrast, there were 26,274 *cizye*-paying households at the end of the war; one would not expect them all to simply move elsewhere (Greene 2000: 52).

Nevertheless, it is worth pointing out that the emergence of a "state-oriented society" on Crete did not result in the erection of a wall between Muslim and Christian society. Certainly European travelers and, later, nationalist historians endorsed the conventional picture of zealous, even murderous, converts, but the court records reveal significant intercommunal ties (Greene 2000: 39). These included marriage, godparentage, Muslim participation in baptism, and witnessing for each other in court.

It is hard to locate the divergences between Trabzon and Crete within a larger historical context, and this is in part because the end of the *devşirme* has received far less attention from historians than has its beginning. What we can say with certainty is that recent converts to Islam continued to join the Ottoman military in large numbers during the tumultuous second half of the seventeenth century, when the Ottomans fought the Venetians for a quarter of a century and then suffered through the disasters of the War of the Holy League for another fifteen. They did not join through the *devşirme*, and the Ottoman military was by then a very different sort of beast; for one thing the line between Ottoman institutions and society had become far more blurred as the Ottomans turned to a more contractual method of military recruitment (Aksan 2011: 81). That must explain the phenomenon, in both places, of Grecophone soldiers who learned Turkish only very gradually, if at all. When we add up all the questions that remain to be explored – the nature and significance of conversion in this period, the relationship between converts and their communities of origin, the proper conceptualization of the post-*devşirme* military, to name only the larger issues – then it seems clearly premature to conclude that the end of the *devşirme* led to non-Muslim alienation from the state.

The War of the Holy League

The siege of Vienna (1683) and the treaty of Karlowitz (1699), which began and ended the War of the Holy League, stand as turning points in Ottoman history. Both required the acceptance of new, and unwelcome, limits. The disastrous defeat at Vienna brought about the downfall of the Köprülü dynasty of vezirs and, in due course, the end of the seventeenth-century attempt to restore Ottoman absolutism (Tezcan 2010: 218). By signing the treaty of Karlowitz the Ottomans had to accept not only massive territorial losses, but also a permanent border in Europe for the first time in their history (Abou-el-Haj 1969). These imperial milestones have received a good deal of attention in the literature, where, particularly in earlier writing on the empire, they have figured prominently in the narrative of Ottoman decline. In part as a corrective, newer studies rightly emphasize the long peace between 1703 and 1770 and the remaking of Istanbul into a city of fountains and pleasure palaces (Hamadeh 2007).[12] The janissary revolts that figure so prominently in the sixteenth and seventeenth centuries are far fewer in the eighteenth century; it is indeed "one of the most peaceful periods of Ottoman history in terms of political protests" (Tezcan 2010: 225).

Without disputing this picture of the imperial center (and perhaps it can be applied to the Anatolian and Arab provinces as well), we can see that it is certainly not an accurate depiction of the Balkan peninsula. It is striking, in fact, how often narratives of the empire do not adequately account for the European provinces. As mentioned earlier, the *celali* revolts overwhelm the narrative of the early seventeenth century, but there were no *celalis* in the Balkans. And then, at the end of the same century, once the losses in the Balkans are swallowed, the (new) emphasis is on the long peace that ensued.[13]

Less attention has been paid to the consequences of the war in the places where it was fought. These were, principally, at the two extremes of the Balkan peninsula. In the south the Venetians wrested the Morea from the Ottomans early on in the war, only to have the latter take it back again in 1715. In the north, the Ottoman loss of Hungary proved to be permanent and the empire had to regroup south of the Danube. Even with the signing at Karlowitz, things remained uneasy along the Habsburg border, and the city of Belgrade went back and forth between the two adversaries several times during the course of the eighteenth century. Unsurprisingly, the results were a disaster for cities that now found themselves on the border. Aleksandar Fotić ends his history of Belgrade as an Ottoman cultural center in 1683, precisely because the consequences of the war for the city proved to be so severe. The city had to rebuild "almost from the ground up" (Fotić 2005: 51). Demographic patterns bear this out. Prior to the war Belgrade's population was something over 50,000; on the eve of the Napoleonic wars it still had no more than 25,000 inhabitants. Skopje was even worse off. Roughly the same size as Belgrade in the seventeenth century, it was set on fire by the invading Habsburg forces and at the end of the following century it could boast no more than 6,000 souls (Stoianovich 1960: 249; Malcolm 1988: 146). The misery wrought by the war was compounded by the flow of Muslim refugees coming in from Hungary, a harbinger of things to come a century later (Gradeva 2001: 154; Finkel 2007: 306). During the war itself local Christians joined with Austrian forces to massacre roughly two-thirds of the Muslim urban residents in the Kosovo region (Zhelyazkova 2002: 238).

Given these developments, it seems likely that relations between Muslims and Christians came out of the war much the worse for wear, as Frederick Anscombe asserts (Anscombe 2006: 6). And indeed, although we lack a general study, there is scattered evidence of a difficult situation. In Vidin in 1718, now directly on the Habsburg border after further territorial losses, Christians were banished from the fortified part of the town and forced to move. With Christians obliged to sell their homes to Muslims, "the two main faiths in the city were spatially separated" (Gradeva 2001: 154). In Bosnia, the large-scale migrations set in motion by the war – migrations that continued into the 1730s – resulted in a peasantry that was more uniformly Christian (both Catholic and Orthodox) than it had been in the seventeenth century. Thus confessional and class boundaries (a Muslim landowning class) came to be conflated in a way they had not been before, and confessional tensions grew accordingly (Hajdarpasic 2008: 91, 93).

But the thesis of deteriorating confessional relations fails in one important aspect, and thus provides only a partial picture of the results of the war years. The situation in the south, in the Morea, was very different. Whereas an embittered tide of Muslim refugees washed over the northern Balkans, in the Morea the Ottoman victory allowed Muslims (or their descendants) who had been displaced in 1683 to return to their ancestral homes. Of critical importance was the fact that in the Morea only the Venetians were viewed as the enemy, not the indigenous Orthodox Christians, and with good reason. The latter had a long and unhappy history under Venetian rule – in Crete, in Cyprus, and elsewhere – and the Ottomans were well aware of this. Therefore they would have assumed that the local population was not happy with

Venice's return to the peninsula, and the limited evidence we have suggests that they were right (Kitromilides 2006: 201; Malliari 2001–2: 424; Alexander 1985: 29). Indeed this attitude toward the Orthodox was a fundamental in deciding the shape of the reconquest (Sakellariou 1939: 41). Ensconced once again in southern Greece, the Venetians returned to their old, punitive religious policies such as trying to cut off all contact between the Orthodox under their control and their clergy elsewhere in the empire. No wonder, then, that in 1688 the patriarch of Jerusalem traveled to Istanbul, where he met with the sultan and the grand vezir and told them he would send letters to the bishops in the Morea, telling them to urge people to return to "the Turks" (Malliari 2001–2: 424). In contrast to the murky situation on the Ottoman–Habsburg border, where some Orthodox clerics were making arrangements with Catholic power, the patriarchs of Jerusalem and of Istanbul were clearly and unequivocally on the side of the Ottoman elites; both wanted the Venetians out of southern Greece. In that sense the Ottoman victory in 1715 was a kind of throwback to earlier centuries, when the sultan's armies steadily drove out the Latins and brought Orthodox populations under patriarchal rule.

This relatively benevolent attitude toward the Greeks is evident in the historical record. Grand Vezir Damat Ali Pasha expelled the Crimean Tartars even before the short, two-month conquest was complete, and threatened with death anyone who killed a Greek. This was starkly different from the reign of terror that the Tartars were allowed to inflict upon Kosovo some twenty years earlier. Some of the Christians who returned to the Morea did so at the invitation of Damat Ali Pasha (Sakellariou 1939: 116–17; Malcolm 1988: 158).

Then there is the extraordinary level of self-government that distinguished the province in the eighteenth century. This must be treated separately from the obviously conciliatory measures taken during and in the immediate aftermath of the conquest, since the origins and development of self-rule in the peninsula are still poorly understood. We do not know, for example, whether such a situation obtained during the first period of Ottoman rule in the Morea (Sakellariou 1939: 87, 94) Nevertheless, the fact that (among other things) two Christians and two Muslims formed the permanent council of the vezir demonstrates a level of Christian empowerment that stands in stark contrast to the case in the northern Balkans (Sakellariou 1939: 89–93).

Now let us turn the lens and view the Balkans from Istanbul, from the Ecumenical Patriarchate at Fener along the Golden Horn. From this vantage point, a new imperial configuration does appear, one that links the northern and southern end of the Balkans, but it concerns not relations between Muslims and Christians but rather a changing balance of power between the Christian communities. What emerges from the war years is a landscape far more favorable to the patriarch in Istanbul and thus to the Greek element more generally in the empire. The Morea was clearly a triumph. Even before the Ottoman victory, Moreot Greek notables were in close touch with patriarchal and other circles in Istanbul despite Venetian attempts at obstruction; when the notables sent a delegation to the Ottoman army in Thebes to offer their submission, they did so in consultation with their co-religionists in the capital (Papastamatiou 2009: 58–9). After 1715 these ties would only grow stronger.

In the north the Catholic population was decimated and the Orthodox areas hardest hit were those populated by Slavic, rather than Greek-speaking, Christians. Famously, the Serbian patriarch at Peć, Arsenije III, fled northward along with about 30,000 Orthodox refugees and, with Habsburg support, established a new metropolitanate at Karlowitz, just inside imperial territory (Malcolm 1988: 161). Just a few years after the collapse of Serbian authority in the northern Balkans, the Romanian boyars of Wallachia and Moldavia lost their position as rulers of the tributary principalities during the short (1710–13) Ottoman war with Peter the Great. Due to perceived disloyalty on the part of the boyars, the Ottomans replaced them with Greeks drawn from the Phanariot circles of Istanbul.

These developments in the principalities are well known and figure prominently in narratives about the rise of the Greeks, particularly the development of Greek culture and intellectual life. Much less remarked is the fact that the war years rendered not just the Romanians but the Serbs, too, suspect in Ottoman eyes (Yerasimos 1992: 149–51). Nor do we know too much about the replacement of Serbian with Greek power in the northern Balkans, although evidence suggests that such a process was taking place in the eighteenth century. The new patriarch appointed to Peć in the wake of Arsenije's flight was probably Greek and, in the second half of the eighteenth century, both Peć and Ohrid would come under the authority of the Ecumenical Patriarchate (Malcolm 1988: 162).

The war years, stretching from 1683 to 1718 in the Balkans, produced much more than the expansion of the Phanariots into the principalities. The devastation of Serbian lands, the flight of the Serbian patriarch, the loss of Hungary – whose acquisition had been so intimately linked to the rise of Serbian power at the highest levels of Ottoman governance –

the Ottoman victory in the solidly Greek Morea, and the fateful choices of the Romanian boyars all combined to ensure that, in the eighteenth century, the only empire-wide Christian patronage network remaining would be dominated by Greek speakers with ties to Istanbul. Only the Ecumenical Patriarchate was powerful enough, and wealthy enough, to extend patronage to ambitious Christians within the empire.

Challenges to Ottoman Christian society would remain, of course, in the eighteenth century. A harbinger of things to come took place during the desperate years of the war. In 1690 the grand vezir Fazil Mustafa Pasha, in a bid to gain French support as he prepared his army to retake Belgrade from the imperial armies, acceded to French requests and restored control of certain key Christian sites in Jerusalem to the Franciscans, thus depriving the Orthodox. It was the first time that the Ottomans had made this change in Jerusalem at the behest of a foreign power, rather than as the result of wrangling within the empire between the Catholic and the Orthodox communities (Finkel 2007: 324). Even as Catholic communities vanished in the Balkans, France emerged as a formidable opponent to the patriarch in Istanbul, since it was both a staunch defender of Catholic interests and the Ottomans' most reliable European ally. But the Orthodox Christian elite, based in Istanbul, now enjoyed far greater control over the vast apparatus of the church than it had been able to manage in the seventeenth century. Given that the church was the most powerful Christian institution in Ottoman society, the consolidation of Greek hegemony over the church, combined with the processes discussed in Chapter 5, paved the way for a remarkable Hellenization of Christian society in the eighteenth century.

Notes

1. Christopher Angell, the author, published his account at Oxford in 1618.
2. Legrand even provides the language used by Greek women when they came looking for the relics: "ἐκεῖνο τό λείψανο ὁποῦ βοῆθα ταῖς γυναῖκε" (that relic that helps women).
3. And the missionaries had to reckon with Ottoman, as well as Orthodox, attitudes. Despite the oft-repeated Arabic phrase used in asserting that the Ottomans were indifferent to divisions within the Christian community – *al-Kufr kullu milla wahida* (unbelief constitutes one nation) – in fact the sultans chose to "support the established traditional church hierarchies in the interests of preserving order." This meant that converts to Catholicism were in an uncertain legal position (Masters 1988: 95).
4. This is how he is presented in the nationalist literature.

5. For the literature on the neo-martyrs see Zachariadou (1990–1: 51–63), Vaporis (2000) and Krstić (2011).
6. What follows is a summary of Anton Minkov's (2004) arguments, as his work is at the time of writing the most recent, and comprehensive, survey of the data.
7. The second fire was "the worst the city had ever experienced" (Baer 2004: 159).
8. Deringil notes that the convert typically remained in contact with his or her community of origin until the arrival of nationalism in the nineteenth century made this impossible (Deringil 2000: 553).
9. Terzioğlu (2013: 111). Terzioğlu situates her work within the broader model of the "age of confessionalization," as does Krstić (2011). See both of these works for a discussion of the concept as it applies to Ottoman society.
10. Krstić (2013: 70–1) records the development of harsher attitudes toward converts in the sixteenth century. The story has not yet been taken up to the seventeenth century.
11. I am aware that this is a controversial point and that there is a growing literature critical of the concept of "crypto-Christianity." My point here is not to enter into this debate but rather to point out how late seventeenth-century conversions had a different character than those that came before. For a critical discussion of "crypto-Christianity" see Türkyilmaz (2009).
12. Tezcan has this to say: "While Ottoman historiography of the nineteenth and twentieth centuries would like us to regard the independence of the janissary corps as a major factor in military decline, and hence the territorial reduction, of the Ottoman Empire in the eighteenth century, it glossed over a very significant point. The eighteenth century also happens to be one of the most peaceful periods of Ottoman history in terms of political protests. Both in the imperial capital and the provinces, there were far fewer rebellions than in the sixteenth and seventeenth centuries" (Tezcan 2010: 225).
13. Edin Hajdarpasic makes the same critique: "It is true that during those decades – roughly from the 1740s to the 1780s – the political elites in Istanbul used the absence of major wars to launch a number of diplomatic and economic initiatives. Nonetheless, this outburst of activity emanating from the capital should not prevent us from perceiving the series of deep and violent upheavals that shook the Ottoman border areas such as Serbia, Wallachia, the Peloponnesus and Bosnia in the eighteenth century" (Hajdarpasic 2008: 79). And Caroline Finkel has noted the difference between Anatolia and the Balkans: "The Balkans offered almost a mirror image of the Anatolian experience, less affected than Anatolia by rebellions during the seventeenth century, more during the eighteenth" (Finkel 2007: 400).

CHAPTER 7

The patriarch's victory

There is a paradox at the heart of historical presentations of the Ottoman eighteenth century, a paradox that has not yet been fully laid out because of persistent subdivisions within the study of the empire.

For a very long time now historians have agreed on the end of the *devşirme* as an important turning point in the empire's history. This was because the ruling institution, once dominated by Christian converts who were slaves of the sultan, underwent a fundamental shift and became the preserve of free-born Muslims (Hathaway 2004: 29–53). Although its roots lay in the seventeenth century, the new reality fully came into its own in the eighteenth. Even a 2010 study, which in many ways presents a radically new paradigm of the post-Süleymanic empire, puts the new-found Muslim ability to enter the state apparatus, and contrast with the *devşirme* past, front and center:

> In contrast to the patriomonial past when the slaves who were handpicked mainly through the *devşirme* system by the administrative-military apparatus constituted the pool from which the ruling class emerged, in the eighteenth century any free Muslim male – that is, any imperial subject endowed with full legal rights granted to the individual under jurists' law – could *theoretically* rise up in the state hierarchy to the highest position. (Tezcan 2010: 236)

Although Tezcan is not focused on the non-Muslim communities of the empire, he is clear about what this development meant for them. An essential dividing line in Ottoman statecraft and society had always been between the tax-paying subjects, the *reaya*, and the tax-collecting ruling class, the *askeri*. As it became possible, at least theoretically, for all Muslims to seize a piece of the state for themselves, the term *reaya*, which previously had not had a religious meaning, came to be associated with the Christian population. Rather than an empire where the slaves of the sultan collected taxes from all tax payers, reguardless of religious identity, the "Second Empire" was one where Muslims ruled over Christians. The result, Tezcan argues, was "the subjection of non-Muslims to second-class status" (Tezcan 2010: 236).

This rather bleak assessment, at least from the Christian point of view, sits rather awkwardly next to the remarkable achievements, both economic and cultural, of Christian, and specifically Greek Christian, society in the same century. We have already discussed the lock that the Greek elites, the Phanariots, secured on all of the offices associated with the Danubian Principalities, and there were others in their portfolio as well (Philliou 2011: 10–11). In the eighteenth century, Greek merchants emerged as a force to be reckoned with across the Balkans and the eastern Mediterranean. The wealth generated by office-holding and trade, as well as of course the holdings of the church, was channeled into the cultural projects, such as schools and book production and translation, that have come to be known as the Greek Enlightenment.

An earlier generation of historians with assumptions about the existence of the "Greek nation," or, at least, its rebirth in the eighteenth century, was able to account for Greek efflorescence during this period.[1] Secure within the walls of the *millet*, a sort of nation within the empire, the Greek community rebuilt itself, with the end result being the national uprising of 1821 that resulted in the establishment, in 1830, of the Greek state. To the extent that the Ottoman context mattered, the Greeks were able to benefit from its difficulties, as they were understood in this narrative. For example, in his seminal article "The Conquering Balkan Orthodox Merchant," Traian Stoianovich wrote,

> At least until 1770, Ottoman landowners imposed only relatively minor deterrents on the trade of merchants selling the grains, cotton and other farm surpluses of their rivals and competitors. Properly bribed customs officials, moreover, even encouraged or shut their eyes to the legally forbidden but widely prevalent export of grains beyond the confines of the Empire. (Stoianovich 1960: 259–60)

This model of the empire, and of the community within the empire, is precisely the sort of paradigm that the new scholarship is pushing against, and there have already been several revisionist accounts of the eighteenth century, accounts that will deeply inform this chapter. Although they write on different aspects of the period, what these accounts have in common is an emphasis on the importance of Ottoman structures in shaping the contours of Greek Orthodox society, as well as the investment of Christian elites in the imperial project.

Ironically, even as a new generation of Greek historians is suggesting the possibility of Greek Orthodox attachment to the empire, those writing the grand imperial narratives are sure that the Greek Orthodox were not wanted. Now these writers, like the nationalist historians of another era, anticipate the Greek exodus long before it happened. Let us return to Tezcan's influential work, and here it is worth quoting at length.

> Although the gradual formation of a collective Ottoman political identity around the category of Muslim in the eighteenth century established the early modern credentials of the Second Empire, it also led toward the path to the eventual dissolution of the Ottoman Empire. Even though the Ottoman polity was a multireligious one, it had always been governed by Muslim rulers. Yet the fact that the dividing line separating the rulers from the ruled had not run along sectarian divisions had made things relatively fair for the ruled. A Muslim peasant belonged just as much to the *reaya*, or the flock of the sultan, as the non-Muslim one; they were both outsiders, or *ecnebis*, as far as the ruling class was concerned. Once certain paths that were closed to the *reaya* started opening up only for upwardly mobile Muslim subjects of the sultan, however, non-Muslim subjects had a legitimate ground for resentment, which the Ottoman state failed to address adequately before it was too late. Non-Muslim Ottoman subjects' expression of political resentment eventually took the form of withdrawal of their political loyalties. (Tezcan 2010: 239)

Karen Barkey's work also has political dissolution in mind. Her chapter on the non-Muslim population in the eighteenth century is titled "On the Road Out of Empire." She writes "The emergence of ethnic and religious antagonism and state distrust of non-Muslim populations dates back to the eighteenth century and can be seen in the changing network associations of non-Muslim and Muslim groups in the empire" (Barkey 2008: 279).[2]

By "changing network associations" Barkey means non-Muslim success in trade with Europe, including their ability to achieve *berath* status, European protection afforded to them as employees of the embassies, which exempted them from many Ottoman obligations. But rather than the supposed demotion of non-Muslims to second-class status, Barkey writes that non-Muslim success created jealously among Muslims in what was, she argues, a century of impoverishment for the latter (Barkey 2008: 279).

The figure of the Greek merchant trading with Europe is often the face of the community, even perhaps the stereotype, for those Ottoman historians whose focus is not the Greek Orthodox. I shall argue that this is a very limited view of what was a variegated social reality, and it obscures the Greek Orthodox position within the empire. Nevertheless, it is worth pausing for a moment on the subject because the most developed arguments for the roots of the Greek exodus from the empire revolve around the topic of commerce.

In a 1999 article on French trade in the 1700s, Edhem Eldem turns his attention at the end to the Ottoman Christian merchants who proved to be such formidable competitors for the merchants of Marseilles. Given the dynamism of these non-Muslim Ottoman merchants Eldem goes on to ask how we can understand the inability of the Ottoman Empire, in the long run, to compete with what proved to be a more powerful western economy. "The problem, we feel, lies mainly in the exclusion and alienation of potential economic forces – a nascent bourgeoisie? – from the mechanisms of power and decision making controlled by the ruling class" (Eldem 1999: 45). One of the clearest illustrations of their exclusion, he continues, was the pursuit by non-Muslim merchants of protected status through European patronage, the so-called *beratli* merchants who leveraged their connection to Europeans into a kind of extraterritorial status. They did this both to gain advantage and to protect themselves against abuse and insecurity. The fact that they behaved in this way means that the state, rather than being their ally, blocked them at every turn. In such a situation, of course, the possibilities for profitable investment of capital were very limited. At the same time, the substantial profits promised through trade with the west were also blocked, at least partially, through a combination of western protectionism and the unwillingness of the Ottomans to grant Ottoman subjects privileges, such as lower import and export duties, that the Europeans enjoyed. Given this situation Eldem concludes his argument in the following way:

> For them, only two options remained: cooperation with the system with all the risks it implied or the expectation of better times which would finally come in the nineteenth century: national liberation and the formation of nation-states in need of their capital and thus ready to co-opt them into the ruling class or total collaboration with the world economy and maximization of profit within the liberal structure imposed upon the Ottoman empire in the second half of the nineteenth century. (Eldem 1999: 45)

This chapter will take up the question of the Greek Orthodox subjects of the sultan in the eighteenth century with this grand narrative in mind and will suggest another, not in its place but running alongside it. To fully articulate this narrative let us remind ourselves of Socrates Petmezas' argument, first mentioned in Chapter 2.

> La formation d'un corps formel de prerogatives et de "privilèges" du patriarche grec-orthodoxe, reconnu par la Sublime Porte, ainsi que la consolidation et l'élargissement de son pouvoir sur ses suffragants ou ses pairs (les autres patriarches et archevêques autocéphales de l'Orient) ont été *l'oeuvre patiente de trois siècles*. (Petmezas 1996a: 490; my emphasis)

Indeed, it was in the eighteenth century that the patriarch in Istanbul, if not fully realizing his goal due to some hesitation on the part of the Ottomans, came closer than he had ever been before to establishing his authority – not just moral, but also civil and in some cases even criminal – over the Orthodox Christian subjects of the sultan. It is in this century, not before and certainly not in 1453, that we can begin to speak of a Greek Orthodox community with the patriarch at its head. This momentous development might seem to dovetail with the argument that the Greek Orthodox were detaching from the empire. But this makes the assumption, unwarranted in my opinion, that a cohesive Christian community would naturally look to exit from the imperial system. In fact one could argue just the opposite: that having finally achieved its objectives the Ecumenical Patriarchate, and those benefitting from its improved position, would be more loyal to the system than ever before. This possibility is also suggested because the new status of the church in the eighteenth century did not develop outside of the imperial framework but was in large part a creation of it. If merchants, perhaps, had reason to be frustrated by the Ottoman state, the church had much to be grateful for in the same period.

There is a second part to this narrative, one that can easily be overlooked if the existence of "the Greek community" is simply assumed rather than investigated. The rights of the patriarch over the Orthodox Christians did not go uncontested by the Orthodox Christians themselves, as we shall see. They could, and did, direct complaints to the Ottoman authorities; in fact petitioning by Christians soared in the eighteenth century, as it did among the Muslim population as well (Bayraktar Tellan 2011: 93; Yaycioğlu 2008: 56). Therefore we can say that, even as they found themselves more and more answerable to church authorities, the Orthodox were still subjects of the sultan. A certain ambiguity remained, then, not unlike the situation in the previous centuries. The difference was that the balance was now tipped in favor of the church.[3]

The increasing authority of the Orthodox Church over the Orthodox Christians of the empire, sometimes accepted and even welcomed and other times resisted, is one of the key developments of the eighteenth-century Ottoman Empire. Any consideration of the place of Christians in the empire that leaves this out – that thinks only of a Christian community and its relationship to the Ottoman state – will misread this critical century. It seems entirely possible (at this point any statement must still be tentative) that both elite and ordinary Christians were far more preoccupied with extending or resisting the authority of the ecclesiastical establishment than they were with their position vis-à-vis religious others. These developments may have been the critical ones in determining their loyalty to the empire.

As we shall see, the consolidation of the Christian community ran through every level of society, from provincial cities all the way up to the patriarch in Istanbul. Let us start with the provinces.

The new urbanism

Mountain towns such as Moschopolis and Ambelakia have figured prominently in older portrayals of the eighteenth century, where their purported isolation from Ottoman society was seen as key to their prosperity.[4] It is true that the eighteenth century saw the further development of the upland communities whose origins lay in the previous century. But if we shift our gaze to lower latitudes, an arguably more dramatic change took shape in the 1700s, and this change has received little attention, especially outside the rather narrow circle of Balkan historians. In city after city the Orthodox population, relative to the Muslims, began to grow, such that, by the nineteenth century, the Orthodox were in the majority in most Balkan cities.[5] Growth was the result of migration from the countryside and it was significant enough that, in some towns, the newcomers outnumbered the already established Christian population. We know this because newcomers were indicated as such (*haymana*) in the local court records (Ivanova 2005: 212) The change in urban centers was not in numbers only. In the cities Christian institutions, incipient in the seventeenth century, came to their full flowering.

Coming across the Balkans on her famous trip in the second decade of the eighteenth century, Lady Mary Wortley Montagu described Sofia as "very large and extremely populous" and "one of the most beautiful towns in the Turkish Empire," and then wrote this about Plovdiv:

> This town is situated on a rising ground near the river Hebrus, and is almost wholly inhabited by Greeks; here are still some ancient Christian churches. They have a bishop and several of the richest

Greeks live here; but they are forced to conceal their wealth with great care, the appearance of poverty (which includes part of its inconveniences) being all their security against feeling it in ernest. (Montagu 1793: 111)

Paul Lucas, a French jeweler and metal engraver (and with many other talents), was sent by the king to the empire to search for precious objects that would enhance the royal collection. Lucas passed through Plovidv just a few years after Montagu, and the Christians appeared very secure to him. He said that, alone among all the towns that he had seen in "Turkey," church bells were routinely rung in Plovdiv to mark the hour (Lucas 1714: 188). At the western edge of the peninsula the French consul in Ioannina in 1707 remarked that the town was as large as Marseilles (Tsimpida and Papageorgiou 2008: 156).

Despite these favorable impressions, Orthodox migration to the cities was not part of a larger process of urban revival, as was the case in the sixteenth century. It was motivated by the wars and the resulting higher levels of insecurity in the countryside (Tsimpida and Papageorgiou 2008: 156). Within the cities themselves the Muslim population level was either stagnant or falling, a fact that contributed to the increasingly Christian character of Balkan urban centers (Sugar 1977: 218).[6] But the Christian community did not emerge, effortlessly, out of the waves of migrants coming into the towns and cities. It had to be created, and in its creation we see the power of Christian elites at work.

Enough scholarship has now accumulated to allow us to state with confidence that, in the eighteenth century, the community became an essential unit of Ottoman provincial governance. By "community" we do not mean simply a group of people residing in a particular territory, but rather groups that had acquired "a legal persona as self-governing bodies" (Yaycioğlu 2008: 143). They grew into this status as a result of changing Ottoman administration and fiscal policies. As the *timar* system slowly crumbled, the authorities turned more and more to local elites to help in the collection of taxes and provision of security. And authority continued to devolve. Well into the seventeenth century the central government was still levying taxes on an individual or household basis, although relying on provincial leaders to do the collecting, but soon that fell away too. Taxes came to be levied on communities, and community leaders then took it upon themselves to apportion the burden among their members (Yaycioğlu 2008: 138). The leaders were known as the *ayan* and they have figured prominently in historiography on the later empire. It is only more recently that historians have turned their attention to the communities that they represented. When they have, issues of Ottoman governance have predominated and their valuable work has contributed to the ongoing project of exploring, and taking seriously, institutional development in the seventeenth and eighteenth centuries.[7] Here I would like to turn the lens slightly and to consider the way in which the state's reliance on communities helped new *Christian* communities to come into existence. Research on town communities in present-day Bulgaria shows that, toward the end of the seventeenth century, the association of specific neighborhoods with the Christian population began to break down.[8] This was because the new migrants – and there were many, as explained above – spread out across each particular town, settling in Muslim *mahalles* (neighborhoods) as well as Christian. Prior to this the demographic realities of Ottoman towns had meant that, in organizing the collection of taxes and other duties through each *mahalle*, the authorities could at one and the same time collect whatever distinct taxes were due from the Christian population. But new settlement patterns made this more difficult, just as the state was relying more heavily on revenues raised from the *mahalles* (Ivanova 2005: 201).

The authorities responded, slowly and not always steadily, by moving toward an intermediary institution, superimposed on the *mahalles*, that would be responsible for the taxes and obligations of all the Christians in a given area, whether they lived in Christian neighborhoods, in Muslim neighborhoods, or on *çiftliks* (farms) on the outskirts of town (Ivanova 2005: 211). This institution, the documents show, was called the *varoş*. The term was an old one, Hungarian in origin, and it originally referred to that area of a town inhabited by Christians. But in the seventeenth century it began to acquire its secondary meaning, which was the Christian community of a place as an institution, with concrete obligations toward the state. Its territorial sense, however, still lingered.

Before going on to the question of who the *varoş* leadership would be, let us look more closely at the *varoş* in the making. A dispute in Sofia has come down to us from the court records there. A number of Christians of "the *mahalles* in the *varoş*" addressed other Christians who lived in Muslim *mahalles* but were, the plaintiffs said, "*reaya* of the *varoş*, from which they have moved out." The plaintiffs complained that they were unable to meet their collective tax obligations and that the defendants must pay with them. Their claim was rejected (Ivanova 2005: 211). Things worked out a little bit differently in Hezargrad, a town in the northeast of present-day Bulgaria. There, some Christians had moved out of their old, Christian neighborhood into a new Muslim one. For a while they continued to pay the collective taxes such as *avarız* assessed on their old neighborhood, but then their new Muslim neighbors complained. "You live in our *mahalle* and you should help us with the *tekalif*," they said (Ivanova 2005: 214). This time around, the authorities decided that the Christians in question would continue paying their taxes in the old neighborhood, despite the fact that they had moved. A slightly different situation obtained in 1723, in Sofia again. A group of Christians identified as "*varoş* infidels" lodged a complaint against three craft guilds. In the past, the plaintiffs said, they had all contributed to the "gift" that was due the *vali* (governor) of Rumeli when he stayed in the city. This time, however, these three guilds were refusing to pay their share. The accused craftsmen protested, saying that they had already made their contribution and they were not going to give a gift together with the "*varoş* infidels" (Ivanova 2005: 211). Most interesting for our purposes is the fact that, along with Muslims, there were many Christians in the three craft guilds. What this means is that, at least when it came to the gift owed to the *vali*, they paid with their guild, not with the *varoş*.

These examples show that the authority of the *varoş* over all the Christians of a given area was not automatic, but in fact had to be wrestled away from other, competing institutions.[9] This struggle may well be behind the growing tendency of guilds in this period to fracture into separate Muslim and Christian branches. Peter Sugar explains this as the result of growing Muslim fanaticism (without, however, any supporting documentation), but Ivanova's alternative explanation is more persuasive and deserves to be quoted:

> altercations which seemed of an inter-confessional nature ... were in fact caused essentially by the financial concerns of Muslim *mahalles* that the tax burden should be shared with their Christian inhabitants, which came into conflict with the interests of the *varoş* as a representative structure of the Christian urban population. (Ivanova 2005: 214)

Even if the emergence of religiously distinct guilds was more about fiscal than religious tensions, this development was part and parcel of a larger trend, namely, the growing overlap between secular and religious institutions, particularly within the Christian community.[10] This overlap was produced when the Ottomans went looking for an already existing institution in order to most efficiently collect taxes and perform other tasks, and church officials (including lay people), seizing the opportunity, stepped into the breach. The leadership of the *varoş* was none other than the members of the episcopal councils who were already managing church business in the towns of the Balkans (Ivanova 2005: 226). Thus in Samokov we see the bishop and his council meeting in the bishop's *konak* (mansion) every year around St. George's day to settle the church accounts. That same group kept a record of expenses incurred for gifts given to Ottoman officials, a municipal responsibility that their Muslim counterparts undertook as well. Those wealthy Christians who were already honored with such traditionally Christian titles as *ktetor* (founder) for their donations to the church moved smoothly into leadership of the *varoş*.

The transformation of Christian communities into Christian institutions was taking place across the empire. Beginning in the seventeenth century, and then picking up speed in the eighteenth, eleven Aegean islands saw fit to draw up constitutive laws for their community. The earliest document, from Mykonos in 1615, says that the islanders, having accepted group responsibility for the taxes owed to the representative of the sultan, now want to put in writing the procedures for determining who shall govern them (Vryonis 1989: 86). The Christian villages nestled on the slopes of Mount Pelion in Thessaly had developed very extensive and detailed record keeping by the late eighteenth century, as Socrates Petmezas' work has shown. Their account books, beginning in 1783, were no doubt preceded by many years of more informal organization (Petmezas 2005: 89). In Smyrna, too, communal institutions were extremely robust, and even in faraway Cappadocia there are eighteenth-century documents that attest to the presence of a community (Vryonis 1989: 110; Iliou 1975; Chatziiosiff 2005: 18).

Most of the studies to date have concentrated on rural or island areas characterized by religious homogeneity. In these milieux one can gain the impression that the process being observed was one of community consolidation. This is what makes Ivanova's urban focus so valuable. In the more complex and religiously mixed cities it becomes clear that other types of institutions could have formed to respond to Ottoman fiscal and administrative needs. If the traditional craft guilds, for example, had been up to the task, then one would have seen municipal institutions that were not defined along religious lines. The experimental nature of provincial governance during this period is made clear by the fact that in 1786, during a brief respite in the wars of the late eighteenth century, the central administration abolished the office of *ayan* and brought back an older office, the city *kethüda* or city steward. The hope was that the office of city steward, with its historic association with the craft guilds, would be occupied by individuals of more modest background who would not, or could not, exploit the urban population in the same fashion as the *ayan*. But just five years later, with the renewal of war and the pressure to extract resources from the population, the *ayan* were brought back.[11]

But in the end it was the Christian *varoş* that triumphed, to such an extent that a study of the Greek community of Smyrna in the early nineteenth century never even hints that the community was a creation of the eighteenth century (Iliou 1975: 305). The ability of the *varoş* to prevail was in part due to Ottoman willingness to delegate tasks to it, but the strength and vitality of Christian society were vital as well (Ivanova 2005: 216, 225–6).

We see this vitality in many areas but one of the most striking, and little recognized within mainstream Ottoman historiography, is the growth of Christian guilds. General narratives of the empire in this period speak of the decline or stagnation of the guilds, but that was true only for the Muslims (Barkey 2008: 284; McGowan 1994b: 697).[12] Among the Christians, guilds were growing in strength and they used that strength to contribute to Christian life in the empire. They were clearly successful because later on in the century guild members would be numbered among the community leaders in towns across the empire, including even the capital city.

The guilds figure prominently in the travel diary of Chrysanthos Notaras, patriarch of Jerusalem (Stathis 1984). In March of 1720 he set off from Istanbul on a mission to collect alms for the church, as was customary for the Orthodox church throughout the Ottoman period. Usually such trips produced only lists of the names of the contributors, as well as the amounts given, but Notaras decided to include some extra details on the places he had been, and guilds, churches, and neighborhoods pepper his account. He traveled throughout the eastern Balkans, across Anatolia as far as Mosul and down to Syria and Palestine. In Plovdiv the *abacis* were his most generous contributors, although he listed many more guilds as well. This makes sense given that the city's *aba* cloth – a light woolen textile – was being sold in Anatolia, the Middle East, and even Calcutta (Lyberatos 2009: 67). The guild, founded in 1685, was associated with St. Dimitrios, a sixteenth-century church in the city. In Pazardzhik, further west, Notaras listed his contributors according to the guild to which they belonged; there were nineteen of them (Stathis 1984: 134–5). If the guilds gave generously to the church, the former also enjoyed the patronage of the latter. In Plovdiv and in Serres, at least, church officials served as guild officials, further accentuating the sectarian nature of these rising urban institutions (Lyberatos 2009: 92).

So far we have been talking about the ability of church officials and lay leaders to consolidate control over the sultan's Christian subjects, thus creating de jure Christian communities. The ability of these officials to do so was directly linked to their participation in Ottoman governance, that is, as leaders of the *varoş*. Now we must add another layer, and that is Hellenization. These municipal communities were often Greek in character, by which I mean the leadership was Greek both in language and in cultural orientation. It is not surprising that the Christian villages on Mount Pelion kept their records in Greek, but so too did the communal leadership in Plovdiv and Tarnavo (Ivanova 2005: 216, 223–4). Harking back to a very old cultural constellation, whereby the cities were centers of Hellenism, Christian in-migration to Balkan towns has been insufficiently appreciated as a factor in the efflorescence of Greek culture in the eighteenth century.[13] We know the Hellenization stories of many of the prominent figures of the age. Iosipos Moisiodax, one of the greatest figures of the Greek Enlightenment, was born in a Vlach-speaking village in today's northern Bulgaria; he was able to procure an education for himself and this brought him into the Greek orbit, since education for Balkan Christians in the eighteenth century meant Greek education (Kitromilides 2013: 20). The Ottoman statesman Stephanos Vogorides (c. 1775–1859) lived through some of the most tumultuous years of imperial history, including the birth of the modern state of Greece. He began life as Stoiko Stoikov in the town of Kotel, in central Bulgaria. The family were Bulgarian-speaking Orthodox Christians. At some point during his childhood the family moved to Arbanasi, a regional trading center near the Wallachian border. It was also the summer residence of a number of Phanariot families. There the family Hellenized their names; his father Stoian became Ioannis, his mother Guna took the name Anna, and young Stoiko became Stephanos. This was the essential first step in ascending the ladder of Phanariot society. Stephanos was soon enrolled in the Princely Academy of Bucharest, the pinnacle of Greek education at the time (Philliou 2011: 38–9).

But the phenomenon was far more widespread than is witnessed by several dozen biographies, and extended to people whose names never entered the historical record. It is in the eighteenth century that a self-styled Christian aristocracy made its appearance in the large towns and cities of the Balkans and along the Anatolian coast. Making their fortunes mostly from long-distance trade (although, as the century wore on, some guild members moved up into their ranks), they joined the clergy in leading the *varoş*. They appropriated the Ottoman title *çelebi* while at the same time assuming Greek nomenclature from the Byzantine past, such as *logothetes* and *ostiarios* (Lyberatos 2009: 82). The use of the Greek language and the acquisition of a Greek education were an essential part of being a *çelebi*. This extended to the female members of the family as well; a new term, *kokona*, began to circulate at this time in order to indicate a kind of female aristocratic status.[14] Before the end of the century, urban Orthodox communities across the empire would establish Greek schools.

Hellenization in the eighteenth century has received a good deal of attention in the literature. But it is usually understood as a process that allowed upwardly mobile individuals to enter into clerical or mercantile networks. This it certainly was, and Hellenization through commerce and the priesthood only picked up steam as the century wore on (Kitromilides 1999). But through Hellenization aspiring Christians could also enter the world of Ottoman governance, as Philliou (2011) has argued. The Phanariot households – and they used the same term, *hanedan*, for their households that elite Muslims used for their own – were not only centers of Hellenic culture, they were also producers of Ottoman bureaucrats. Through joining them, an aspiring young Christian could acquire Greek culture, Greek language, and a position in the Ottoman bureaucracy (Philliou 2011: 17, 28). This argument can be extended even further. Opportunities for governance also developed at the more modest level of municipal affairs and, as we have seen, those Christians in the Balkans and Anatolia who took charge of community institutions also entered the sphere of Greek culture and education.

From patriarch to patriarchate

At the same time that the bishops and the *çelebis* were putting a Greek stamp on urban Christian society, the patriarch in Istanbul, always the bearer par excellence of Greek Christian culture, was amassing a series of privileges that extended in many directions. That is, not only was the patriarch securing more and more privileges in his relationship to Ottoman authority; that same authority was also giving him greater power over his clergy, ordinary Christians, and elites – both Christian and Muslim – who might be tempted to interfere in the church's affairs. Alongside these concrete stipulations the status of the church improved. For a time in the second half of the seventeenth century patriarchs had not even been able to present themselves to the sultan. Now, in the eighteenth, they were once again able to secure audiences, "a clear sign that the post had gained respectability and importance" (Bayraktar Tellan 2011: 91). Ottoman bureaucratic language also changed quite dramatically in this period. At the beginning of the century *kefere* (infidel) was still the preferred term for Christians. Then it was *zimmi* (protected non-Muslim subject) and, finally, *nasrani* (Christian), ironically enough a reverse journey back to fifteenth-century norms (Lowry 2002: 129).

We can hear the new assertiveness of the patriarch vis-à-vis the empire's Orthodox Christians by dipping into the stream of petitions sent to the Sublime Porte. Up through the seventeenth century the clergy could do no more than threaten an ordinary Christian (that is, not a member of the clergy) with excommunication. Punishment rested with the Ottomans. Not so in the eighteenth. In 1754 the patriarch asked that a certain *zimmi* be sent to the galleys until he reformed himself; he was, Patriarch Kyrillos wrote, evil and a deceiver (Bayraktar Tellan 2011: 153). In response to another petition sent by the same patriarch, the *kadi* of Kayseri, assisted by an imperial officer, was directed to return Thomas, his wife, and his brother Anastasios to Kayseri, their place of origin, from Istanbul. Apparently they were causing disturbances in the capital city. In that same year two other men, also residents of Istanbul, were exiled to the castle of Limni, again upon the request of the patriarch.[15] These cases stand in contrast to an incident recorded in 1672. There, *reaya* of Zile (in today's north central Turkey) complained to the *kadi* that a certain monk was disturbing their peace. The *kadi* informed the patriarch, who, as the wielder of ecclesiastical justice, had the monk dismissed. But it was the *kadi*, not the patriarch, who wrote to the sultan in order to secure the monk's dismissal from the community. A century later the patriarch was more likely to intervene between Christians on the one hand, both clerical and lay, and the Porte (Bayraktar Tellan 2011: 158).

Moving beyond the sphere of punishment, it was in the eighteenth century, too, that the long-established church practice of arbitration on behalf of Christians moved out of the shadows, in the sense that the Ottoman authorities recognized church arbitration in the *berats* that they issued to members of the clergy. The agreements reached could now be submitted to the *kadi* court and other judicial venues (Kermeli 2007: 175–6). The proviso on arbitration was just one of many new clauses that were added in the eighteenth century as *berats* issued to the clergy became lengthier and lengthier. Many of them – such as the stipulation that *zimmis* could be married up to three times but could not be married to more than one woman simultaneously – were designed to give the clergy what it wanted: greater control over the lives of ordinary Christians (Bayraktar Tellan 2011: 143). To that end, church authorities also tried to move beyond their traditional purview of family law into cases of civil law and by the end of the eighteenth century they had largely succeeded in this endeavor. Thus in 1788 Theofilos, bishop of Campania in Macedonia, could write with satisfaction:

> At the times of the Christian kingdom (alas) the prelates governed only the priesthood and matters of the church and did not interfere with the civil ones ... But now ... the prelates in the provinces accept the mundane lawsuits and trials, for inheritance, for debts and almost all that deal with the Christian civil law, which even now is in favour of the royal external (Ottoman) orders, according to which, when they judge and decide on the basis of our law, and punish the disobedient ones with penance, not one of the external authorities is opposed to them. (Kermeli 2007: 181)

In his "patient work of three centuries" (Petmezas 1996b: 490) the patriarch had to worry not only about the assertion of his authority over ordinary Christians, but also about the exclusion of those who were in a position to interfere in his project. Again, the *berats* of the eighteenth century make it clear that, with the sultan's help, the patriarch was determined to prevent provincial elites across the empire from meddling in the business of the church. To that end, in the course of collecting taxes from the Christians, the patriarchs' representatives were to be allowed to change clothes and to carry arms (this itself was an innovation) in dangerous areas; local notables (*ehl-i örf*) were not to interfere. If a priest performed a marriage in violation of canon law he would be excommunicated and no *kadi* or anyone else could interefere. No outsiders (*taraf-i âherden*) could interfere in the appointment of metropolitans and bishops; if someone complained about the dismissal and exile of clerics, no attention should be paid to them. Powerful people (*ba'zi zi-kudret kimesneler*) (Bayraktar Tellan 2011: 137, 144–5) must not interfere in marriages by "forcing priests to perform illegal marriages or changing the priests of churches" (Bayraktar Tellan 2011: 146). In Crete the struggles of the upper clergy for control extended even to encroachment on the private churches of the island (Bayraktar Tellan 2011: 147).

In the opening of this chapter I mentioned the resistance of some Christian communities to the growing reach of ecclesiastical authority. The clearest evidence for this comes from the Aegean islands, where, due to the peculiarities of their conquest in the sixteenth century, community rule remained largely intact (Kermeli 2007: 183) Thus, in documents from Santorini the islanders stated "the ecclesiastical authorities should not interfere in the affairs of the community." And in Naxos in 1810 the community decided to put down in writing that "no clergyman should be accepted in communal courts and that they should restrict themselves to their judicial boundaries" (Kermeli 2007: 182).

It is almost certainly impossible to arrive at a global statement about the attitude of ordinary Christians toward the expansion of ecclesiastical authority in the eighteenth century. All that can be said, and admittedly this is a rather banal statement, is that some welcomed while others resisted it, for a variety of factors in both cases. But, for our purposes, that is not the point. What is important is the fact that the power of the patriarch and the upper clergy was growing and this development calls into question two narratives. The first, which fewer and fewer scholars adhere to but which still persists in the general narrative, is that the patriarchate remained essentially unchanged over the many centuries of Ottoman rule. The second (and more interesting) point is that it challenges the narrative of Christian alienation from the empire in two ways. First, it suggests that, more than at any other previous time in Ottoman history, the church was able to extract from the Ottoman authorities the kind of authority over the empire's Orthodox Christians that it had always coveted. Second, struggles over the emerging shape of the Christian community were as much of a preoccupation as, if not more so than, any supposed exclusion from what some have argued was a power structure that increasingly identified itself as Muslim.

Why were the Ottomans willing to grant the eighteenth-century patriarchs greater authority over the empire's Christians? The explanation is little different than that already discussed for the provinces. Changes in administrative and financial practices meant a search for new imperial partners, and church elites seized on the opportunity. At the very pinnacle of the Orthodox Church the patriarch became *mültezim* (tax farmer) in chief, as it were. The tight link between the patriarch and the tax-farming system as a whole is demonstrated by, once again, the *berats*. From 1714 onward the office of patriarch was granted for life, as opposed to the renewable three-year terms that had been the norm. This was just a few years after the implementation of *malikane*, or life-term tax farms, in the empire as a whole (Bayraktar Tellan 2011: 132–3). Along with delivering taxes, the empire's tax farmers also appear to have assumed responsibility (whether directly or through delegation) for law and order in the areas where their revenues were located. The patriarchs clearly grasped this concern as they routinely referred to threats to order (*nizam*) in their petitions to the sultan (Bayraktar Tellan 2011: 86, 150, 222). In other words, it is not that the Ottomans were interested in creating a Christian community per se. Rather they were willing to rely on the church for certain key functions and the church hierarchy used this opportunity to expand its authority in other areas. As Kermeli points out, "no work has been done on whether the Ottomans were aware of, and fully supported such developments" (Kermeli 2007: 206). The conversion of the office of patriarch into a lifelong appointment was not the only privilege that the sultan granted in the eighteenth century. Indeed it was not even the most significant. Through a series of concessions dating from the middle of the century the church gained recognition, for the first time in Ottoman history, as an institution. From a patriarch, a patriarchate emerged.

These concessions can be traced in the *berats* issued over a twenty-year period between the 1740s and the 1760s. What they show is a steady rise in the power of the metropolitans vis-à-vis the patriarch. It might seem paradoxical that the patriarchs in this period also supported this development (with a few notable exceptions), but they did so because the Orthodox elite in Istanbul shared a common goal. That goal was to obtain and then to defend a set of routine bureaucratic procedures that would protect the highest offices of the church (and thus the church as a whole) from abuse. We see this concern in the petition from 1741 submitted by twenty-three metropolitans that marks off the beginning of this period. They complained that certain "stranger" priests had been submitting complaints against the patriarchs with the goal of replacing them; some even managed to do so (Bayraktar Tellan 2011: 225–6). The remedy for this was to expand and to formalize the number and the role of the people involved in the running of the church, to move beyond the single office of the patriarch inhabited by one person. This was what the metropolitans managed to do. By the 1760s there was a permanent synod, consisting of five metropolitans, whose rights were consistently laid out in the *berats*. These rights initially clustered around the election of the patriarch himself. The patriarch would not be removed without their consent, complaints against the patriarch from outsiders would not be entertained, and so on and so forth. If the metropolitans wished to dismiss the patriarch, they had to issue a written request and each would be examined to see the truth of their claims (Konortas 1998: 218). There was also a series of measures to put the finances of the church in order, such as the 1759 reform whereby candidates for the office of patriarch were to pay for the post out of their own funds rather than the common funds of the church (Bayraktar Tellan 2011: 229). Over time, all the rights that the patriarch had acquired over ordinary Christians came to be shared with the metropolitans. These included the appointment and dismissal of church officials, decisions over the punishment and imprisonment of clerics, the right to receive the receipts from taxes that had been collected, and the management of the affairs of the other Orthodox patriarchs (Bayraktar Tellan 2011: 235–6). The last petition submitted to the sultan solely by the patriarch was in 1763; after that his seal was divided into four. One part was held by the patriarch, the other three by the metropolitans, and all four parts had to come together to present a petition to the sultan (Konortas 1998: 138–9). This system of power sharing, which lasted well into the nineteenth century, has come to be known in the literature as γεροντισμός, or rule by the elders, in contrast to an earlier period of absolutism (απολυταρχικό) on the part of the patrarich (Konortas 1998: 125).

The impulse behind all of these petitions was clearly reformist. At the same time, expanded participation in the running of the church also reflected the growing power of lay elites in the capital, specifically the Phanariots and the guilds (Konortas 1998: 133). They were wealthy – the guilds of Istanbul paid an astounding 60 percent of a tax levied on the Orthodox community of the capital in 1788 – and with their wealth they supported the church (Konortas 1998: 146). Naturally enough, these lay elites then expected to have a say.

The question of Ottoman motivation remains. If in the case of tax farming the explanation is fairly straightforward, the same cannot be said for the institutionalization of the church. After all, not only the sultan but all the creditors of the various candidates for church office – a group that included powerful players such as the janissaries and the Muslim foundations (*evkaf*) of the city – benefitted from a rapid turnover of office-holders (Bayraktar Tellan 2011: 226). Here we must admit straightaway that the research has not yet been done that would allow us to answer this question. Nevertheless, certain general observations can, and should, be made. Konortas gives us the rather global explanation of Ottoman decline. The increasing legal recognition given to the church from the end of the sixteenth century onward, he writes, was due to the rise of the Orthodox community and the growing weakness of the Ottoman state (Konortas 1998: 359). This is unsatisfactory not only because Ottoman decline has been extensively rethought as a useful concept over the last several decades. It is also unsatisfactory because it resurrects the old paradigm whereby the flourishing of the Greek Orthodox community required the weakening of Ottoman sovereignty. Empirically, this does not work since, as we have seen, Orthodox Christians petitioned the sultan in greater numbers than ever in the eighteenth century and some were unhappy with the expansion of the church's jurisdiction. Certainly the political influence of the Phanariots is an essential part of the explanation. Throughout the eighteenth century the European border of the empire was a volatile one and Phanariot diplomacy was more essential than ever.

But we must also look beyond the Greek community when thinking about the institutionalization of the church. Within Armenian society, too, we see the rise of a wealthy elite – the *sarrafs* – who, in a manner very similar to that of the Phanariots, used their wealth to support the church (Konortas 1998: 143). It would be well worth it to compare the history of the two churches in Istanbul in the eighteenth century to see whether similar *berats* were pursued and obtained by Armenian elites. This work has not yet been done. Moving on to Ottoman society more broadly, it is striking how the story of the Orthodox Church in this period lines up with two essential features of the eighteenth century, namely the emergence of an estate society and the expanding number of people who were able to claim a role in imperial governance (Yaycioğlu 2008; Tezcan 2010; Zilfi 1988).

By "estate society" Ottoman scholars mean the way in which groups such as the janissaries and the *ulema*, coming out of the upheaval of the seventeenth century, were able to stabilize their position and their privileges within society in the century that followed. Thus we see the rise of an "*ulema* aristocracy" in which a small number of families achieved a monopoly over the highest offices in the empire (Zilfi 1988: 46). Among the janissaries the right of a father to pass on part of his salary to his son was officially recognized (Tezcan 2010: 184).

The appearance of new actors in Ottoman governance, especially in the provinces, has long been recognized. In the seventeenth and eighteenth centuries, after all, Ottoman commentators themselves condemned the participation of *ecnebis* (understood here as "outsiders") in tasks that had previously been reserved for the sultan's slaves, his *kuls*, alone. Supporters of the decline theory picked up on this critique and condemned the developments of the later centuries as illegitimate deviations. More recently, Ottoman scholars have pointed out how the proliferation of offices and responsibilities – the *ayan*, the deputy governors, the tax farmers, the tax-collecting communities, and the retinues that served them all – created a large group of people, participants in imperial governance, who identified with the Ottoman system. There was a thickening, if you will, of Ottoman governance as people attached themselves to the streams of revenue that ran across the empire in every direction.

Viewed this way, the Ecumenical Patriarchate is in perfect alignment with eighteenth-century trends. The church was able to extract and to retain a number of privileges over the course of the century, such that by the end of the period it was a far more solid institution than it had been in earlier centuries. At the same time, the number of people with a stake in the running of the Ecumenical Patriarchate rose. Behind the metropolitans who formed the synod were the Phanariots and the guilds, and they, too, had their retinues, which they directed from their mansions in the capital city.

The links between these developments and broader developments in Ottoman society remain, of course, to be investigated. What is certain, however, is that any explanation of changes in church governance in the eighteenth century must consider changing patterns of Ottoman governance more broadly. What I have outlined here suggests that it is incorrect to conclude that the Ecumenical Patriarchate "came into its own" as Ottoman power declined. Rather, its history in this period can be, and must be, profitably comparted to other Ottoman institutions that were transforming themselves at this time as well.

We have described the Hellenizing project of the Christian aristocracy that came to power in the towns and cities of the Balkans in the eighteenth century. The Ecumenical Patriarchate, of course, was synonymous with Hellenization and it, too, scored a notable victory of its own in this period when the patriarchate finally realized the dream of control over the whole of the Balkans. The Serbian church never recovered from the devastation of the wars at the turn of the century and, in 1766 and 1767 respectively, the autocephalic archbishoprics of Peć and Ohrid were abolished and joined to the Ecumenical Patriarchate. The Phanariots had begun moving in long before this formal change. In 1739, during yet another Ottoman–Habsburg war, the (Serbian) archbishop of Peć fled to Hungary and the Ottomans, suspicious of the Serbs since the wars of the late seventeenth century, supported the appointment of Ioannikou Karatza, of the Phanariot Karatza family, as archbishop of Peć. Karatza brought his Greek Istanbul entourage with him and served in Peć until 1746; in the 1760s he became patriarch (Konortas 1998: 219).

Exactly in line with what we have been discussing, the sultan recognized and institutionalized the changed status of Peć and Ohrid. The the two archbishoprics were abolished through an imperial order (a *hatt-ı şerif*) that the patriarch solicited. In so doing the patriarch made explicit reference to the sultan as the "legal emperor" who, as such, had the right to rearrange ecclesiastical boundaries. This right came directly out of the Byzanto-Roman tradition, to which reference was made in the imperial order (Konortas 1998: 220).

The provincial century

In the beginning of this chapter we outlined the argument for the eighteenth century as the Muslim century par excellence. This frame sits alongside another long-standing, indeed venerable, understanding of the same time period, which is the rise of provincial society. The former has clear implications for the empire's Christians, as discussed earlier. What about the latter?

Briefly put, the rise of provincial society refers to the increasing role that provincial actors came to play in imperial governance. There were three points of entry into the system (Yaycıoğlu 2008: introduction). First, imperial officers – particularly governors – began to appoint locally prominent people as their deputies to act in their stead. The key office here was the *mütesellim* or deputy governor. Over time, this position came to be monopolized by certain provincial families. Tax farming was another opportunity. Increasingly, revenues belonging to the imperial fisc were farmed out and these, too, came to be controlled by a select number of provincial elites. Deputy-ship was reserved for Muslims. Large-scale tax farmers who sat at the pinnacle of a descending series of smaller contracts were known as *muhassıl* or *voyvoda* and they were also Muslim.

At the district level, provincial notables dominated the market in tax-farming contracts and here Christians did participate. One such Christian tax farmer was Panayiotes Benakes, the leading Christian notable in the district of Kalamata, in the southwest corner of the Peloponnese (Papastamatiou 2009: 68). Active in the middle of the century, Benakes sometimes acted alone while on other occasions he bought tax-farming contracts together with local Muslim notables. His contracts, which included the taxes due on salt, silk, and olive oil, were not restricted to the district of Kalamata but extended to neighboring districts as well (Papastamatiou 2009: 137–8).

These provincial notables were known as the *ayan*. They were by far the largest group to enter into a relationship with the state and thus they have come to define the century, which is commonly referred to as "the age of the *ayan*." Based in the towns and operating at the district level, the *ayan* included many Christians as well, although they tended to go under different names – *kocabaşis*, *çorbacis*, and *knez* (Yaycioğlu 2008: 57). Whether Christian or Muslim, they shared a common economic profile across the empire. They grew wealthy through a combination of land-holding, trade, money-lending, and tax farming, and they operated at the level of the *kaza* rather than an entire province.

The origins of the *ayan* are difficult to trace and have been the subject of much discussion; suffice it to say that they emerged out of the communities that they came to represent.[16] As taxes came to be levied on communities, the *ayan* took it upon themselves to apportion the burden among their members (Yaycioğlu 2008: ch. 3). Outside of the Arab provinces, the *ayan* as community leaders have been eclipsed by the far more spectacular *ayan* as regional power brokers, even though the latter were far fewer in number and did not come into their own until the disturbances of the last quarter of the eighteenth century.[17] This is significant because an emphasis on the family dynasties of Anatolia, such as Karaosmanoğlu, or on a strongman such as Ali Pasha in the Balkans has given a Muslim flavor to the class of provincial notables that is misleading, particularly for earlier in the eighteenth century. Wherever Christian communities emerged, through processes similar to the ones described earlier in this chapter, Christian community leaders came to the fore and carved out a space for themselves in the evolving fiscal machinery of the empire.

Because of Ivanova's research, we can compare Christian community leaders to their Muslim counterparts in the same place. The similarities are striking; Ivanova, in fact, calls the one "the mirror image" of the other (Ivanova 2005: 233). In the towns and cities of the Ottoman Balkans, both Christian and Muslim leaders came out to receive state emissaries. Together, they provided the collective gifts to various functionaries on special occasions that were an essential aspect of provincial etiquette. The Christian leadership, like its Muslim counterpart, was called upon to render numerous services to the imperial center, such as providing ox-carts for the transportation of the army, as well as to respond to municipal needs such as the repair of bridges, streets, and water-pipes. When problems arose, the Christian leaders joined together and penned petitions to the authorities. There were differences. Among the Muslim notables several were commonly singled out and given an official appointment as *ayan* (Ivanova 2005: 234). This was not done with the *varoş* leaders, whose authority was always more informal, as was the authority of most of the Muslim notables; the latter were called *iş erleri* rather than *ayan* (Ivanova 2005: 238). This does not mean that the responsibilities of the *varoş* leaders were any less real (Petmezas 2005: 80–1). In addition, the Muslim *ayan* were sometimes called upon to represent the entire town in a way that did not happen with the *varoş* leaders.

Studies of Christian versus Muslim notables in more rural settings have made very similar arguments, Both grew out of the same fiscal and administrative processes and had comparable economic profiles, but Muslim elites were able to operate on a wider stage (Petmezas 2005: 111; Anastasopoulos 2005: 267). This opportunity differential brings us back to the questions that began the chapter but now, having outlined the salient developments of the eighteenth century, we are in a better position to evaluate the position of Muslims and Christians within the imperial project.

Imperial dynamics crossed the religious divide. Whether Muslim *ayan* or Christian *kocabaşı* (one of many terms), communal leaders came to the fore in the eighteenth century because the community became an essential unit within the fiscal system. In addition, the central bureaucracy was willing to institutionalize, albeit somewhat tentatively, the structures that were emerging. This was the case with the *ayan* and it was also true for the communities that they represented.[18] We have seen this at work, too, in the patriarchate. In the second half of the eighteenth century both lay and clerical elites secured from the sultan formal recognition of their role in running the affairs of the church. It is misleading, then, to present the eighteenth century as the century when the fates of Muslim and Christian elites diverged, since a common process created both.

On alienation

The difficult question of alienation remains. Let us approach it by first considering the assumptions underlying assertions of alienation, and then suggesting some evidence that can point to an answer.

Even if it is true that by the eighteenth century the term *reaya* had come to be synonymous with non-Muslim, this only mattered if the critical distinction remained that between the *reaya* and the *askeri*.[19] Yet that is not self-evidently the case, particularly in the provinces.[20] The new elites occupied a rather grey area, one that resisted definition throughout the period. One could object that, even if the new elites rendered obsolete the old *reaya/askeri* distinction, Muslims could still rise higher than Christians. But is that necessarily the comparison that Christian guild leaders and communal leaders, Christian tax farmers and the circles around the patriarchate, would be making? It seems equally plausible that their focus would be on the new opportunities opening up, across the empire, as Christian communities became units of governance. Men of wealth and ambition moved swiftly to take control of these entities, and to thus secure for themselves the numerous economic and social benefits that flowed from communal leadership. In addition to the opportunities, church elites must have been gratified by the increasingly distinct lines of a Christian community, as the maintenance of religious boundaries had always been important to them (Zilfi 2000: 298). And all of these positions, from the metropolitans in Istanbul to the *varoş* officials in Balkan towns, received at least some measure of recognition from the central government.

Having raised this theoretical possibility, the task remains of trying to identify attitudes. Because of educational gains and a boom in publishing, there are more Greek voices in the eighteenth century than in previous ones. We shall consider those in the final chapter. Here let us look at two aspects of material culture: clothing and housing.

The rising wealth of Greek elites translated into rising levels of consumption and displays of wealth. This phenomenon has received a fair amount of attention and has been interpreted as westernization, an argument that fits in well with the traditional emphasis on Greek merchants and their trade with Europe when discussing the Ottoman eighteenth century; contact with Europe led to an identification with European values (Göçek 1996: 97). After all, it was Ottoman Christians, particularly in Istanbul where the Greek element was always dominant, who were the first to begin wearing "Frankish" clothes (Göçek 1996: 93; Jirousek 2000: 228).

But the image of Greeks as precocious westernizers, leaving a hidebound society behind, is problematic. The vectors of influence and emulation were multidirectional and extended well beyond clothing. Lists of goods seized from high Ottoman officials show that elite Muslims, too, were avid consumers of western goods including clocks, watches, shawls, chairs, telescopes, and flatware (Göçek 1996: 99–100). From official edicts condemning the practice we know that, in Istanbul again, Muslim women were imitating the novel sartorial styles of Christian women (Zilfi 2000: 299). This suggests, too, a contestation over meaning; a practice that official elites saw as a challenge to established hierarchies, Muslim women saw rather differently, perhaps through the prism of fashion. And if in this case Muslims were imitating Christians, European portraiture from the period makes clear the high prestige that non-Muslims attached to Ottoman official dress. In painting after painting wealthy Christian men and women, most of them connected to international trade, have bedecked themselves in the furred robes and luxurious turbans of the Ottoman elite for this moment of memorialization (Zilfi 2000: 302; Koller 2008: 123).

In housing and domestic life, too, there is a clear imitation of Ottoman style on the part of Greek elites. These wealthy homes (known in Greek as *archontika*), which archeologists have named "the international Ottoman architectural style," were two to three stories high with a lower stone base and a higher level (or levels) made of wood and plaster, with large and continuous windows all around. The upper stories protruded outward, over the lower stone edifice. This type of housing was most predominant in what is today's northern Greece; these were areas that were close to the main trade routes and to the capital of the empire, where this style was in full flourish. But it trickled down to the Greek populations of western Anatolia, Cyprus, and even the southernmost parts of Greece, including Crete, as well as further north in the Balkans (Sigalos 2003: 219). Even domestic gender arrangements drew from Islamic culture, with elite homes possessing a *haremlik* as well as screened areas where females could listen and observe while remaining invisible to male visitors (Bintliff 2012: 461). At the same time the *archontika* also borrowed features from central and western Europe in both the exterior and interior, much as architectural structures in Istanbul in the eighteenth century also experimented with styles from both east and west (Hamadeh 2007: *passim*). In the words of one archeologist, "they were attempting to distinguish themselves from the rest of the population *by means of the symbols of distinction that were available to them*" (Sigalos 2003: 220; my emphasis). Condemnation of these very same practices in the eighteenth century suggests just how entrenched they were. Orthodox clerics criticized Christians, and especially wealthy Greek merchants, for imitating Muslim lifestyles, particularly their practice of keeping their wives and daughters in harems.[21]

Merchants, reconsidered

Let us end this chapter by returning to that elite figure that has been so prominent in the historiography, the Greek Orthodox merchant. It has not been the intent of this chapter to downplay his extraordinary successes. From the Greek colonies in the Habsburg lands to the massive inroads into the Mediterranean trade as a result of the Seven Years War (1756–63), Greek commerce grew by leaps and bounds in the eighteenth century and funded the intellectual production of the Greek Enlightenment. But future studies of the Greek merchant should consider him in the context of other important trends in Greek society that I have outlined in this chapter. These trends were: the increasing institutionalization of the church; the emergence of Christian communities as essential units of governance; and the opportunities this afforded to Christian elites across the empire, not just among the Phanariot elites, of a renewed Hellenization project and yet, at the same time, an embrace of Ottoman elite culture. The Greek merchant's relationship to all of these developments – and not just his relationship with Europe – must be investigated. We already know that the Greek merchants who obtained *berats* through their association with the Europeans were the very same people who used their new-found wealth to associate themselves with the status symbols of Ottoman society. At the more narrowly economic level, the profits that accrued from international trade must be balanced against other sectors where Greeks were active, such as tax farming and the relatively understudied arena of trade within the empire (Papastamatiou 2009: 40; Pamuk 2004: 241). Thus it is well known that Plovdiv developed a flourishing trade with central Europe and the Danubian Principalities, but its very strong commercial ties with Anatolia and the Arab provinces do not appear in the standard narrative, even though the *abaci* guild's production was so closely tied to markets in Anatolia and the Middle East that even the names of the masters – Arabastanis, Amasyalis, Chaleplis – reflected this orientation (Lyberatos 2009: 61, 73).

Similarly absent is the large state factory for the dying of *aba* cloth that was located in the city; two local notables, Michalaki Kyrou and Yannakis Doulgeroglu, were in charge of it (Lyberatos 2009: 93). Even when it comes to shipping, traditionally seen as the quintessentially Greek activity, a 2008 study levies the following criticism: "Mainstream Greek historiography in particular has ignored the Ottoman political and economic framework within which the Ottoman Greek shipowners and captains were active" (Harlaftis and Laiou 2008: 1).

These future tasks should concern not just those historians who write more narrowly on the Greeks, but Ottoman historians more generally as well. There is agreement, I believe, that a more integrated empire emerged in the eighteenth century, in the sense that a larger number of people were engaged in governance and, in so doing, began to identify with the elites. Thus, something called Ottoman culture, beyond the confines of the palace and the upper reaches of the bureaucracy, came into being. The burning question is whether this development was confined to the sultan's Muslim subjects. Those who would assert that it was need to engage more deeply with the Christian experience and with the Greeks in particular, since (for reasons that I have explained) Christian elites took on a decidedly Hellenic hue in the eighteenth century. The evidence assembled here suggests that, for the Christians as well, the future still looked imperial.

Notes

1. See Vacalopoulos (1976) for a classic in this genre. The very title makes clear his suppositions.
2. Faroqhi, too, speaks of disloyalty. "As non-Muslims increasingly benefitted from their contacts with Europeans and were less inclined to accept their subordinate status, they were probably perceived as potentially disloyal" (Faroqhi 1995: 96).
3. "This ambiguity about rights and responsibilities allowed the patriarchate to take the lead and establish an undisputed authority from the mid eighteenth century not only in the traditional accepted area of family law, but also civil law" (Kermeli 2007: 206).
4. "Hidden in a mountain fastness and thus long secure from the envy of outlaws and Ottoman officials, the citizens of Moschopolis grew rich through the sale of products of their flocks – wool, hides and cheese – to Jewish buyers of Salonika and to Italian merchants" (Stoianovich 1960: 252, and see 257 for a very similar explanation of Ambelakia's prosperity).
5. Argo (2008: 268). To give just two examples, in 1655 just 1 percent of Sarajevo's population was Christian, and in Banja Luka that number was 6 percent. In 1807 those percentages had risen to 25 percent and 80 percent respectively (Stoianovich 1960: 251).
6. This was true even as cities became the central node in the fiscal management of provincial communities (Yaycioğlu 2008: part I, ch. III).
7. By this I mean a rejection of the old declinist model that saw institutions in this period as only the corrupt and illegitimate shadows of their sixteenth-century selves.
8. The following discussion relies heavily on Ivanova's (2005) article. Her research covers a number of town communities in present-day Bulgaria, and relies on the documents, in both Bulgarian and Greek, that these communities produced.
9. In other cases it seems that Christian communities resisted the involvement of the clergy in tax collecting, preferring a direct relationship with the Ottoman authorities themselves (Ursinus 1994: 244).
10. As Christians fell away, it is possible that Muslim guilds also became

more Muslim. But what that would look like is not clear, given the more diffuse nature of religious authority in the Islamic tradition. The question remains to be investigated. Another major question is what appears to be a difference between guilds in Istanbul and guilds in the provinces. Based on limited, but very suggestive, research, Bayraktar Tellan seems to argue that "In the eighteenth century, the major link between certain groups of craftsmen in eighteenth century Istanbul was *hemşherilik* rather than religion." *Hemşherilik* translates, roughly, as "being from the same hometown." And yet just a few pages later she refers to the "Christian guilds of Istanbul" (Bayraktar Tellan 2011: 99–101).

11. Yaycioğlu (2008: 165). The repercussions of this policy shift for the Christian elite have not yet been investigated.
12. Yaycioğlu's very extensive discussion of municipal governance in the eighteenth century, while not defined in religious terms, is concerned first and foremost with Muslim institutions, and guilds do not figure in his discussion at all.
13. This process was still going on in the nineteenth century (Karakasidou 1997).
14. The term comes from the Romanian word *cocoana*, and its appearance is probably a testimony to the influence of Romanian culture, filtered through the Phanariots, in the Orthodox Christian world at this time. I thank Michael Konaris for his assistance with the word.
15. See Bayraktar Tellan (2011: 153–6) for many other examples. These also include the pardoning of Christians upon the patriarch's request.
16. Yaycioğlu (2008: 135) writes that "the main difference between the tax-famer and the *ayan* was that the *ayan* was expected to be an elected or designated representative of his community, whereas tax-farming positions were for sale."
17. "From the ranks of these local notables, there in time emerged a second, more select group, also misleadingly known as *ayans*. In fact, since they often seized power by force and formal quasi-feudal networks, they were closer to being warlords. The crucial period for their emergence was the war of 1768–1774, even though some, such as the Bustali family of Albania, already were carving out fiefdoms for themselves years earlier" (McGowan 1994a: 662–3).
18. This is an argument made most strongly by Yaycioğlu. The central government, he says, was interested in securing "the active role and consent of the community" as a counterbalance to the *ayan* (Yaycioğlu 2008: 160). This was why, for example, it decreed in 1784 that account books must be kept by the community and sent to Istanbul for inspection. In Petmazas' work on the records kept by the Christian communities on Mount Pelion, however, there is no indication that community records were ever sent to Istanbul.
19. This is often asserted but, in the absence of a systematic study

of Ottoman usage of the terms during this period, it remains an assertion.
20. "While the two-fold structure of the Ottoman imperial system between the governing imperial elite (*askeri*) and the tax-paying communities (*re'aya*) was dissolving, a third category, the provincial elite/notables (*ayan* and *eşraf*) which belonged neither to *askeri* nor to *re'aya* was being consolidated as the primary power in provincial politics and governance" (Yaycioğlu 2008: 2).
21. Gradeva (1997: 51): "This suggests that the integration of Christians within Ottoman society continued into the eighteenth century even in matters closely associated with religion."

CHAPTER 8

The Ottoman court and the Greek Enlightenment

The geography of the Greek Enlightenment is well known and it begins at the University of Padua.[1] In the early modern period Padua became the center of a flourishing Neo-Aristotelianism, thanks in part to the Greek texts brought to Italy by scholars fleeing the Ottoman advance. Greek students flocked to the university, which, being part of the Venetian Republic, was free from the pressures of Rome and the Counter-Reformation. From Padua the students, now scholars, returned to the Ottoman Empire and brought the intellectual verve of their education home with them. The Athenian Theophilos Korydaleus (1570–1646) is credited with introducing Neo-Aristotelianism to the Greek world when Patriarch Loukaris asked him, in 1624, to reorganize the Patriarchal Academy. Loukaris was already an advocate of religious humanism – the revival of learning based on the study of the texts of antiquity – and the two projects were very compatible. After a long lull, due to the difficult circumstances of the seventeenth century, the graduates of Padua took up once again the task of intellectual and educational revival and the turn of the eighteenth century saw the founding of numerous schools, the most famous being those in Bucharest and Jassy (Nicolaidis 2011: 136–7). In addition to the Danubian Principalities, Ioannina and Smyrna also grew into prominent centers of Greek education and cultural activity in the eighteenth century, due to their strong commercial ties with the west, ties that facilitated the diffusion of Enlightenment ideas. And of course it was the commercial cities that produced the merchants who funded the schools and the publication programs – both translations and original works – that were so characteristic of the Greek Enlightenment. Over the course of the eighteenth century Vienna emerged as another important center of Greek commerce and, thus, as an additional support for the strengthening of Greek culture, particularly in the central and northern Balkan towns that lay on the trade routes to central Europe.

This story, as it is told, is first and foremost a story of the Danubian Principalities, where the Phanariot princes oversaw a remarkable revival of Greek learning. Layered on to that are the scattered Greek communities united by the peripatetic careers of the clerical educators – either graduates of Padua or trained by them – who moved from school to school, bringing new texts and new ideas to their students. In most narratives, this outpouring of intellectual activity is still understood as a project of national revival with the aim of liberating the Christians from Ottoman rule (Dvoicenco-Markov 1971: 383).

The Ottoman court, naturally enough given the presuppositions, is absent from this story, except as facilitator in the sense that the sultan's decision to turn over the thrones of Wallachia and Moldavia to the Phanariots created the conditions for the full flowering of Greek culture. But more recent research has begun to reveal that the rivers of knowledge that flowed out of Padua took many routes and not all of them poured directly into the empire's Greek communities, although the Greek connection was often present. Nuh Efendi, the chief physician (*hekimbaşı*) who served from 1695 to 1707, spanning the reigns of Mustafa II and Ahmet III, was a Cretan by birth. Born in 1627, he went to Padua to study medicine at age seventeen and then to Istanbul. He advanced quickly in his medical career and converted to Islam. By the mid-1670s he was serving in the palace (Bayat 1999: 20). Nuh's advancement was certainly due to his Paduan education. As we shall see, the Neo-Aristotelian approach to medicine that was taught at Padua found favor in the court of Ahmet III, just as it did in more exclusively Greek circles, and physicians with this kind of training – both Christian and Muslim – were prominent in the educated circles of early eighteenth-century Istanbul.

Then there is the figure of Esad Efendi, prominent at the court of Ahmet III, who translated the work of Johannes Cottunius, a Greek professor of philosophy at Padua, from Latin into Arabic. Europeans called Esad "the most erudite man in the Ottoman Empire" (Küçük 2013: 134). He was a native of Ioannina, where he must have learned his Greek.[2] Rising to become Ahmet III's librarian in 1719, his circle included the most illustrious Greek intellectuals of his day. Alexander Mavrokordatos and Chrysanthos Notaras, the patriarch of Jerusalem, were his patrons and Alexander's son, Nicholas, was his student. Demetrius Cantemir learned his Turkish from Esad (Küçük 2012: 73, 133).

These connections and overlaps – and there are others – suggest that it is high time to consider not only the Ottoman context of the Greek Enlightenment, but even what was Greek about the historical developments that are usually subsumed under that name. For instance, it is still common to understand the intellectual trends of the seventeenth and eighteenth centuries, Neo-Aristotelianism and religious humanism, as part of a project of national revival (Dialetis, Gavroglu, and Patiniotis 1999: 47). But a consideration of the Ottoman context renders this less certain, since "Paduan Aristotelianism, Cartesianism and chemical philosophy were Ottoman movements and had Turkish and Greek speaking proponents" (Küçük 2012: 36).

In the end I will not go as far as a 2013 article that conceives of the Greek Enlightenment as a part of a greater Ottoman whole.[3] Rather, it seems that there were two projects, one of which we can call the Ottoman and the other the Greek or Neo-Hellenic Enlightenment.[4] Certain individuals appear in both and the intellectual content of the two was broadly similar, although not identical. But just as the movements could converge so, too, could they diverge and it seems likely that they did so after 1730. A story of convergence and divergence is not only historically valid; it also encourages us to think about what Ottoman elites shared across religious lines and what was distinct about their historical experience in the empire. An essential difference, I shall argue, is that the Greek Enlightenment was a more diffuse phenomenon and this made it more resilient. The Ottoman Enlightenment was narrower; it was intimately tied to the capital city and to the Ottoman court in particular.

The Greek Enlightenment

Let us begin with a more extensive discussion of the Greek Enlightenment. We have already mentioned the founding of schools, the establishment of printing presses, and the ambitious program of translation and original scholarship. To what end?

Here we must distinguish between two phases of the Enlightenment, perhaps one could even say two Enlightenments. In the early phase, which started in the late seventeenth century and extended to at least 1730, and possibly later, the Enlightenment must be understood as an elite project. Its adherents were social elites, most often clerics, who had studied philosophy, theology, mathematics, and physics. They had been educated in western Europe, usually Italy, and they wrote in Attic or Archaic Greek. The new learning was supported, more or less, by the church, and the pursuit of knowledge was funded through elite patronage. Courtly life – in Jassy, in Bucharest, and in Istanbul – was vital to the survival of these new intellectual ventures. By the second half of the eighteenth century, and certainly after 1770, intellectual life had moved out of the control of the elites and of the church. The many merchant colonies established in Europe – now often as not in central Europe rather than Italy – meant a generation of educated Greeks were directly influenced by the French Enlightenment. They took it upon themselves to popularize the new experimental science (as opposed to the older Aristotelianism) with the goal of bringing it to as many Greeks within the empire as possible. They wrote in a more vernacular Greek (Nicolaidis 2011: 164).

These distinct profiles already point to some reasons for a divergence in Ottoman and Greek projects later on in the century; we shall return to that point later on. But for now the task is to characterize the earlier period. First, it is not always sufficiently appreciated that the appearance of schools in Ottoman territory – including places without a prior tradition of learning, such as Kastoria or Milies in Pelion – is related, in ways that are not yet well understood, to diminished opportunities in Italy. Possibly Greek scholars were pushed out; economic difficulties at the Greek College in Rome (the traditional stepping-stone to Padua) in the 1660s and 1670s had the result of reducing the number of Ottoman Greeks who were admitted (Fyrigos 1983: 197–9). Possibly they chose to retreat, due to a growing disconnect between the kind of education they favored and the new natural philosophy that was coming to the fore in the Europe of the Scientific Revolution (Dialetis et al. 1999: 50–1). For whatever reason, Greek education increasingly shifted to the Greek lands themselves, although wealthy students continued to find their way to Padua (Küçük 2013: 144–5). This shift was noted at the time by one of the most brilliant figures of the Greek Enlightenment, Nicholas Mavrokordatos himself, in his philosophical novel *Philotheou Parerga*.

> Greece is no longer completely dispossessed of learned men; She at last guards the relics of her ancient grandeur. Over the years excellent scholars in all fields have returned from the illustrious Academies of Rome and Padua. They enrich their nation in both foreign knowledge and Greek philosophy. (Küçük 2013: 150)

Thus did the Neo-Aristotelianism of Padua come to not only learned Greek circles in the Ottoman Empire, but to Greek education as well (Kitromilides 2013: 27). What did Neo-Aristotelianism mean in the Ottoman context? Here we must describe, briefly, what it is that Korydaleus brought back to the empire. First, pride of place was given to philosophy. Philosophy did not depend upon theology, and philosophical questions could be debated without reference to theology.

The physical, rather than the metaphysical, aspect of the universe was the proper subject of study (Nicolaidis 2011: 133). Second, the Neo-Aristotelians proclaimed a strong link between philosophy and virtue. Cottunius told his students that the study of the orderly operation of nature imparted "justice, fortitude, temperance, prudence, liberality, munificence and every conceivable virtue" to those who studied it (Küçük 2013: 138) and Korydaleus agreed – "the happiness of man consists of study" (Nicolaidis 2011: 133). The writings of Nicholas Mavrokordatos, and the Phanariot class more generally, are shot through with a keen interest in the question of virtue.[5]

Finally, the utility of knowledge was valued. This was particularly pronounced in the treatises written by medical doctors, many of whom had trained at Padua. The doctors were wedged somewhere between Neo-Aristotelianism and the emerging practices of experimental science; the latter was still fairly controversial in the empire whereas the former was not. Alexander Mavrokordatos, a Neo-Aristotelian in many other aspects, put his faith in human judgment rather than the authority of ancient texts in his University of Padua dissertation on the circulation of the blood (Kitromilides 2013: 30). A preoccupation with utility is also very clear in that consistently favored genre of the Greek Enlightenment, namely texts on political and ethical issues.

What explains the appeal of these new values? Why the interest in virtue and utility? And why did intellectuals want theology to take a back seat to philosophy? Here the rise of the Phanariot class is absolutely central. As the Phanariots secured their hold on vital Ottoman offices in both the Danubian Principalities and Istanbul – including domination of the medical positions within the palace – they developed a strong and abiding interest in the qualities of a ruler. Both Alexander Mavrokordatos and his son Nicholas wrote extensively on the virtuous prince (Kitromilides 2013: 28–35). The Neo-Aristotelian contemplation of nature was valuable not only, or perhaps not even principally, for the production of scientific knowledge, but for the qualities it developed in the individual.[6]

If the relationship between virtue and utility on the one hand and the rise of a new Greek elite on the other is clear enough, other connections, I would argue, are less so, even though they are frequently asserted. Kitromilides describes the Phanariots as a "secular" elite, and others imply that they were anti-clerical because their rise undermined the monopoly of the clergy (Kitromilides 2013: 28; Dialetis et al. 1999: 49). The study of philosophy without regard for theology, then, is understood as an act directed against the church, at least in part. This is overstating the case, for several reasons. Clerics were very prominent in the Greek Enlightenment. In the earlier part of the century they were the vast majority of those who were producing the new thinking and implementing the new curricula in the schools. Of course it is true that opposition, at times very harsh indeed, such as the excommunication of Methodios Antrhakitis (himself a clergyman), also came entirely from within the ranks of the church. There is no surprise here. Since the intellectual life of the Greeks within the empire was dominated by the church, it makes sense that it is there that the Enlightenment would be both produced and opposed. Yes, the church was wary of the Copernican system, but at the same time the first person to describe the new cosmology was the future metropolitan of Athens (Nicolaidis 2011: 136).

It is also the case (and is generally acknowledged) that, overall, church opposition to the new thinking was rather mild. Here we must consider the argument about national revival (an argument that figures prominently as an explanation) since it is central to our own concerns. The historian of science Efthymios Nicolaidis writes:

> Little by little, the hierarchy of the Orthodox Church came around to the idea of teaching ancient natural philosophy independently of the teaching of Creation. This acceptance was prepared by the idea – increasingly widespread in the 17th century – that Orthodox believers were the heirs of Greek splendor and learning. This idea was a comfort to the Orthodox of the Ottoman Empire who felt subjugated to the Muslim state and, at the same time, threatened by the specter of Uniates. (Nicolaidis 2011: 136)[7]

Thus does the reception of the new philosophical ideas go right back to the question of belonging and to the nature of the empire, the same question that began the previous chapter. Therefore it is time to turn to the court of Ahmet III.

An Ottoman Enlightenment?

Unlike the Greek Enlightenment, which is an established historical topic, the existence of an Ottoman Enlightenment rests on very recent arguments about the early eighteenth century, such that one cannot even begin to speak of a consensus among historians.[8] For the purposes of our argument we can remain agnostic on the question of terminology. The real value of the work that has been done is that it provides an alternative, or an additional, way of thinking about the early Greek Enlightenment.

The frame of the Ottoman Enlightenment places Greek intellectual life within the context of the court of Ahmet III (1703–30). Ahmet's court has long attracted the attention of many historians as a center of reform and innovation. After a very long absence, the sultan returned the seat of the court to Istanbul from Edirne. The palace then initiated the greatest wave of building projects since the sixteenth century, projects that were novel in both their form and function. Suburban waterfront palaces and public gardens and fountains allowed for a new kind of public sociability, as people picnicked and promenaded in the new spaces. The new worldly atmosphere in Istanbul charmed European visitors. Lady Mary Wortley Montagu wrote "Tis true their Magnificence is of a different taste from ours, and perhaps of a better. I am allmost [sic] of opinion they have a right notion of life; while they consume it in Music, Gardens and Wine, and delicate eating" (Evin 1980: 141).

Ahmet's court was not only about parties at Saadabad, the famous palace of Ahmet's luxury-loving grand vezir, Damat Ibrahim Pasha. The sultan and his grand vezir initiated a number of military reforms, sent a famous embassy to Paris to "study the means of civilization and education there," funded a number of translation and publishing projects, and set up the first printing press to use the Arabic script (Evin 1980: 135). Taken together, these innovations and this period (1718–30 in particular) are subsumed under the name of "the Tulip Age," a historiographical convention that is well known to all Ottoman historians. It refers to the passion for cultivating tulips that seized the capital during these years and is a synecdoche for the spirit of reform and innovation that characterized these years. The phrase has come in for severe criticism due to the fact that it was not used at the time but was coined, with obvious ideological intent, in the early twentieth century. Historians have been similarly critical of the original assumption that the Tulip Age was all about westernization (Erimtan 2006). A sustained debate, then, has formed over the meaning and significance of Ahmet's court. And yet, with one notable exception, no Ottoman historian has thought to compare the preoccupations of Ahmet's court with those of the Greek Enlightenment, nor have Greek historians engaged with the extensive literature on the Tulip Age.[9]

Despite the extensive literature on the reign of Ahmet III, it is only very recently that this court has been considered as a site of intellectual production (Küçük 2012). This was of course a traditional role for courts, and attention has been lavished on the intellectual patronage practiced at earlier courts – particularly those of Fatih Mehmet and Süleyman – but this is an unfamiliar role both for Ahmet and for his grand vezir, no doubt in part, at least, because the eighteenth century has been considered a time of intellectual stagnation. When viewed from this unexpected angle, both Ahmet's court and the Greek Enlightenment look rather different. For example, when Chrysanthos Notaras, patriarch of Jerusalem, went to Paris his first goal was to see a telescope. He spent a week at the Paris Observatory with Jacques Cassini (Stathis 1999: 89). In the same period Grand Vezir Damat Ibrahim Pasha ordered three telescopes and two microscopes from Paris through the French ambassador in Istanbul (Küçük 2012: 173). Nicholas Mavrokordatos received his first telescope from Notaras, who had it sent to him (Stathis 1999: 165).

Notaras' stargazing is conventionally understood as the earliest rumblings of a national revival. Damat Ibrahim Pasha's fascination with the telescope is folded into the larger project of modernizing the state, which is held to have originated in a sense of crisis following the loss of territory with the treaty of Karlowitz (1699). This explains the willingness to reform and to innovate during the Tulip Age.[10] Viewed this way, the two men seem to share nothing beyond the coincidence of an interest in the telescope. But if we understand that both men were members of the Istanbul elite that developed after 1703, it is very plausible that their enthusiasm for the telescope (and other western devices) grew out of a shared interest in natural philosophy, an interest that animated so many members of Ahmet's court.[11]

The court of Ahmet III

By the time Ahmet came to the throne in August 1703, the sultanate had hit an unprecedented low. Ahmet's brother, Mustafa II, had been forced to abdicate, the empire had suffered stinging military defeats, and the coffers of the state were empty. In the middle of all the chaos the janissaries set up a temporary government in Istanbul in 1703 and there was talk of doing away with the sultan all together (Küçük 2012: 60). Faced with this crisis Ahmet decided to make a decisive break with the ways of his immediate predecessors. The move back to Istanbul and the rebuilding of the city have already been mentioned. He also made a concerted, and largely successful, effort to build up a brilliant court, and he filled it with new allies, leaving behind the Köprülü and other households that had figured so prominently in the second half of the seventeenth century.[12] In addition to the members of the imperial family, which included his Cretan-born mother, the convert Gülnüş, who had negotiated skillfully to bring her son to the throne, he turned to the bureaucrats, men who, when analyzing the problems that confronted the empire, turned to Aristotelian natural philosophy rather than to the moral explanations that had been favored by the *kadizadeli*. As the bureaucrats saw it, it was the misplaced enthusiasm for *jihad* that had led to the defeat at Vienna in 1683 and the subsequent disasters. It was time for more sober minds to put the empire on a firmer footing.

Esad Efendi, the good friend of Chrysanthos Notaras, was typical of the new type of scholar/bureaucrat who was favored at Ahmet's court. The direct beneficiary of Damat Ibrahim Pasha's patronage, he had none of the training in traditional Islamic theology and philosophy that had been an essential aspect of a successful scholar's education in the sixteenth century, despite having secured a position at a *medrese* in prestigious Eyup.[13] Instead, he interested himself in philosophical movements that were outside of the *medrese* system, chief among them the Neo-Aristotelianism that was so favored at Padua (Küçük 2012: 78).

All of these trends – a new and more public court, an appreciation of natural philosophy, transformations in scholarly education, and an interest in effective rulership – opened up space for the Greek elite and for what we can call Greek learning at Ahmet's court. So, too, did the emphasis on improving the empire's public finances because the Phanariots were essential as financiers in the new *malikane* regime, which brought steady income into the treasury throughout the first half of the eighteenth century (Küçük 2012: 62, 70). Here we should note that the Greek ascent at the Ottoman court began long before Ahmet came to the throne, with the arrival of Phanariots and physicians (whether Greek Orthodox or Greek converts to Islam) in the second half of the seventeenth century. Both groups brought with them the intellectual movements that they had absorbed in Padua and thus we can say that natural philosophy and medical humanism and the like were there, percolating, even at Mehmet's rustic court in Edirne. But it was in Ahmet's cosmopolitan Istanbul that the Paduan Greeks emerged as familiar faces in the new social world that was so much part of the Ahmedian regime. The Phanariots were regular attendees at the parties at the summer palaces, along with Europeans, both Catholic and Protestant, and the worldly Muslim bureaucrats who staffed the offices of state (Küçük 2012: 12–13). Like their elite Muslim counterparts, the Phanariots too built villas along the Bosphorus in the eighteenth century (Philliou 2009: 172). In his discussion of Nicholas Mavrokordatos' philosophical novel *Philotheou Parerga*, Kitromilides notes that the novel depicts "an international group of cultured gentlemen promenading in an exquisite garden and discussing psychology, society and culture from a shared social and moral values" (Kitromilides 2013: 34). He calls this, rather vaguely, cosmopolitanism. But when one is aware of the celebration of the garden in eighteenth-century Ottoman poetry, as well as the valorization of philosophical speculation at Ahmet's court, it is clear that Mavrokordatos' novel is a product of the Istanbul milieu (Hamadeh 2007: 281).

The luminaries of the early Greek Enlightenment then, men such as Chrysanthos Notaras, the Mavrokordatoi, and Demetrius Cantemir, were not only the princes of Moldavia and Wallachia or office-holders in the Orthodox Church. They were also members of Istanbul court society. Cantemir, after all, dedicated his justly famous study of Ottoman music to Ahmet III (Dvoicenco-Markov 1971: 389). Who were their Muslim associates and what interests did they share? Here we must admit that it is easier to answer the second than the first question. There is strong evidence of shared intellectual interests and worldviews, such as just mentioned above with *Philotheou Parerga*. But the relationships that (presumably) existed between Christian and Muslim intellectuals in Istanbul at this time are difficult to document.[14]

Esad Efendi is the exception to the rule, no doubt in part because of his very high profile in Ahmedian Istanbul. His ties to so many prominent Greek intellectuals, mentioned above, are well known and have been the subject of several studies. There were connections, too, to less well-known, but well-educated, Greeks. For example, when he embarked on the translation of Cottunius, the sultan provided him with two Greek scholars to assist him. One of them was the librarian at the patriarchate (Küçük 2012: 154). Esad Efendi's prominence is also clear from the fact that when the first Ottoman Turkish printing press finally came into being, he edited the press's first books (Stathis 1986: 58). Surviving letters between Esad Efendi and Notaras testify to the deep friendship between the two men (Stathis 1986). We know very little about how these relationships came to be but Esad Efendi's facility with the Greek language must have been a key facilitator. He was born in Ioannina and, although information on his early years is sparse as well, we do know that the Muslim community of Ioannina retained the Greek language to an unusual extent; not only were they Greek speaking but the literate among them also wrote in Greek (Kotzageorgis 1997; 2009). Ioannina was a center of Greek education with strong connections to Padua and it is possible that some of this filtered through to Esad Efendi. This, however, is entirely speculative (Küçük 2013: 141).

Esad Efendi and Notaras shared a deep interest in astronomy but Esad Efendi was not Notaras' only correspondent on these matters; from the patriarch's letters it is clear that he sought out other astronomers at court and that he had their deep admiration, including that of the head astronomer (Stathis 1986: 66). There were other Greek-speaking Muslim scholars active at this time. Hezarfen Hüseyin Efendi was a Greek speaker from Chios who wrote a history of Istanbul using Byzantine sources. Another scholar, who had served as a judge in Athens for twenty years, wrote a history of that city that he called *A History of the City of Philosophers*, using both modern and ancient Greek sources (Küçük 2013: 150).

And then there were the converts. Nuh Efendi, the chief physician, and Gülnüş Sultan, the sultan's mother, were the most prominent. Both were from Crete and Cantemir tells us that they were close friends (Küçük 2012: 119). At the palace, converts were particularly prominent within the community of physicians. Padua was a great center of medical education and many of those who had converted from Christianity either were graduates of Padua or had received a Padua-like education within the Ottoman lands. They were visible enough that an opponent of theirs, a Muslim practitioner of chemical medicine, fulminated against the "Greek physicians [who] are plotting to make medicine subservient to their natural philosophy" (Küçük 2012: 122).

This picture of the elites circling within the orbit of Ahmet's court is fragmentary. Nevertheless, it is enough to show that any discussion of intellectual production in the early eighteenth century that simply assumes separate and self-contained linguistic and religious communities is problematic. Elites routinely crossed both religious and linguistic boundaries. Phanariot Greeks studied Arabic, Persian, and Turkish while Greek-speaking Muslims – a group about whom we know next to nothing – brought Greek sources into the world of Ottoman scholarship.[15] Demetrius Cantemir certainly knew the Ottoman chronicle tradition since his history of the Ottoman Empire, *The History of the Growth and Decay of the Ottoman Empire*, drew extensively from the chronicle of Saadi Effendi, presented to Sultan Mustafa in 1696 (Dvoicenco-Markov 1971: 395). Both groups knew Latin and translation projects, into Turkish, Arabic, and Greek, were routine (Küçük 2013: 126). Then there is the open question of the relationship between Greek converts and Greeks who remained Christian. Alexander Mavrokordatos and Nuh Efendi both studied medicine at Padua and both were Greek. They would seem to have had an affinity for each other, and they must have known each other, but we know nothing about their actual relationship. Indeed it is striking that, in the early eighteenth century, we are confronted with the same phenomenon (although certainly on a smaller scale) that we saw in the days of Mehmet the Conqueror: a court filled with both powerful Greek Christians and powerful Greek converts, as well as the same uncertainty over how to understand the relationship between the two groups.

We are on much firmer footing when it comes to the interests and attitudes that united the elites around Ahmet's court. The evidence for a shared spirit of the age is quite remarkable, in fact. Sociability, freedom of inquiry, virtue, and liberation from the constraints imposed by religion were values held in common. The willingness to come into conflict with church doctrine, for example, was mirrored in a Muslim elite that dispensed with the study of theology and took up disciplines, most prominently natural philosophy, that were not part of the *medrese* curriculum. Contemporaries frequently remarked on the religious skepticism of men such as Damat Ibrahim Pasha (Küçük 2012: 16). And yet – and this is equally striking – neither group was interested in launching an attack on religion. What they wanted to be able to do was to pursue their own intellectual interests free of interference from those who might take it upon themselves to object.[16] Part of the appeal of Johannes Cottunius' work – which Ahmet III commissioned and Esad Efendi translated – was its agnosticism. It was neither markedly religious nor impious, a quality that gave it a broad appeal (Küçük 2012: 153).

Muslim intellectuals drew the same connections between the study of philosophy and virtue that figure so prominently in Phanariot writing. The ethics that animated Alexander Mavrokordatos' *On Duties* were echoed in works penned by Muslim members of Ahmet's court, where the cultivation of virtuous rulership was a widely shared preoccupation during this time (Küçük 2012: 74).

Shared values were reflected in common intellectual projects, such as astronomy, natural philosophy, and the exploration of new scientific instruments such as the telescope. In *Philotheou Parerga* Nicholas Mavrokordatos deplored the dearth of modern books that could initiate the Ottomans into the natural sciences (Bouchard 1981: 122, 124). This dearth was exactly the motivation behind Ahmet's founding of the printing press in 1727 (Küçük 2012: 162). It is also the case that Greek translation projects must not be viewed in isolation; the same French texts that were selected for translation into Greek also attracted Turkish translators (Küçük 2012: 33–4).

Finally, let us pause for a minute on one aspect of the intellectual landscape of early eighteenth-century Istanbul that must be of interest in any consideration of the place of the Greeks within the empire. Here I am referring to hints, and they are only hints at this point, that some elite Ottomans were attracted to another Paduan project, which was the separation of a Greek identity from its confessional identification with Greek Orthodoxy. This project was manifest in, once again, Johannes Cottunius' *Commentarii*, the work that Esad Efendi translated for Ahmet III. Cottuniuswas a convert to Catholicism. For him Greekness was enshrined not in the Christian religion but in ancient Greek language and philosophy. In Venice he patronized a book that catalogued all the ancient Greek busts that were extant in the city, and at the Greek college that he established all the students were given a rigorous education in classical literature (Küçük 2013: 143).

Moving ahead several decades, Chrysanthos Notaras' law professor in Padua was one Nicholas Komnenos. Komnenos was a convert to Catholicism but this did not stop him from developing the greatest admiration for his brilliant new pupil. Komnenos described himself as 'Ἕλλην αλλ' οὐ φωτιανός' (Stathis 1999: 84). By this he seemed to mean that he was Greek (using the term "Hellene," with its association with antiquity) but not Orthodox.[17]

We know that the essentials of a Paduan education were transferred to the Ottoman lands as Greek educational institutions opened up in the empire. It makes sense that this line of thought would have made the journey as well. Could this explain why Esad Efendi and other court intellectuals took the rather extraordinary step of referring to the (modern) Greeks as *Yunani* rather than the traditional *Rumi*, with its inevitable Christian connotation (Küçük 2013: 145)? In the autograph copy of his translation of Cottunius' *Commentarii*, Esad Efendi said that his goal was to unite Islamic and *Yunani* learning (Küçük 2012: 158). This is a clear indication that for him at least *Yunani* offered the possibility of an intellectual project that could cross, or at least overlook, religious divides. As for those other Muslim scholars who used Greek sources both ancient and modern in their work, we do not yet know how they positioned themselves vis-à-vis the Greek heritage.

Esad Efendi's *Yunani* project obliges us to look again at Mavrokordatos' statement about the return of scholars to Greece in *Philitheou Parerga*. On the surface his references fit easily into a conventional understanding of Greece and the Greek heritage and his statement can be seen as an early sign of national revival. But Esad Efendi was his teacher and the Phanariot must have been aware of his views on *Yunani* learning. Therefore it is at least possible that Mavrokordatos, too, had a more expansive view of Greece, Greek philosophy, and the Greek heritage in general than a national interpretation would admit. Nicolaidis writes that, beginning in the seventeenth century, the idea spread that "the Orthodox believers were the heirs of Greek splendor and learning" (Nicolaidis 2011: 136). Certainly that idea was there. But evidence from the early eighteenth century suggests that this was a project whose boundaries could expand and contract. Other, additional heirs were possible.

Enlightenment reconsidered

In his study of the early figures of the Greek Enlightenment, Paschalis Kitromilides can barely contain his disappointment. Neo-Aristotelianism "ossified" Greek education and the Neo-Aristotelians themselves turned into the "relentless enemies" of modern philosophy and scientific learning. Alexander Mavrokordatos' dissertation on the circulation of the blood was (appropriately) scientific in its approach but this did not last. "Soon, however, his interests as a writer were, characteristically, adapted to the prevailing intellectual conventions of the Greek East." Mavrokordatos' values, Kitromilides continues, were prudence and realism. These are explained by "the instinct for survival that a social group rising under the aegis of despotism felt necessary to cultivate" (Kitromilides 2013: 31). Nicholas Mavrokordatos fares a bit better since, in Kitromilides' interpretation, his thought is at least moving toward "revolutionary Neohellenic consciousness" (Kitromilides 2013: 33).

In Kitromilides' thought, the Ottomans are defined by their conservatism and thus any Phanariot attachment to the house of Osman – which Kitromilides readily concedes – is by definition a conservative stance. But this is to ignore the concrete historical significance of Ahmet's court and to insist on interpreting the Greek Enlightenment outside of its Ottoman context. The Phanariots, along with their Muslim counterparts, were the "new men" of Ahmet's court. By that I mean they were part of a larger group of courtiers who were deliberately cultivated by Ahmet in order to re-establish the authority of the sultanate in the face of many challengers. The Mavrokordatoi and others were loyal not so much to the Ottomans in general as to this political project. And their loyalty was secured in part by Ahmet's patronage of a novel kind of elite sociability that was open to non-Muslims. These elites prided themselves on their realism, which was reflected in their embrace of Neo-Aristotelianism as opposed to metaphysics, as well as their insistence on diagnosing the problems of the empire on the basis of sound thinking. Regardless of their religious identity, the men of Ahmet's court despised what they saw as superstition and fanaticism. Kitromilides speaks of the Phanariots' cosmopolitanism but, unsurprisingly, he locates the cosmopolitan world outside the empire, in Europe, and fails to recognize that Ahmet's court itself was a center of cosmopolitan thinking (Kitromilides 2013: 33).

Mavrokordatos' prudence and realism, then, were not the defensive stance of a cringing minority.[18] They were the hallmark of the virtuous man as defined in the age of Ahmet III. Similarly, the unwillingness to fully embrace new scientific ideas cannot be wholly explained by a capitulation to the "prevailing intellectual conventions of the Greek East" since, as we have seen, Muslim elites behaved very similarly. They were eager to forge new intellectual paths but were unwilling to directly take on the religious tradition. This moderation, if we can reframe it this way, might be explained as a consequence of the emphasis on sociability and conviviality that was so evident at Ahmet's court.

In the historiography the events of 1730, known as the Patrona Halil rebellion, bring an end to the Tulip Age. As mentioned earlier, the concept of the Tulip Age is itself controversial and the tendency in writing about the eighteenth century now is to point to trends that continued beyond 1730, while not denying the drama of the events of that year. For one thing, Ahmet was forced to abandon the throne (although he did not lose his life). Stability and reform continued to be favored over war, for example, and thus the well-educated bureaucrat was still preferred over the military leaders of an earlier age.[19] Building projects, so closely identified with Ahmet and his grand vezir, never ceased. The destruction of Saadabad is perhaps the most iconic moment of the supposed end of the Tulip Age, but in fact the palace was repaired in subsequent decades and it continued to be a place of pagaentry; an embassy from Vienna to ratify the treaty of Belgrade in 1739 was entertained there (Finkel 2007: 365).

Did the end of Ahmet's reign end the prominence of Greek letters at the Ottoman court? Major players in the story we have been telling died right around the same time. Damat Ibrahim Pasha actually lost his life in the uprising of 1730. Esad Efendi died the same year and Chrysanthos Notaras followed one year later. At the very least, existing patronage networks must have been severely disrupted. But it is difficult to say more than that. As Finkel has observed, the second half of the eighteenth century (starting, I would argue, in 1730) is one of the least known periods in Ottoman history (Finkel 2007: 372). How much more is our ignorance compounded when we consider intellectual production at the Ottoman court, a topic that, as noted before, has barely been considered even for the relatively well-researched Tulip Age. But one thing can be said, and it is suggestive.

In the intellectual history of the Greek Enlightenment the middle years of the eighteenth century are identified with the second generation of thinkers, of whom the greatest is Eugenios Voulgaris. These writers and educators, still members of the clergy, moved Greek thought ahead (here again is the movement toward the nation that is omnipresent in writing on the Greek Enlightenment) by finally abandoning Neo-Aristotelianism and embracing the new European science (Nikolaidis 2011: 156). In the battle between the Ancients and the Moderns, the former had finally lost.

Ottoman philosophical thinking followed the same chronology. Among the very first things published by the Müteferrika press in the early 1730s were two pamphlets that introduced Cartesian philosophy to an Ottoman readership. Cartesianism was the sworn enemy of Neo-Aristotelian thought, and palace sponsorship of the pamphlets' publication signaled the end of the court's patronage of the Neo-Aristotelians.[20] As with the Greeks, experimental science also made its way into Ottoman intellectual life at this time (Küçük 2012: 171–2). Again, it is easier to trace similar intellectual paths than it is to uncover the relationships between Greek and Ottoman elites at this time. But it seems likely that the proponents of experience and experiment knew each other. One of the Europeans responsible for bringing the new science to the Ottoman court (and to the printing press) in this period was Johann Friedrich Bachstrom, a German missionary who came to Istanbul in 1728. His way into the court came through John Mavrokordatos, the son of Nicholas Mavrokordatos. Through him he met Mehmet Said, the curator of the printing press (Küçük 2012: 176).

The move from Neo-Aristotelianism to the more radical methods of experimental science, then, cannot be told solely as a story of the Greek Enlightenment, since similar trends can be detected at the Ottoman court. As with the earlier period so too in the middle of the century; the meaning and the context of Greek literary efforts, from translation to commentaries and original writings, must be reconsidered since their preoccupations were not peculiar to them, but were shared by others.

Education

We have met Chrysanthos Notaras the astronomer and Chrysanthos Notaras the dear friend of the Ottoman courtier Esad Efendi. But there is another Notaras, and that is Notaras the educator. According to his biographer, nothing was closer to his heart. Throughout his lifetime the bulk of his energies were devoted not to philosophical musings, but to the perhaps more mundane tasks of founding schools, supporting students, recruiting and paying teachers, and collecting the books and manuscripts that would support the education of the Greek Orthodox (Stathis 1999: 166).

Notaras' devotion to education is a useful way to introduce the other face of the Greek Enlightenment. And this face does properly belong to the Greeks. When it comes to the philosophical ideas and the elite figures who have figured so prominently in intellectual histories of the Greek Enlightenment, the overlap with elite Muslim society – in particular the people around Ahmet's court – is great enough that we must question the narrative that understands this as an exclusively Greek phenomenon. Not so when it comes to the educational advances made within Greek Orthodox society in the eighteenth century. These were particular to the Greeks, they were dramatic, and they were rooted in social and economic changes that proved to be self-perpetuating. Although we cannot be certain, it seems that Ahmet's abdication ended, at least for a time, a period of intellectual efflorescence (Küçük 2012: 201). This in turn suggests that cultural and intellectual innovation was still dependent upon courtly patronage. The founding of Greek Orthodox schools and the publication projects of the various Greek presses, by contrast, went on steadily throughout the eighteenth century. Moreover, they were the result of a decentralized process that thrived on local initiative rather than dictates handed down from Istanbul (Dialetis et al. 1999: 59). This is not to say that the church did not involve itself in educational matters, because of course it did. But it is to say that a new social group, the merchants, was absolutely vital in the spread of educational opportunities and the church had to accommodate itself to the new social forces, at least to a certain extent. Thus as early as 1723 the clergyman and philosopher Methodios Anthrakites turned for support to the lay commercial leadership of Ioannina and Kastoria. Prior to his excommunication by the Holy Synod in 1723, in a struggle over the content of his teaching, Anthrakites had taught philosophy in the schools in both of these towns.[21]

Of course the merchants would be deeply interested in Anthrakites' fate, as well as his teaching, because it was the merchants themselves who had created these schools.

We can take as our example the "First School of Ioannina," as it was known, whose history shows both the critical role of merchants and the ties that linked the provinces to the imperial center. The school was founded in 1680 by Emmanuel Leontari Gyuma, a merchant with strong ties to Venice.[22] He appointed the director and, at the same time, solicited a patriarchal letter that forbade any interference in the school on the part of the local elites. The head teacher was a monk named Vyssarion, from Istanbul, who had studied with Alexander Mavrokordatos. When a second school was established, in 1690, the head teacher there had been Vyssarion's student (Aravantinos 1857: 276–9). Thus we see how wealthy merchants provided the institutional support that allowed for the spread of the new philosophical thinking from the capital to the provinces.

Between 1620 and 1821 twenty-two centers of Greek higher education came into being, almost all of them within Ottoman territory.[23] The best-known, such as the Princely Academies at Bucharest and Jassy, were founded by political elites but the rest, such as the First School of Ioannina, were the creation of philanthropic merchants. These merchants are still relatively unknown to us and have not been studied to the same extent as have the educators and clerics who created the texts of the Greek Enlightenment. The schools must have been relatively successful in their intellectual endeavors because in the second half of the eighteenth century a significant reading public emerged. Their subscriptions supported the ever-increasing activities of the Greek presses (unlike the schools, these were located outside of the empire). Between 1749 and 1821 these presses produced roughly 120,000 volumes in the Greek language, most of them translations of European works. Publication soared in the final decades of the eighteenth century but even earlier the numbers were still impressive. Between 1749 and 1767 three presses in Venice and one in Leipzig published 1,482 volumes combined. Subscriber lists show that there were over a hundred communities of readers, in an area stretching from Livorno to Kayseri. The major centers of literacy were Smyrna, Istanbul, Vienna, Bucharest, Jassy, Trieste, and Athos. All of these cities had strong ties to one, two, or all three of the social groups that formed the backbone of the Greek Enlightenment, that is the church, the Phanariots, and the merchants (Iliou 1975: 164).

Let us remember that Ahmet III and the men around him, men who had close ties to Greek elites, had very similar goals for the printing press he founded in the late 1720s. He hoped that the greater availability of books would lead to the spread of learning within Ottoman Muslim society. But these hopes were to be sorely disappointed. Unlike its Greek counterparts, the Müteferrika press (named after the Hungarian convert who was in charge of it) proved to be very short-lived and did not survive beyond Müteferrika's death in the 1740s. Nor did any new printing press replace it. The establishment and the demise of the Müteferrika press have attracted a lot of scholarly attention over the years and, in the past, provided the occasion for sweeping statements about the conservatism and even fanaticism of Ottoman society. More recent and careful studies have tackled the social realities that made printing in the Arabic script a difficult project, and these make for an interesting comparison with the Greek case.

Müteferrika's books were fairly expensive, for one thing, and the small size of the reading public made expansion difficult (Sabev 2007: 73, 76). Changes in Greek society made for a very different reality. Philanthropic merchants were willing to provide books for needy students, thus making the printing presses financially viable, and the reading public was continuously expanding. In addition, much has been made of the (very real) opposition of the *ulema* to the printing press. Here we must turn away from vague references to Islam and consider instead what the printing press meant to the religious establishment in 1730. The threat to the livelihood of calligraphers, and to all of those who were attached to a manuscript culture, has long been recognized. But the threat was bigger than that. The printing press looked to be another encroachment on the authority and autonomy of the *ulema*. We have already noted that under Ahmet III men without all the credentials of a *medrese* education, men such as Esad Efendi, were able to become influential members of the *ulema*. Now, with the printing of books under the control of palace circles, the sultan was set to interfere with the *medrese* itself. It is rarely noted that, at the same time that he was authorizing the printing press, the sultan was also setting up a new, official examination that members of the *ulema* would have to take if they aspired to the top positions within the learned hierarchy (Küçük 2013: 167).

In short the *ulema* were facing a challenge to their control over access to knowledge and to Muslim education in the empire, a challenge that – unsurprisingly – they fought tooth and nail.[24] This tug of war between the palace and the *ulema* (a war that the palace lost) serves to highlight the very close cooperation, despite some famous battles such as the excommunication of Anthrakitis, among the various stakeholders in Greek education, particularly between the Greek merchants who funded Greek education and the clergy who staffed and oversaw the schools.

Historians' accounts of the Greek Enlightenment often reflect the frustration of the more radical thinkers whom they study. Particularly by the end of the eighteenth century men such as Iosipos Moisiodax could be relied upon to decry what they saw as the moribund state of Greek education. This critique has overshadowed the tremendous enthusiasm for education, however it was understood, within Greek society at the time. And the voices of intellectuals have been allowed to predominate, whereas other social groups had their own ideas about the significance of education. By bringing in other voices I am not trying to overthrow the existing narrative of the Greek Enlightenment and replace it with another. My goal is rather to thicken the narrative by including, alongside the battle of ideas, the social changes and new social actors who were also a vital part of the landscape.

For all these reasons it is worth considering, as just one example of an underrepresented voice, the following excerpt from a letter written by Christian merchants from Kastoria, now settled in Istanbul, in the late seventeenth century. They wrote to their compatriots back home about the matter of establishing a school in their city.[25] It had come to their attention, they begin, that one Manolakis from Kastoria – "born and brought up in our exalted town" – had become a man of distinction and was busy establishing schools of Greek learning "in diverse and many places," since "learning is the light and the life of man." And they continued: "We are perplexed as to why others, strangers, should be nourished by one of our own while our own homeland remains thirsty and in the darkness of ignorance." The letter writers then proceeded to ask their compatriots to approach this Manolakis about establishing a school in Kastoria, and, should he resist, they were to say the following in order to persuade him.

> It is unsuitable and sinful and a shame that we consume ourselves in the struggle to realize our worldly and material goals, while neglecting this great good [education] which would be of great benefit to all of us as well as a source of great pride for our homeland. And consider how all the places near us worked and founded [schools], that is, Ioannina, Arta, Anatolikon, Athens and Thessaloniki. It is shameful, then, that our homeland should remain behind these places. (Kournoutos 1953: 428–9)

Two things are of particular note in this passage. First, there is the sense of an unstoppable social momentum. As town after town built its school, places without a school come to seem deficient. Second, there is a very powerful attachment to one's place of origin; identity is local before it is anything else. Of course the letter writers of Kastoria were part of the Greek Enlightenment. But the sentiments in the letter (and there are many others like them) can also be linked to other eighteenth-century developments, although that work has yet to be done. Like the Ecumenical Patriarchate in the same century, it seems that the Christian communities of the sultan's domains were finding their place in the empire. When the merchants of Kastoria looked out across the Balkans and parts of Anatolia they saw Christian schools proliferating, one after the other, and they were anxious that their town not be left out. The fact of having a school, it seems to me, must have counted just as much as the curriculum itself, and this was a new development.

Countless writers have associated Greek society with a strong sense of localism. But it seems likely that the Ottoman context is just as important in understanding the merchant-philanthropists of the eighteenth century. As we saw in the last chapter, this was the provincial century par excellence. It was also a time of community consolidation and the adoption of aristocratic titles – *çelebi*, *logothetes*, and *kokona* – by the Christian elite that assumed leadership of provincial Christian society. Founding a school had certainly become an essential part of *noblesse oblige* in the nineteenth-century Ottoman Empire. The impulse could well have been similar as early as 1700.

The return of war

As with more general narratives of the Greeks in the eighteenth century, exit from the empire hangs over much of the writing on the Greek Enlightenment. And exit did become an explicit program, at least for some, in the last quarter of the eighteenth century. But many things changed after the war with Russia (1768–74) as the empire entered an extended period of turmoil that upended many long-standing arrangements, including those that governed the lives of the empire's Christians. The provincial unrest that generated first the Serbian revolt in 1804 and then, of course, the Greek Revolution was in no way confined to the sultan's Christian subjects or even to the Balkans. Faced with the wars of the late eighteenth century, the leadership in Istanbul targeted long-standing fiscal arrangements between the center and the provinces in an attempt to fill the coffers of the state. This was met with resistance across the empire (Salzmann 1993: 406–7). At the same time there is evidence that the government began to move against Christians in particular. For example, after the so-called "Orlov Revolt" of 1770 in the Peloponnese, the sultan moved to take offices away from the Christian notables who had held them for the better part of a century and to give them either to local Muslims or to state-appointed officers (Gündoğu 2014: 80).

Faced with these challenges, the robust educational advances of nearly a century paid off in terms of a new generation of leaders who were well equipped to understand and seize the opportunities presented by a changing world. But it is misleading to understand Greek intellectual and educational activity prior to 1770 within the context of the very volatile world that prevailed in the last quarter of the century. One of the problems created by such anachronistic thinking is that Greek intellectuals – who were the ones, after all, producing the material that constitutes what is known as the Greek Enlightenment – are judged as either revolutionaries (although often thwarted) or conservative apologists for their Ottoman masters who ruled over a moribund empire. In this and the previous chapter I have tried to argue for a different narrative. In the long peace of the eighteenth century the Greeks settled in and hammered out a place for themselves in the empire that was more institutionally distinct, and more distinctly Christian, than what had existed prior. In this they were not unlike other, elite Muslim groups of the same period – such as the *ayan* and the *ulema* – who also sought the articulation and the protection of their privileges. The greater cohesiveness of Christian society, in turn, must have contributed to the desire for a general program of education and improvement to be undertaken among the Christian communities of the empire. Unsurprisingly, greater investment in the Christian community also led to fights over what kind of a community it should be. These efforts, and the quarrels that ensued, are often subsumed under what we call the Greek Enlightenment. Viewed this way, the Greek Enlightenment should not be understood first and foremost as the product of either alienation from or marginalization within the empire. Instead it reflected the confidence of a community that felt secure enough to take up the task of tending to its own garden.

Notes

1. Not everyone agrees that the first half of the eighteenth century belongs to the Enlightenment. Stathis (1999) calls Notaras the forerunner (πρόδρομος) of the modern Greek Enlightenment.
2. See Stathis (1986) for the extent of Esad Efendi's knowledge of Greek.

3. "A comprehensive assessment of the intellectual life of Istanbul, one that looks beyond linguistic, ethnic and confessional boundaries, may suggest that what has so far been presented as the Neo-Hellenic Enlightenment was part of a broader Ottoman movement" (Küçük 2013: 77).
4. This is for analytical purposes only. It is not clear that the participants would have made these distinctions.
5. "What carried the understanding that natural philosophy was a means to moral self-improvement to Istanbul were the Ottoman Greeks" (Küçük 2012: 128).
6. See the very interesting discussion in Dialetis et al., where they argue that, whereas in Europe during the scientific revolution the role of scientists was to produce scientific knowledge, in the periphery (such as the Greek lands) scientists saw their role as educational. It was their task to disseminate this knowledge through the educational structures (Dialetis et al. 1999: 44).
7. The Enlightenment as national revival, even in this early period, runs throughout the literature. See Dialetis et al. (1999: 47).
8. This chapter draws very heavily on Küçük's pioneering 2012 dissertation, to the extent that this chapter would not have been possible without it. Aware of the novelty of his interpretation, Küçük feels obliged to justify his idea of an Ottoman Enlightenment. "Why am I writing about an early Enlightenment movement in Istanbul? What is my investment in a debate that is specific to what happened in Europe and not the Ottoman Empire in the eighteenth century?" (Küçük 2012: 6).
9. Penelope Stathis, in her biographical study of Chrysanthos Notaras, does situate his life within the context of the Tulip Period (Stathis 1999: 40).
10. "The quest for secular knowledge was prompted by the need to assess the position of the Empire under new conditions resulting from change in the balance of power" (Evin 1980: 135).
11. In a letter written in 1714 to Chrysanthos Notaras, Esad Efendi provides his comments on the former's book on astronomy, Εἰσαγωγὴ εἰς τά Γεωγραφικὰ καὶ Σφαιρικά [Introduction to Geography and to the Spheres] (Stathis 1986: 65).
12. In this analysis I am drawing heavily on the arguments made by Küçük (2012).
13. Stathis (1986: 58). See Küçük (2012: ch. 3) for the reasons behind the break with Islamic theology and philosophy in the eighteenth century.
14. Küçük asserts a number of relationships but does not always provide evidence to back up his claim. For example, he says that Panayiotes Nikousios, the first Phanariot to hold the position of grand dragoman, was an important patron for Greek speaking Ottoman scholars, but he provides no source for this claim (Küçük 2013: 147).
15. Stathis takes note of Notaras' deep interest in the east, which existed alongside his admiration for things western and especially French. He

wrote a study on the holy cities of Mecca and Medina and his astronomical writings were deeply informed by the Arab tradition. All of this, she says, was the result of his very close intellectual ties with the Muslim scholars of Ahmet's court (Stathis 1999: 167).

16. Dialetis notes "a conscious policy to avoid a rupture with the strictly theological approach to nature and to human affairs" and Küçük argues that "theology died a natural not a violent death." Theology was not targeted; simply, the new ideas prevailed (Dialetis et al. 1999: 49; Küçük 2012: 81).
17. The phrase means, literally, "a Hellene but not a follower of Photios," Photios being a patriarch who was particularly associated with the schism between Catholicism and Orthodoxy. I thank Teresa Shawcross for helping me understand the meaning of this phrase.
18. This is not to deny that politics continued to be an extremely hazardous pursuit during the reign of Ahmet III. But it was not more hazardous for Christians than for others (Küçük 2012: 72–3).
19. "While Aristotle went out of fashion with the printing press, what remained were the values Esad and his fellow peripatetics had nurtured. After 1730 grand viziers were expected to be accomplished thinkers. And, Ottoman reformism of the high eighteenth century was a direct consequence of the intellectualization of the imperial administration" (Küçük 2012: 201).
20. For the reasons behind this shift see Küçük (2012: ch. 6).
21. He was allowed to return to teaching a few years later, but had to promise that he would not deviate from Aristotelianism (Kitromilides 2013: 36, 38).
22. Ἐμμανουὴλ Λεωντάρη Γκιοῦμα (Aravantinos 1857: 276).
23. See the map at http://dlab.phs.uoa.gr/ellinomnimon/schools.htm.
24. The Orthodox Church would react the same way, to the same challenge, at the end of the eighteenth century.
25. Even the geographical framework of this epistolary exchange is little known in the historiography, where little has been written about Greek migration to Istanbul in the seventeenth and eighteenth centuries. Kitromilides' comment on the sociological dimension of the Greek Enlightenment is very welcome. He writes, "The geographical pattern of the Greek Enlightenment points at its sociological dimension as well. The regions in which novel ideas and imported cultural outlooks could find a certain receptivity were those where new social groups had emerged as a result of incipient changes in relations of production and exchange in local society." But he is adamant about locating social and intellectual change in areas that were far from Ottoman power (Kitromilides 2013: 56).

Timeline

1354	Ottomans occupy Gallipoli, their first conquest in Europe
1369	Ottomans conquer Adrianople (Edirne) and make it their new capital
1387	Conquest of Thessaloniki
1402	Battle of Ankara; collapse of Bayezit I's empire
1403–13	Ottoman civil war
1430	Second conquest of Thessaloniki
1438–45	Council of Florence-Ferrara works for unification of the churches
1453	Mehmet II (Fatih) conquers Istanbul
1459	Conquest of the Morea
1461	Conquest of Trabzon
1522	Conquest of Rhodes
1526	Battle of Mohacs; conquest of Hungary
1557	Establishment of Serbian patriarchate at Peć
1570	Conquest of Cyprus
1586	Patriarchate relocates to Fanar in Istanbul
1669	Panayiotes Nikousios, a Phanariot, becomes grand dragoman; Ottoman conquest of Crete
1683–99	War of the Holy League
1686	Venetians conquer the Morea
1699	Treaty of Karlowitz; Ottomans surrender Hungary
1711	Phanariot rule in Wallachia and Moldavia begins
1715	Ottomans regain the Morea
1730	Patrona Halil rebellion; end of the Tulip Age
1766–7	Archbishoprics of Ohrid and Peć are joined to the Ecumenical Patriarchate
1768–74	Ottoman–Russian War

Guide to Further Reading

For surveys of Ottoman history see:

Faroqhi, S. N. (ed.) (2006), *The Cambridge History of Turkey: The Later Ottoman Empire, 1603–1839* (New York: Cambridge University Press).
Fleet, K. (ed.) (2009), *The Cambridge History of Turkey: Byzantium-Turkey, 1071–1453* (New York: Cambridge University Press).
Fleet, K. and Faroqhi, S. N. (eds) (2012), *The Cambridge History of Turkey: The Ottoman Empire as a World Power, 1453–1603* (New York: Cambridge University Press).
İnalcık, H., with Quataert, D. (eds) (1994), *An Economic and Social History of the Ottoman Empire, 1300–1914* (Cambridge: Cambridge University Press).

There is one general survey in English – by now quite dated – of the Greeks under Ottoman rule. The reader may wish to consult it:

Vakalopoulos, A.E. (1976), *The Greek Nation: The Cultural and Economic Background of Modern Greek Society*, trans. Ian and Phania Moles (New Brunswick, NJ: Rutgers University Press).

There is no general survey of the sultan's Christian subjects as a whole. But there are a few general studies of the Balkans during the Ottoman period that devote a considerable amount of space to the experience of the Christian populations:

Mazower, M. (2000), *The Balkans: A Short History* (New York: Modern Library).
Stavrianos, L.S. (2000), *The Balkans since 1453* (New York: New York University Press).
Sugar, P. (1977), *Southeastern Europe under Ottoman Rule, 1354–1804* (Seattle: University of Washington Press).

It is interesting that general surveys of the Ottoman Jewish experience do exist, as well as several studies of Christians and Jews in the Arab provinces. The reader may find it useful to consult these for a comparative perspective:

Benbassa, E., and A. Rodrigue (2000), *Sephardi Jewry: A History of the Judeo-Spanish Community, Fourteenth to Twentieth Centuries* (Berkeley: University of California Press).
Levy, A. (1992), *The Jews in the Ottoman Empire* (Princeton: Darwin Press).
Masters, B. (2001), *Christians and Jews in the Ottoman Arab World: The Roots of Sectarianism* (Cambridge: Cambridge University Press).

Bibliography

Abou-el-Haj, R. A. 1969."The Formal Closure of the Ottoman Frontier in Europe, 1699–1703." *Journal of the American Oriental Society* 89(3).
Aksan, V. 2011. "Ottoman Ethnographies of Warfare 1500–1800," in *Empires and Indigenes: Intercultural Alliance, Imperial Expansion, and Warfare in the Early Modern World*, ed. Wayne E. Lee. New York: New York University Press.
Alexander, John. 1985. *Brigandage and Public Order in the Morea 1685–1806*. Athens: s.n.
Alexander, John. 1983. "The Monasteries of Meteora during the First Two Centuries of Ottoman Rule." *Jahrbruch der Österreichischen Byzantinistik* 32(3).
Alexiou, Stylianos. 1985. *Η Κρητική λογοτεχνία και η εποχή της: μελέτη φιλολογική και ιστορική* [Cretan Literature and its Age: A Philological and Historical Study]. Athens: Stigme.
Anastasopoulos, Antonis. 2005. "The Mixed Elite of a Balkan Town: Karaferye in the Second Half of the Eighteenth Century," in *Provincial Elites in the Ottoman Empire*, ed. Antonis Anastasopoulos. Rethymnon: University of Crete Press.
Anscombe, Frederick. 2006. "Introduction," in *The Ottoman Balkans 1750–1830*, ed. Frederick Anscombe. Princeton: Markus Wiener.
Aravantinos, P. 1857. *Χρονογραφία της Ηπείρου* [Chronology of Epirus], vol. 2. Athens: S. K. Vlastou.
Arbel, Benjamin. 1995. *Trading Nations: Jews and Venetians in the Early-Modern Eastern Mediterranean*. Leiden: Brill.
Argo, Charles. 2008. "The Ottoman Balkan City: The Periphery as Center in Punitive Spectacle," in *Secondary Cities and Urban Networking in the Indian Ocean Realm c. 1400–1800*, ed. Kenneth R. Hall. New York: Lexington Books.
Argyriou, Asterios. 1987. *Les exégèses grecques de l'apocalypse à l'époque turque (1453–1821)*. Thessaloniki: Institute for Macedonian Studies. Asdrachas, Spyros I. 2007. *Greek Economic History: 15th–19th Centuries. Vol. 2: Sources*, ed. Eutychia D. Liata. Athens: Piraeus Bank Group Cultural Foundation.
Athenagoras, Metropolitan of Paramythia and Parga. 1929. *Νέος κουβαρᾶς, ἤτοι χρονικὰ σημειώματα ἀναφερόμενα εἰς τήν πόλιν ἰδίᾳ τῶν Ἰωαννίνων, εἰς μονὰς αὐτῆς καὶ τὰς ἐπαρχιας αὐτῆς* [Notes from Chronicles Concerning the City of Ioannina, its Monasteries and its Vicinity]. Ioannina: Epirotika Chronika.
Babinger, Franz. 1978. *Mehmed the Conqueror and His Time*, trans. Ralph Manheim. Princeton: Princeton University Press.
Baer, Marc David. 2008. *Honored by the Glory of Islam: Conversion and Conquest in Europe*. New York: Oxford University Press.
Baer, Marc David. 2004. "The Great Fire of 1660 and the Islamization of Christian and Jewish Space in Istanbul." *International Journal of Middle East Studies* 36(2).

Ballian, Anna. 2005. "Silver and Gold: Church Plate and Liturgical Veils of the Sixteenth to Eighteenth Century," in *From Byzantium to Modern Greece: Hellenic Art in Adversity, 1453–1830: From the Collections of the Benaki Museum, Athens*. New York: Alexander S. Onassis Public Benefit Foundation in association with the Benaki Museum, Athens.

Barkan, O. L. 1957. "Essai sur les données statistiques des registres de recensement dans l'empire ottoman aux XVe et XVI siècles." *Journal of the Economic and Social History of the Orient* 1.

Barkey, Karen. 2008. *Empire of Difference: The Ottomans in Comparative Perspective*. Cambridge: Cambridge University Press.

Barkey, Karen. 1994. *Bandits and Bureaucrats: The Ottoman Route to State Centralization*. Ithaca, NY: Cornell University Press.

Bayat, Ali Haydar. 1999. *Osmanlı Devlet'inde Hekimbaşılık ve Hekimbaşılar* [The Palace Doctors and the Ottoman State]. Ankara: Atatürk Kültür Merkezi Başkanlığı Yayınları.

Bayraktar Tellan, Elif. 2011. *The Patriarch and the Sultan: The Struggle for Authority and the Quest for Order in the Eighteenth Century Ottoman Empire*. PhD dissertation: Bilkent University.

Behar, Cem. 2003. *A Neighborhood in Ottoman Istanbul: Fruit Vendors and Civil Servants in the Kasap İlyas Mahalle*. Albany: SUNY Press.

Beldiceanu, N. 1983. "Thessalie entre 1454/5 et 1506." *Byzantion* 53.

Belin, M. 1872. *Histoire de l'Église Latine de Constantinople*. Paris: Jules Le Clere.

Bintliff, John. 2012. *The Complete Archaeology of Greece: From Hunter-Gatherers to the 20th Century A.D.* Chichester: Wiley-Blackwell.

Bouchard, Jacques. 1981. "Nicolas Mavrocordatos et l'époque des tulipes." Ἐρανιστής 17.

Bryer, Anthony. 1980. "The Tourkokratia in the Pontos: Some Problems and Preliminary Conclusions," in *The Empire of Trebizond and the Pontos*, ed. Anthony Bryer. London: Variorum Reprints.

Bryer, Anthony. 1979. "The Late Byzantine Monastery in Town and Countryside," in *The Church in Town and Countryside: Papers Read at the Seventeenth Summer Meeting and the Eighteenth Winter Meeting of the Ecclesiastical History Society*, ed. D. Baker. Oxford: Blackwell.

Bryer, Anthony. 1965. "Trebizond and Serbia." *Archeion Pontou* 27.

Camariano-Cioran, Ariadna. 1974. *Académies princières de Bucarest et de Jassy et leurs professeurs*. Thessaloniki: Institute for Balkan Studies.

Canbakal, Hülya. 2007. *Society and Politics in an Ottoman Town: 'Ayntāb in the 17th Century*. Boston: Brill.

Canbakal, Hülya. 2004. "Some Questions on the Legal Identity of Neighborhoods in the Ottoman Empire." *Anatolia Moderna* X.

Casale, Giancarlo. 2010. *The Ottoman Age of Exploration*. Oxford: Oxford University Press.

Chatziiosiff, Christos. 2005. Συνασός: Ιστορία ενός τόπου χωρίς ιστορία [Synasos: History of a Place without History]. Rethymnon: University of Crete Press.

Çizakça, Murat. 1995. "Cash Waqfs of Bursa, 1555–1823." *Journal of the Economic and Social History of the Orient* 38(3).

Costantini, Vera. 2008. "Old Players and New in the Transition of Cyprus to Ottoman

Rule," in *Living in the Ottoman Ecumenical Community: Essays in Honour of Suraiya Faroqhi*, ed. Vera Costantini and Markus Koller. Leiden: Brill.

Ćurčić, Slobodan. S. 2010. *Architecture in the Balkans from Diocletian to Süleyman the Magnificent*. New Haven: Yale University Press.

Darling, Linda. 1994. "Public Finances: The Role of the Ottoman Centre," in *An Economic and Social History of the Ottoman Empire*, ed. Halil İnalcık with Donald Quataert. Cambridge: Cambridge University Press.

Dávid, G. 1995. "Administration in Ottoman Europe," in *Süleyman the Magnificent and His Age: The Ottoman Empire in the Early Modern World*, ed. Metin Kunt and Christine Woodhead. New York: Longman.

Deringil, Selim. 2000."There is No Compulsion in Religion: On Conversion and Apostasy in the Late Ottoman Empire: 1839–1856." *Comparative Studies in Society and History* 42(3).

Dialetis, Dimitris, Kostas Gavroglu, and Manolis Patiniotis. 1999. "The Sciences in the Greek Speaking Regions during the 17th and 18th Centuries," in *The Sciences in the European Periphery during the Greek Enlightenment*, ed. K. Kavroglu. Dordrecht: Kluwer.

Doxiadis, Evdoxios. 2011. *The Shackles of Modernity: Women, Property, and the Transition from the Ottoman Empire to the Greek state (1750–1850: Cultural Politics, Socioaesthetics, Beginnings*. PhD dissertation: Harvard University.

Dvoicenco-Markov, Demetrius. 1971. "Demetrius Kantemir and Russia." *Balkan Studies* 12(2).

Eldem, Edhem. 1999. "French Trade and Commercial Policy in the Levant in the Eighteenth Century." *Oriente Moderno* n.s. XVIII(LXXIX).

Erdoğru, M. Akif. 1996. "The Island of Rhodes under Ottoman Rule: Military Situation, Population, Trade and Taxation." *Arab Historical Review for Ottoman Studies* 13–14.

Erimtan, Can. 2006. "The Sources of Ahmed Refik's Lale Devri and the Paradigm of the 'Tulip Age': A Telelogical Agenda," in *Essays in Honour of Ekmeleddin Ihsanoğlu*, ed. H. Eren, M. Kacar, and Z. Durukal. Istanbul: IRCICA.

Evin, Ahmet. 1980. "The Tulip Age and Definitions of 'Westernization'," in *Social and Economic History of Turkey 1071–1920*, ed. Halil Inalcık and Osman Okyar. Ankara: Meteksan.

Evliya Çelebi. 1999–2006. *Seyahatnamesi*, vol. 8. Beyoğlu: YKY.

Faroqhi, Suraiya. 2012. "Ra'iyya," in *Encyclopedia of Islam*, 2nd edn, ed. P. Bearman, T. Bianquis, C. E. Bosworth, E. van Donzel, and W. P. Heinrichs. Leiden: Brill. http://referenceworks.brillonline.com/entries/encyclopaedia-of-islam-2/ra-iyya-COM_0905?s.num=14&s.f.s2_parent=s.f.book.encyclopaedia-of-islam-2&s.q=Faroqhi (last accessed December 5, 2014).

Faroqhi, Suraiya. 2005. "An Orthodox Woman Saint in an Ottoman Document," in *Syncrétismes et hérésies dans l'Orient seldjoukide et ottoman (XIVe–XVIIIe siècle)*, ed. G. Veinstein. Paris: Peeters.

Faroqhi, Suraiya. 1995. "Ottoman Guilds in the Late Eighteenth Century: The Bursa Case," in Suraiya Faroqhi, *Making a Living in the Ottoman Lands, 1480–1820*. Istanbul: Isis.

Faroqhi, Suraiya. 1994a. "Making a Living," in *An Economic and Social History of the Ottoman Empire, 1300–1914*, ed. Halil İnalcık with Donald Quataert. Cambridge: Cambridge University Press.

Faroqhi, Suraiya. 1994b. "The Ruling Elite between Politics and 'the Economy'," in *An*

Economic and Social History of the Ottoman Empire, 1300–1914, ed. Halil İnalcık with Donald Quataert. Cambridge: Cambridge University Press.

Findley, Carter Vaughn. 1980. *Bureaucratic Reform in the Ottoman Empire: The Sublime Porte, 1789–1922*. Princeton: Princeton University Press.

Finkel, Caroline. 2007. *Osman's Dream: The Story of the Ottoman Empire, 1300–1923*. New York: Basic Books.

Finlay, Robert. 1998. "Prophecy and Politics in Istanbul: Charles V, Sultan Süleyman, and the Habsburg Embassy of 1533–1534." *Journal of Early Modern History* 2(1).

Fleischer, Cornell. 1990. "The Lawgiver as Messiah: The Making of the Imperial Image in the Reign of Süleyman," in *Soliman le Magnifique et son temps: Actes du Colloque de Paris Galeries Nationales de Grand Palais, 7–10 Mars*, ed. Gilles Veinstein. Paris: Le Documentation Française.

Fodor, Pal. 2001. "The Ottomans and their Christians in Hungary," in *Frontiers of Faith: Religious Exchange and the Constitution of Religious Identities, 1400–1750*, ed. Eszter Andor, Francisco Bethencourt, and István György Toth. Budapest: Central European University.

Fotić, Aleksandar. 2005. "Belgrade: A Muslim and Non-Muslim Cultural Center (Sixteenth–Seventeenth Centuries)," in *Provincial Elites in the Ottoman Empire*, ed. Antonis Anastasopoulos. Rethymnon: University of Crete Press.

Frazee, Charles. 1983. *Catholics and Sultans: The Church and the Ottoman Empire, 1453–1923*. Cambridge: Cambridge University Press.

Fyrigos, Antonis, ed. 1983. *Il Collegio Greco di Roma: richerche sugli alunni, la direzione, l'attività*. Rome: Pontificio Collegio Greco S. Atanasio.

Gara, Eleni. 2007. "Η πόλη και η περιοχή της Βέροιας στους οθωμανικούς χρόνους" ["The City and District of Veroia during the Ottoman Period"], in *Ημαθίας Μελετήματα*. Veroia: Friends of the Byzantine Museum of Veroia.

Gara, Eleni. 2005/6. "Neo-Martyr without a Message." *Archivum Ottomanicum* 23.

Gara, Eleni. 1998. "In Search of Communities in Seventeenth Century Ottoman Sources: The Case of the Kara Ferye District." *Turcica* 30.

Göçek, F. M. 1996. *Rise of the Bourgeoisie, Demise of Empire: Ottoman Westernization and Social Change*. Oxford: Oxford University Press.

Goffman, Daniel. 1990. *Izmir and the Levantine World, 1550–1650*. Seattle: University of Washington Press.

Gradeva, Rossitsa. 2005. "Towards a Portrait of the Rich in Ottoman Provincial Society: Sofia in the 1670s," in *Provincial Elites in the Ottoman Empire*, ed. Antonis Anastasopoulos. Rethymnon: University of Crete Press.

Gradeva, Rossitsa. 2001. "War and Peace along the Danube: Vidin at the End of the Seventeenth Century." *Oriente Moderno* n.s. XX(LXXXI).

Gradeva, Rossitsa. 1997."Orthodox Christians in the Kadi Courts: The Practice of the Sofia Sheriat Court, Seventeenth Century." *Islamic Law and Society* 4(1).

Gradeva, Rossitsa. 1995. "Turks and Bulgarians: Fourteenth to Eighteenth Centuries." *Journal of Mediterranean Studies* 5(2).

Greene, Molly. 2010. *Catholic Pirates and Greek Merchants: A Maritime History of the Mediterranean*. Princeton: Princeton University Press.

Greene, Molly. 2007. "Trading Identities: The Sixteenth Century Greek Moment," in *A Faithful Sea: The Religious Cultures of the Mediterranean, 1200–1700*, ed. Adnan Ahmed Husain and K. E. Fleming. Oxford: Oneworld.

Greene, Molly. 2000. *A Shared World: Christians and Muslims in the Early Modern Mediterranean*. Princeton: Princeton University Press.

Greenwood, T. 1988. *Istanbul's Meat Provisioning: A Study of the Çelepkeşan System*. PhD dissertation: University of Chicago.

Gregoriou, P. 1958. *Σχέσεις Καθολικών και Ορθοδόξων* [Catholic–Orthodox Relations]. Athens: Ioannou Rossolatou & Sia.

Gudziak, Borys. 1998. *Crisis and Reform: The Kyivan Metropolitanate, the Patriarchate of Constantinople, and the Genesis of the Union of Brest*. Cambridge: Ukrainian Research Institute, Harvard University Press.

Gündoğu, B. 2014. "A Boiling Cauldron of Conflicts and Cooperation: The Question of Two Distinct Societies During and After the Morea Rebellion of 1770." *International Journal of Turkish Studies* 20(1/2).

Hadrovics, L. 1947. *Le peuple serbe et son église sous la domination turque*. Paris: Presses Universitaires de France.

Hajdarpasic, Edin. 2008. *Whose Bosnia? National Movements, Imperial Reforms and the Political Re-Ordering of the Late Ottoman Balkans, 1840–1875*. PhD dissertation: University of Michigan.

Haldon, John. 1986. "Limnos, Monastic Holdings and the Byzantine State ca. 1261–1453," in *Continuity and Change in Late Byzantine and Early Ottoman Society*, ed. Anthony Bryer and Heath Lowry. Washington, DC: University of Birmingham.

Hamadeh, Shirine. 2007. *The City's Pleasures: Istanbul in the Eighteenth Century*. Seattle: University of Washington Press.

Harlaftis, Gelina, and Sophia Laiou. 2008. "Ottoman State Policy in Mediterranean Trade and Shipping, c. 1780–1820: The Rise of the Greek-Owned Ottoman Merchant Fleet," in *Networks of Power in Modern Greece: Essays in Honor of John Campbell*, ed. John Campbell and Mark Mazower. New York: Columbia University Press.

Hathaway, Jane. 2004. "Rewriting Eighteenth Century Ottoman History." *Mediterranean Historical Review* 19(1).

Hathaway, Jane. 1995. "The Military Household in Ottoman Egypt." *International Journal of Middle East Studies* 27(1).

Hathaway, Jane, with Karl Barbir. 2008. *The Arab Lands under Ottoman Rule, 1516–1800*. New York: Pearson Longman.

Hering, Gunnar. 1992. *Οικουμενικό πατριαρχείο και ευρωπαϊκή πολιτική, 1620–1638* [The Ecumenical Patriarchate and European Politics, 1620–1638]. Athens: Cultural Foundation of the National Bank.

Herrin, Judith. 2007. *Byzantium: The Surprising Life of a Medieval Empire*. London: Allen Lane.

Hill, George Francis. 1972. *A History of Cyprus*. Cambridge: Cambridge University Press.

Hupchick, Dennis. 1983. "Seventeenth Century Bulgarian Pomaks: Forced or Voluntary Converts to Islam?" in *Society in Change: Studies in Honor of Bela K. Kiraly*, ed. Steven Bela Vardy and Agnes Huszar Vardy. New York. Columbia University Press.

Hütteroth, Wolf-Dieter. 2008. "Ecology of the Ottoman Lands," in *The Cambridge History of Turkey. Vol. 3: The Later Ottoman Empire, 1603–1839*, ed. Suraiya N. Faroqhi. Cambridge: Cambridge University Press.

Hypsilantis, A. K. 1870. *Τὰ μετὰ τὴν Ἅλωσιν, 1453–1789* [The Events After the Fall], ed. G. Afthonidos. Athens: I. A. Vretou.

Iliou, P. 1975. "Luttes sociales et movement des lumières à Smyrne en 1819," in

Structure sociale et développement culturel des villes sud-est européennes et adriatiques aux XVIIe–XVIIIe siècles. Bucharest: Association Internationale d'Études du Sud-Est Européen.

Imber, Colin. 2002. *The Ottoman Empire, 1300–1650: The Structure of Power.* New York: Palgrave Macmillan.

Imber, Colin. 1997. *Ebu's-Su'ud: The Islamic Legal Tradition.* Stanford: Stanford University Press.

Imber, Colin. 1990. "Süleyman as Caliph of the Muslims: Ebu Suud's Formulation of Ottoman Dynastic Ideology," in *Soliman le Magnifique et son temps: Actes du Colloque de Paris Galeries Nationales de Grand Palais, 7–10 Mars,* ed. Gilles Veinstein. Paris: Le Documentation Française.

Imber, Colin. 1979. "The Persecution of the Ottoman Shi'ites according to the Muhimme Defterleri 1565–1585." *Der Islam 56.*

İnalcık, Halil. 2012."Istanbul," in *Encyclopedia of Islam,* 2nd edn, ed. P. Bearman, T. Bianquis, C. E. Bosworth, E. van Donzel, and W. P. Heinrichs. Leiden: Brill. http://referenceworks.brillonline.com/entries/encyclopaedia-of-islam-2/istanbul-COM_0393?s.num=164&s.start=160 (last accessed December 5, 2014).

İnalcık, Halil. 1998. "The Status of the Greek Orthodox Patriarch under the Ottomans," in Halil İnalcık, *Essays in Ottoman History.* Istanbul: Eren.

İnalcık, Halil. 1993. "Greeks in the Ottoman Economy and Finance," in *To Hellenikon: Studies in Honor of Spyros Vryonis, Jr,* ed. Jelisaveta Stanojevich Allen et al. New Rochelle: Aristide D. Karatzas.

İnalcık, Halil. 1991. "Ottoman Galata 1453–1533," in *Première rencontre internationale sur l'Empire Ottoman et la Turquie moderne, Institut National des Langues et Civilisations Orientales, Maison des Sciences de l'Homme, 18–22 janvier 1985,* ed. Edhem Eldem. Istanbul: Isis.

İnalcık, Halil. 1989. *The Ottoman Empire: The Classical Age,* trans. Norman Itzkowitz and Colin Imber. New Rochelle: Aristide D. Karatzas.

İnalcık, Halil. 1980. "Military and Fiscal Transformation in the Ottoman Empire, 1600–1700." *Archivum Ottomanicum 6.*

İnalcık, Halil. 1979. "Ottoman Policy and Administration in Cyprus after the Conquest," in Halil İnalcık, *The Ottoman Empire: Conquest, Organization and Economy.* London: Variorum Reprints.

İnalcık, Halil. 1975. "The Socio-Political Effects of the Diffusion of Fire-Arms in the Middle East," in *War, Technology and Society in the Middle East,* ed. Vernon J. Parry and Malcolm Yapp. Oxford: Oxford University Press.

İnalcık, Halil. 1969–70. "The Policy of Mehmed II toward the Greek Population of Istanbul and the Byzantine Buildings of the City." *Dumbarton Oaks Papers 23–5.*

İnalcık, Halil. 1954. "Ottoman Methods of Conquest." *Studia Islamcia 2.*

İnalcık, Halil. 1953. "Stefan Duşan'dan Osmanlı İmparatorluğuna: XV. Asırda Rumeli'de Hıristiyan Sipahiler ve Menşeleri" ["From Stefan Duşan to the Ottoman Empire: The Origins of the Christian Cavalrymen in the Fifteenth-Century Balkans"], in *Fuad Köprülü Armağanı.* Istanbul: Osman Matbaası.

Iorga, Nicolae. 1935. *Byzance après Byzance: continuation de l'Histoire de la vie byzantine.* Bucharest: L'Institut d'Etudes Byzantines.

Ivanova, Svetlana. 2005. "*Varoş*: The Elites of the *Reaya* in the Towns of Rumeli, Seventeenth–Eighteenth Centuries," in *Provincial Elites in the Ottoman Empire,* ed. Antonis Anastasopoulos. Rethymnon: University of Crete Press.

Janos, Damien. 2005/6. "Panaiotis Nicousios and Alexander Mavrocordatos: The Rise of the Phanariots and the Office of Grand Dragoman in the Ottoman Administration in the Second Half of the Seventeenth Century." *Archivum Ottomanicum* 23.

Jirousek, Charlotte. 2000. "The Transition to Mass Fashion System Dress in the Later Ottoman Empire," in *Consumption Studies and the History of the Ottoman Empire, 1550–1922*, ed. Donald Quataert. Albany: SUNY Press.

Kafadar, Cemal. 2007. "A Rome of One's Own: Reflections on Cultural Geography and Identity in the Lands of Rum." *Muqarnas* 24.

Kaldellis, A. 2007. *Hellenism in Byzantium: The Transformation of Greek Identity and the Reception of the Classical Tradition*. Cambridge: Cambridge University Press.

Karakasidou, Anastasia. 1997. *Fields of Wheat, Hills of Blood: Passages to Nationhood in Greek Macedonia, 1870–1990*. Chicago: University of Chicago Press.

Karamustafa, Ahmet. 1994. *God's Unruly Friends: Dervish Groups in the Islamic Later Middle Period, 1200–1550*. Salt Lake City: University of Utah Press.

Kermeli, Eugenia. 2008. "Central Administration vs. Provincial Arbitrary Governance: Patmos and Mount Athos Monasteries in the 16th Century." *Byzantine and Modern Greek Studies* 32(2).

Kermeli, Eugenia. 2007. "The Right to Choice: Ottoman Justice vis-à-vis Ecclesiastical and Communal Justice in the Balkans, Seventeenth–Nineteenth Centuries," in *Studies in Islamic Law: A Festschrift to Colin Imber*, ed. A. Christmann and R. Gleave. *Journal of Semitic Studies* suppl. 23.

Khoury, Dina. 1997. *State and Provincial Society in the Ottoman empire: Mosul, 1540–1834*. Cambridge: Cambridge University Press.

Kiel, Machiel. 1996. "The Rise and Decline of Turkish Boeotia, 15th–19th Century," in *Recent Developments in the History and Archaeology of Central Greece: Proceedings of the 6th International Boeotian Conference*, ed. J. L. Bintliff. Oxford: Archaeopress.

Kiel, Machiel. 1990. "Central Greece in the Süleymanic Age: Preliminary Notes on Population, Growth, Economic Expansion and its Influence on the Spread of Greek Christian Culture," in *Soliman le Magnifique et son temps: Actes du Colloque de Paris Galeries Nationales de Grand Palais, 7–10 Mars*, ed. Gilles Veinstein. Paris: Le Documentation Française.

Kiel, Machiel. 1988. "The Spread of Islam in Bulgarian Rural Areas in the Ottoman Period (15th–18th Centuries): Colonization and Islamization," in *Musulmanskata kultura po balgarskite zemi Izsledvaniya*, ed. R. Gradeva and S. Ivanova. Sofia: IMIR.

Kiel, Machiel. 1985. *Art and Society of Bulgaria in the Turkish Period*. Assen: Van Gorcum.

Kiel, Machiel. 1979. "Some Reflections on the Origins of Provincial Tendencies in the Ottoman Architecture of the Balkans," in *Islam in the Balkans: Persian Art and Culture of the 18th and 19th Centuries*, ed. Jennifer Scarce. Edinburgh: Royal Scottish Museum.

Kitromilides, Paschalis. 2013. *Enlightenment and Revolution: The Making of Modern Greece*. Cambridge, MA: Harvard University Press.

Kitromilides, Paschalis. 2006. "Orthodoxy and the West: Reformation to Enlightenment," in *The Cambridge History of Christianity. Vol. V: Eastern Christianity*, ed. Michael Angold. Cambridge: Cambridge University Press.

Kitromilides, Paschalis. 1999. "Orthodox Culture and Collective Identity in the Ottoman Balkans during the Eighteenth Century." *Oriente Moderno* n.s. 18(79).

Koller, Markus. 2008. "The Istanbul Fur Market in the Eighteenth Century," in *Living

in the Ottoman Ecumenical Community: Essays in Honor of Suraiya Faroqhi, ed. Vera Constantini and Markus Koller. Leiden: Brill.
Kolovos, Elias. 2007. "Insularity and Island Society in the Ottoman Context: The Case of the Aegean Island of Andros." *Turcica* 39.
Kolovos, Elias. 2005a. "Το Άγιον Όρος και η συγκρότηση της οθωμανικής αυτοκρατορίας" ["Mount Athos and the Making of the Ottoman Empire"], in *1453: Η άλωση της Κωνσταντινούπολης και η μετάβαση από τους μεσαιωνικούς στους νεώτερους χρόνους* [1453: The Fall of Constantinople and the Transition from the Medieval to the Modern Period], ed. Tonia Kioussopoulou. Rethymnon: University of Crete Press.
Kolovos, Elias. 2005b. "Negotiating for State Protection: Çiftlik Holding by the Athonite Monasteries (Xeropotamou Monastery, 15th–16th Centuries)," in *Frontiers of Ottoman Studies: State, Province and the West*, vol. II, ed. Colin Imber, Keiko Kiyotaki, and Rhoads Murphey. London: I.B. Tauris.
Kolovos, Elias, Marinos Sariyannis, and Antonis Anastasopoulos. 2008. "The Ottoman Empire and the Greek Lands," in *Ottoman Architecture in Greece*, ed. Ersi Brouskari, trans. E. K. Fowden. Athens: Hellenic Ministry of Culture.
Konortas, Paraskeuas. 1998. *Οθωμανικές θεωρίες για το Οικουμενικό πατριαρχείο: Μπεράτια για τους προκαθημένους της μεγάλης εκκλησίας, 17ος-αρχές 20ου αιώνα* [Ottoman Views of the Ecumenical Patriarchate: Berats Issued to the Primates, 17th to the 20th Century]. Athens: Ekdoseis Alexandreia.
Kotzageorgis, Fokion. 2011."Τα μοναστήρια ως οθωμανικές τοπικές ελίτ" ["Monasteries as Provincial Elites"], in *Μοναστήρια: Οικονομία και πολιτική από τους μεσαιωνικούς στους νεώτερους χρόνους* [Monasteries: Economy and Politics from the Middle Ages to Modern Times], ed. Elias Kolovos. Rethymnon: University of Crete Press.
Kotzageorgis, Fokion. 2009. "Pour une definition de la culture ottoman: le cas des Tourkoyanniotes." *études Balkaniques* 16.
Kotzageorgis, Fokion. 1997. *Το Ισλάμ στα Βαλκάνια: ένα ελληνόφωνο μουσουλμανικό χειρόγραφο από την Ήπειρο του 18ου αιώνα* [Islam in the Balkans: A Greek language Muslim Manuscript from Eighteenth-Century Epirus]. Athens: Σύνδεσμος τῶυ ἐν Αθήναις μεγαλοσχολιτῶν.
Kournoutos, G. P. 1953. "Σχολεῖα τῆς τουρκοκρατούμενης Καστοριᾶς" ["Schools in Kastoria during the Turkish Period"], in *Γέρας Ἀντωνίου Κεραμοπούλου*. Athens: Myrtide.
Krstić, Tijana. 2013. "Conversion and Converts to Islam in Ottoman Historiography of the Fifteenth and Sixteenth Centuries," in *Writing History at the Ottoman Court: Editing the Past, Fashioning the Future*, ed. H. Erdem Çıpa and Emine Fetvacı. Bloomington: Indiana University Press.
Krstić, Tijana. 2011. *Contested Conversions to Islam: Narratives of Religious Change in the Early Modern Ottoman Empire*. Stanford: Stanford University Press.
Krstić, Tijana. 2007. "Review of *Conversion to Islam in the Balkans: Kisve Bahası Petitions and Ottoman Social Life, 1670–1730*, by Anton Minkov." *Journal of the Economic and Social History of the Orient* 50(1).
Krstić, Tijana. 2004. "The Politics of 'Ambiguous Sanctuaries': F. Hasluck and Historiography on Syncretism and Conversion to Islam in 15th and 16th Century Ottoman Rumeli," in *Archaeology, Anthropology and Heritage in the Balkans and Anatolia: The Life and Times of F. W. Hasluck*, ed. D. Shankland and K. Hopewood. Istanbul: Isis.

Küçük, Bekir Harun. 2013. "Natural Philosophy and Politics in the Eighteenth Century: Esad of Ioannina and Greek Aristotelianism at the Ottoman Court." *Journal of Ottoman Studies* XLI.

Küçük, Bekir Harun. 2012. *Early Enlightenment in Istanbul*. PhD dissertation: University of California, San Diego.

Kunt, Metin. 1982. "Transformation of *Zimmi* into *Askeri*," in *Christians and Jews in the Ottoman Empire. Vol. 1*, ed. Benjamin Braude and Bernard Lewis. New York: Holmes and Meier.

Laiou, Sophia. 2011. "Σχέσεις μοναχών και χριστιανών λαϊκών κατά την οθωμανική περίοδο" ["The Relationship among Monks and the Christian Laity during the Ottoman Period"], in *Μοναστήρια: Οικονομία και πολιτκή από τους μεσαιωνικούς στους νεότερους χρόνους* [Monasteries: Economy and Politics from the Middle Ages to Modern Times], ed. Elias Kolovos. Rethymnon: University of Crete Press.

Laiou, Sophia. 2007. "Christian Women in an Ottoman World: Interpersonal and Family Cases Brought before the Shari'a Courts in the Seventeenth and Eighteenth Centuries (Cases Involving the Greek Community)," in *Women in the Ottoman Balkans: Gender, Culture and History*, ed. Amila Butorović and Irvin Cemil Schick. London: I.B. Tauris.

Lane, Winthrop. 1923. "Why Greeks and Turks Oppose Being 'Exchanged'." *New York Times Current History* 86.

Legrand, E. 1869. *Relations de la Compagnie de Jésus en Levant*. Paris: Maisonneuve.

Lopasic, Alexander. 1994. "Islamization of the Balkans with Special Reference to Bosnia." *Journal of Islamic Studies* 5(2).

Lowry, Heath. 2009. *The Islamization and Turkification of the City of Trabzon (Trebizond) 1461–1583*. Istanbul: Isis.

Lowry, Heath. 2003. *The Nature of the Early Ottoman State*. Albany: SUNY Press.

Lowry, Heath. 2002. *Fifteenth Century Ottoman Realities: Christian Peasant Life on the Aegean Island of Limnos*. Istanbul: Eren.

Lowry, Heath. 1995. "The Ottoman *tahrîr defterleri* as a Source for Social and Economic History: Pitfalls and Limitations," in *Türkische Wirtschafts- und Sozialgeschichte (1071–1920)*, ed. Hans Georg Majer and Raoul Motika. Wiesbaden: Harrassowitz.

Lucas, Paul. 1714. *Voyage du Sieur Paul Lucas, fait par ordre du roi dans la Grèce, l'Asie Mineure, la Macedoine et l'Afrique*. Amsterdam: Aux depens de la Compagnie.

Luttrell, Anthony. 1987. "Greeks, Latins and Turks on Late Medieval Rhodes." *Byzantinische Forschungen* 11.

Lyberatos, A. 2009. *Οικονομία, πολιτική και εθνική ιδεολογία: Η διαμόρφωση των εθνικών κομμάτων στη Φιλιππούπολη του 19ου αιώνα* [Economy, Politics and National Ideology: The Formation of the National Parties in Nineteenth Century Phillipoupolos]. Rethymnon: University of Crete Press.

Malcolm, Noel. 1988. *Kosovo: A Short History*. New York: New York University Press.

Malliari, Alekse. 2001–2. "Η Τουρκική εισβολή στη βενετική Πελοπόννησο (1715)" ["The Turkish Invasion of the Venetian Peloponnesos"], in *Πρακτικά του έκτου Διεθνούς Συνέδριου Πελοποννησιακών Σπουδών* [Proceedings of the Sixth International Congress of Peloponnesian Studies]. Athens: Εταιρεία Πελοποννησιακών Σπουδών.

Mantzana, T. 2008. "Trikala in the Ottoman Period," in *Ottoman Architecture in Greece*, ed. Ersi Brouskari, trans. E. K. Fowden. Athens: Hellenic Ministry of Culture.

Masters, Bruce Alan. 2001. *Christians and Jews in the Ottoman Arab World: The Roots of Sectarianism*. New York: Cambridge University Press.

Masters, Bruce Alan. 1988. *The Origins of Western Economic Dominance in the Middle East: Mercantilism and the Islamic Economy in Aleppo, 1600–1750.* New York: New York University Press.

Matschke, Klaus-Peter. 2002. "Research Problems Concerning the Transition to Tourkokratia: The Byzantinist Standpoint," in *The Ottomans and the Balkans: A Discussion of Historiography*, ed. Fikret Adanir and Suraiya Faroqhi. Leiden: Brill.

Mauroeidi, Phani. 1992. *Ο Ελληνισμός στο Γαλατά (1453–1600): Κοινωνικές και οικονομικές πραγματικότητες* [Hellenism in Galata 1453–1600: Social and Economic Realities]. Ioannina: University of Ioannina.

Mauroeidi, Phani. 1976. *Συμβολὴ στὴν ἱστορὶα τῆς ἑλληνικῆς ἀδελφότητας Βενετίας στὸ ΙΣΤ΄ αἰώνια, 1533–1562* [A Contribution to the History of the Greek Fraternity of Venice in the Sixteenth Century, 1533–1562]. Athens: Βιβλιοπωλεῖον Νότη καραβια.

Mazower, Mark. 2004. *Salonica, City of Ghosts: Christians, Muslims and Jews, 1430–1950.* London: HarperCollins.

McGowan, Bruce. 1994a. "The Elites and their Retinues," in *An Economic and Social History of the Ottoman Empire, 1300–1914*, ed. Halil İnalcık with Donald Quataert. Cambridge: Cambridge University Press.

McGowan, Bruce. 1994b. "Merchants and Craftsmen," in *An Economic and Social History of the Ottoman Empire, 1300–1914*, ed. Halil İnalcık with Donald Quataert. Cambridge: Cambridge University Press.

McGrew, William. 1992. *The Mountains of the Mediterranean World: An Environmental History.* Cambridge: Cambridge University Press.

Meeker, Michael E. 2002. *A Nation of Empire: The Ottoman Legacy of Turkish Modernity.* Berkeley: University of California Press.

Minkov, A. 2004. *Conversion to Islam in the Balkans: Kisve Bahası Petitions and Ottoman Social Life, 1670–1730.* Leiden: Brill.

Montagu, Lady Mary Wortley. 1793. *Letters of the Right Honourable Lady Mary Wortley Montagu. Written during her Travels in Europe, Asia and Africa.* London: s.n.

Murphey, Rhoads. 2012. "Woynuk," in *Encyclopedia of Islam*, 2nd edn, ed. P. Bearman, T. Bianquis, C. E. Bosworth, E. van Donzel. and W. P. Heinrichs. Leiden: Brill. http://referenceworksbrillonline.com/browse/encyclopaedia-of-islam-2/alphaRane/Wo%20–%20Wu/W (last accessed December 5, 2014).

Murphey, Rhoads. 1996. "Patterns of Trade along the Via Egnatia in the 17th Century," in *The Via Egnatia under Ottoman rule (1380–1699): Halcyon Days in Crete II: A Symposium Held in Rethymnon 9–11 January 1994*, ed. Elisavet A. Zachariadou. Rethymnon: University of Crete Press.

Necipoğlu, Gülrü. 2005. *The Age of Sinan: Architectural Culture in the Ottoman Empire.* Princeton: Princeton University Press.

Necipoğlu, Gülrü. 1991. *Architecture, Ceremonial and Power: The Topkapı Palace in the Fifteenth and Sixteenth Centuries.* Boston: MIT Press.

Necipoğlu, Nevra. 2009. *Byzantium between the Ottomans and the Latins: Politics and Society in the Late Empire.* Cambridge: Cambridge University Press.

Necipoğlu, Nevra. 1995. "Byzantine Monasteries and Monastic Property in Thessalonike and Constantinople during the Period of Ottoman Conquests." *Journal of Ottoman Studies* 15.

Necipoğlu, Nevra. 1990. *Byzantium between the Ottomans and the Latins: A Study of Political Attitudes in the Late Palaiologan Period, 1370–1460*, PhD dissertation: Harvard University.

Nicol, Donald. 1963. *Meteora: The Rock Monasteries of Thessaly*. London: Chapman and Hall.

Nicolaidis, Efthymios. 2011. *Science and Eastern Orthodoxy: From the Greek Fathers to the Age of Globalization*, trans. Susan Emanuel. Baltimore: Johns Hopkins University Press.

Odorico, Paolo. 1996. "Texte et Traduction," in *Conseils et mémoires de Synadinos, prêtre de Serrès en Macédonie (XVIIe siècle): Textes, documents, études sur le monde byzantin, néohellénique, et balkanique*, ed. Paolo Odorico and Spyros I. Asdrachas. Paris: Editions de l'Association Pierre Belon.

Ozil, A. 2009. *The Structure of Community: Orthodox Christians of the Ottoman Empire in North-Western Asia Minor, c. 1860–1910*. PhD dissertation: Birkbeck College.

Page, Gill. 2008. *Being Byzantine: Greek Identity before the Ottomans*. Cambridge: Cambridge University Press.

Pamuk, S. 2004. "Institutional Change and the Longevity of the Ottoman Empire." *Journal of Interdisciplinary History* 35(2).

Papademetriou, Anastasios G. 2001. *Ottoman Tax Farming and the Greek Orthodox Patriarchate: An Examination of State and Church in Ottoman Society (15th–16th Century)*. PhD dissertation: Princeton University.

Papadopoulos, Stelios A. 1972. *The Greek Merchant Marine (1453–1850)*. Athens: National Bank of Greece.

Papastamatiou, Dimitrios. 2009. Οικονομικοκοινωνικοί μηχανισμοί και το προυχοντικό φαινόμενο στην οθωμανική Πελοπόννησο του 18ου αιώνα: Η περίπτωση του Παναγιώτη Μπενάκη [Socioeconomic Mechanisms and the Notable Phenomenon in the Eighteenth Century Ottoman Peloponnese: The Case of Panayiotis Benakes]. PhD dissertation: Thessaloniki, University of Thessaloniki.

Pappas, N. C. 1991. *Greeks in Russian Military Service in the Late Eighteenth and Early Nineteenth Centuries*. Thessaloniki: Institute for Balkan Studies.

Pashley, Robert. 1989. *Travels in Crete*. Athens: D. N. Karavias Reprints.

Patrinelis, Christos. 1991–2. "Ὁ ἑλληνισμὸς κατὰ τὴν πρώιμη Τουρκοκρατία (1453–1600): Γενικὲς παρατηρήσεις καὶ συσχετισμοὶ μὲ τὴν ιστορικὴ ἐξέλιξη τῆς μεταβυζαντινῆς τέχνης" ["Hellenism during the first Tourkokratia (1453–1600): General Observations and Connections to the Historical Development of post Byzantine Art"]. *Δελτίο τῆς Χριστιανικῆς Ἀρχαιολογικῆς ἑταιρείας* 16.

Patrinelis, Christos. 1973. "Κρητικοὶ ἔμποροι Ἀ στὴ Μολδαβία καὶ τὴν Πολωνία κατὰ τον 16 αἰώνα" ["Cretan Merchants in Moldavia and Poland in the Sixteenth Century"], in Πεπραγμένα του τρίτου Διεθνούς Κρητολογικού Συνέδριου [Proceedings of the Third International Cretan Symposium], ed. Georgios I. Manousakas and M. I. Kourmoules. Athens: *s.n.*

Patrinelis, Christos. 1966. "The Exact Time of the First Attempt of the Turks to Seize the Churches and Convert the Christian People of Constantinople to Islam," in *Actes du Premier Congrès international des études Balkaniques et Sud-Est européennes*. Sofia: Académie bulgare des sciences.

Peirce, Leslie. 2003. *Morality Tales: Law and Gender in the Ottoman Court of Aintab*. Berkeley: University of California Press.

Petmezas, Socrates. 2005. "Christian Communities in Eighteenth- and Early Nineteenth-Century Ottoman Greece: Their Fiscal Functions." *Princeton Papers: Interdisciplinary Journal of Middle Eastern Studies* XI.

Petmezas, Socrates. 1996a. "La région et la ville de Serrès sous les Ottomans," in *Conseils et mémoires de Synadinos, prêtre de Serrès en Macédonie (XVIIe siècle): Textes, documents, études sur le monde byzantin, néohellénique, et balkanique*, ed. Paolo Odorico and Spyros I. Asdrachas. Paris: Editions de l'Association Pierre Belon.

Petmezas, Socrates. 1996b. "L'organisation ecclésiastique sous les Ottomans," in *Conseils et mémoires de Synadinos, prêtre de Serrès en Macédonie (XVIIe siècle): Textes, documents, études sur le monde byzantin, néohellénique, et balkanique*, ed. Paolo Odorico and Spyros I. Asdrachas. Paris: Editions de l'Association Pierre Belon.

Pfeiffer, Helen. 2014. *To Gather Together: Cultural Encounters in Sixteenth-Century Ottoman Literary Sources*. PhD dissertation: Princeton University.

Philliou, Christine May. 2011. *Biography of an Empire: Governing Ottomans in an Age of Revolution*. Berkeley: University of California Press.

Philliou, Christine May. 2009 "Communities on the Verge: Unraveling the Phanariot Ascendancy in Ottoman Governance." *Comparative Studies in Society and History* 51(1).

Pizanias, Petros. 2013. "Ο κόσμος της 'θαλασσας των βουνῶν': Ο αρματολισμός από τον 16º αιώνα έως το 1821" ["The World of the Sea of Mountains: The Armatole Institution from the Sixteenth Century through 1821"]. *Νεα Εστία* 173 (857).

Ploumides, G. 1972. "Considerazione sulla populazione greca a Venezia nella seconda meta del 1500." *Studi Veneziani* 14.

Rossi, E., and W. J. Griswold. 2012. "Martolos," in *Encyclopedia of Islam*, 2nd edn. ed. P. Bearman, T. Bianquis, C. E. Bosworth, E. van Donzel, and W. P. Heinrichs. Leiden: Brill. http://referenceworks.brillonline.com./entries/encyclopaedia-of-islam-2/martolos-SIM_4974?s.num=476&s.start=460 (last accessed December 7, 2014).

Sabev, Orlin. 2007. "The First Ottoman Turkish Printing Enterprise: Success or Failure?" in *Ottoman Tulips, Ottoman Coffee: Leisure and Lifestyle in the Eighteenth Century*, ed. Dana Sajdi. New York: I.B. Tauris.

Sadat, Deena. 1972. "Rumeli Ayanlari: The Eighteenth Century." *Journal of Modern History* 44(3).

Sakellariou, M. 1939. *Ἡ Πελοπόννησος κατά τήν δευτέραν Τουρκοκρατίαν (1715–1821)* [The Peloponnese during the Second Period of Turkish Rule (1715–1821)]. Reprint 1978. Athens: Hermeis.

Salakidis, Georgios. 2004. *Η Λάρισα (Yenişehir) στα μέσα του 17ου αιώνα κοινωνική και οικονομική ιστορία μίας βαλκανικής πόλης και της περιοχής της με βάση τα Οθωμανικά ιεροδικαστικά έγγραφα των ετών 1650–1652* [Larissa/Yenişehir in the Middle of the 17th Century: Social and Economic History of a Balkan City and its Hinterland in the Years 1650–1652, on the Basis of the Ottoman Judicial Records]. Thessaloniki: Antonis Stamoulis.

Salzmann, A. 1993. "An Ancien Régime Revisited: 'Privatization' and Political Economy in the Eighteenth Century Ottoman Empire." *Politics and Society* 21.

Sariyannis, M. 2005/6. "Aspects of 'Neo-Martyrdom': Religious Contacts, Blasphemy and Calumny in Seventeenth Century Istanbul." *Archivum Ottomanicum* 23.

Savvides, A. 1994."Τα προβλήματα για την Οθωμανική κατάληψη και την εξάπλωση των κατακτητών στο θεσσαλικό χώρο" ["Issues Concerning the Ottoman Conquest of and Expansion in Thessaly"]. *Θεσσαλικό Ημερολόγιο* 28.

Sdrolia, S. 2008. "Larisa in the Ottoman Period," in *Ottoman Architecture in Greece*, ed. Ersi Brouskari, trans. E. K. Fowden. Athens: Hellenic Ministry of Culture.

Sedlar, Jean W. 1994. *East Central Europe in the Middle Ages, 1000–1500*. Seattle: University of Washington Press.

Sfyroeras, V. 1968. *Τα Ελληνικά πληρώματα του τουρκικού στόλου* [The Greek Crews of the Turkish Fleet]. Athens: *s.n.*

Shapiro, Henry. 2011. *Diverse Views on the Legitimacy of Ottoman Rule in Fifteenth and Sixteenth Century Greek Chronicles*. MA thesis: Sabanci University.

Shawcross, Teresa. 2013. "A New Lycurgus for a New Sparta: George Gemistos Plethon and the Despotate of Mystra," in *Viewing the Morea: Land and People in the Late Medieval Peloponnese*, ed. S. Gerstel. Washington, DC: Dumbarton Oaks Research Library and Collection.

Shawcross, Teresa. 2009. *The Chronicle of Morea: Historiography in Crusader Greece*. Oxford: Oxford University Press.

Sigalos, Lefteris. 2003. "Ottoman, Greek or European? Reflections of Identity in Housing Architecture from Mid-Eighteenth to Early Twentieth Centuries," in *Constructions of Greek Past: Identity and Historical Consciousness from Antiquity to the Present*, ed. H. Hokwerda. Groningen: Egbert Forsten.

Slot, B. J. 1982. *Archipelagus turbatus: Les Cyclades entre colonisation latine et occupation ottomane c. 1500–1718*. Istanbul: Nederlands Historisch-Archaeologisch Instituut te Istanbul.

Spanakes, Stergios G. 1940. "Relazione del Nobil Huomo Zuanne Mocenigo ritornato provveditore generale del regno di Candia presentata nell'eccellentissimo consiglio 17 Aprile 1589," in *Μνημεῖα τῆς κρητικῆς ἱστορίας* [Monuments of Cretan History], vol. 1, ed. Stergios G. Spanakes. Herakleion: Candia.

Stathis, Penelope. 1999. *Χρύσανθος Νοταρᾶς πατριάρχης Ἱεροσολύμων: Πρόδρομος τοῦ νεοελληνικοῦ διαφωτισμοῦ* [Chrysanthos Notaras, Patriarch of Jerusalem: Forerunner of the Greek Enlightenment]. Athens: Σύνδεσμος τῶν ἐν Ἀθήναις μεγαλοσχολιτῶν.

Stathis, Penelope. 1986. "'Ὁ 'σοφώτατος Ἐσάτ Ἐφέντης' φίλος καὶ ἀλληλογράφος τοῦ Χρύσανθου Νοταρᾶ" ["The 'Most Wise Esad Efendi': Friend and Correspondent of Chrysanthos Notaras"]. *Ὁ Ἐρανιστῆς* 18.

Stathis, Penelope. 1984. "Τό ἀνέκδοτο Ὁδοιπορικό τοῦ Χρύσανθου Νοταρᾶ" ["The Traveling Journal of Chrysanthos Notaras"]. *Μεσαιωνικὰ καὶ Νέα Ἑλληνικὰ* 1.

Stavrides, T. 2001.*The Sultan of Vezirs: The Life and Times of the Ottoman Grand Vezir Mahmud Pasha Angelovic 1453–1474*. Leiden: Brill.

Steele, R., ed. 1715. *An Account of the State of the Roman-Catholick Religion throughout the World. Written for the Use of Pope Innocent XI by Monsignor Cerri*. London: *s.n.*

Stoianovich, Traian. 1960. "The Conquering Balkan Orthodox Merchant." *Journal of Economic History* 20(2).

Strauss, Johann. 2002. " Ottoman Rule Experienced and Remembered: Remarks on Some Local Greek Chronicles of the Tourkokratia," in *The Ottomans and the Balkans: A Discussion of Historiography*, ed. Fikret Adanir and Suraiya Faroqhi. Leiden: Brill.

Strauss, Johann. 1996. "Graeco-turcica: Die Muslime in Griechenland und ihr Beitrag zur osmanischen Kultur," in *Die Kultur Griechenlands in Mittealter und Neuzeit*, ed. R. Lauer and P. Schreiner. Göttingen: Vandenhoeck und Ruprecht.

Subrahmanyam, Sunjay. 2003. "Turning the Stones Over: Sixteenth Century Millenarianism from the Tagus to the Ganges." *Indian Economic and Social History Review* 40(2).

Sugar, Peter. 1977. *Southeastern Europe under Ottoman Rule 1354–1804*. Seattle: University of Washington Press.

Terzioğlu, Derin. 2013. "Where *Ilm-I Hal* Meets Catechism: Islamic Manuals of

Religious Instruction in the Ottoman Empire in the Age of Confessionalization." *Past and Present* 220.

Tezcan, Baki. 2010. *The Second Ottoman Empire: Political and Social Transformation in the Early Modern World*. New York: Cambridge University Press.

Thiriet, Freddie. 1959. *Romanie vénitienne au Moyen Age: Le développement et l'exploitation du domaine colonial vénitien XVIIe–XVe siècles*. Paris: Editions de Boccard.

Todorov, Nikolai. 1983. *The Balkan City, 1400–1900*. Seattle: University of Washington Press.

Topping, Peter. 1986. "Latins in Limnos before and after 1453," in *Continuity and Change in Late Byzantine and Early Ottoman Society*, ed. Anthony Bryer and Heath Lowry. Washington, DC: University of Birmingham.

Triandafyllidou, Konstantinos. 1897. Ἀκολουθία καὶ βίος τοῦ ἐν ἁγίος ηατρὸς ἡμῶν Βησσαρίωνος ἀρχιεπισκόπου Λαρίσσης [Holy Service and Life of Saint Bessarion, Archbishop of Larissa].) Athens: *s.n.*

Tsampouras, Theocharis. 2013a. "The Mount Grammos Painters' Contribution in the Formation of a Common Artistic Language in the 17th-Century Balkans: An Extraordinary Example of Balkan Heritage," in *Fifth International Graduate Student Conference in Modern Greek Studies*. Princeton University (unpublished).

Tsampouras, Theocharis. 2013b. *Τα καλλιτεχνικά εργαστήρια από την περιοχή του Γράμμου κατα το 16° και το 17° αιώνα: Ζωγράφοι από το Λινοτόπι, τη Γράμμοστα, τη Ζέρμα και το Μπουρμπουτσικό* [The Artistic Workshops of the Grammos Area in the Sixteenth and Seventeenth Centuries: Painters from Linotopi, Grammosta, Zerma and Bourboutsiko]. PhD dissertation: University of Thessaloniki.

Tselatka, A. M. 2011. "Η αντίστροφη πορεία: Οι Μουσουλμάνοι πρόσφυγες" ["The Reverse Path: Muslim Refugees"]), in Το *1922 και οι πρόσφυγες: Ηια νέα ματιά* [1922 and the Refugees: A New Perspective], ed. A. Liakos. Athens: Nefeli.

Tsimpida, E. and Papageorgiou, N. 2008. "Ioannina in the Ottoman Period," in *Ottoman Architecture in Greece*, ed. Ersi Brouskari, trans. E. K. Fowden. Athens: Hellenic Ministry of Culture.

Türkyilmaz, Z. 2009. *Anxieties of Conversion: Missionaries, State and Heterodox Communities in the Late Ottoman Empire*. PhD dissertation: University of California at Los Angeles.

Ursinus, Michael. 1994. "Petitions from the Orthodox Church Officials to the Imperial Diwan, 1675." *Byzantine and Modern Greek Studies* 18(1).

Vacalopoulos, A. E. 1976. *The Greek Nation, 1453–1669: The Cultural and Economic Background of Modern Greek Society*. New Brunswick, NJ: Rutgers University Press.

Vaporis, N. M. 2000. *Witnesses for Christ: Orthodox Christian Neo-Martyrs of the Ottoman Period 1437–1860*. New York: St. Vladimir's Seminary Press.

Varnalidis, S. L. 1979. "Ό φιλενωτικὸς ἀρχιεπίσκοπος Ἀχρίδος Πορφύριος Παλαιολόγος καὶ ἡ συμμετοχὴ αὐτοῦ εἰς τὰς συνωμοτικὰς ἐνεργείας ἐναντίον Κυρίλλου τοῦ Λουκάρεως" ["The Unionist Archbishop of Ohrid Porfirios Palaiologos and his Participation in Conspiratorial Activity against Kyrillos Loukares"]. Μακεδονικά 19.

Vatin, Nicolas, and Gilles Veinstein. 2004. *Insularités ottomane:, Collection passé ottoman, présent turc*. Paris: Maisonneuve & Larose.

Vogiatzis, S. 1995. *Συμβολή στην ιστορία της εκκλησιαστικής αρχιτεκτονικής της κεντρικής ελλάδος κατά τον 16ος αιώνα* [A Contribution to the History of Church Architecture in Central Greece in the 16th Century]. PhD dissertation: Athens.

Vyronis, Speros. 1989. "Local Institutions in the Greek Islands and Elements of

Byzantine Continuity during Ottoman Rule." *Annuaire de l'Université de Sofia: Centre de Recherches Slavo-Byzantines Ivan Dujčev* 83(3).

Vryonis, Speros. 1981. "The Byzantine Legacy and Ottoman Forms," in *βυζαντινὰ καὶ Μεταβυζαντινὰ. Vol. 2: Studies on Byzantium, Seljuks and Ottomans*. Malibu: Undena.

Vryonis, Speros. 1980. "Decisions of the Patriarchal Synod in Constantinople as a Source for Ottoman Religious Policy in the Balkans Prior to 1402." *Recueil des Travaux de l'Institut d'Études Byzantines* 19.

Vryonis, Speros. 1972. "Religious Changes in the Balkans 14th through 16th Centuries," in *Aspects of the Balkans: Continuity and Change*, ed. Henrik Birnbaum and Speros Vryonis. The Hague: Mouton.

Vryonis, Speros. 1971. *The Decline of Medieval Hellenism in Asia Minor and the Process of Islamization from the Eleventh through the Fifteenth Century*. Berkeley: University of California Press.

Ware, Timothy. 1964. *Eustratios Argenti: A Study of the Greek Church under Turkish Rule*. Oxford: Clarendon Press.

White, Sam. 2013. "The Little Ice Age Crisis of the Ottoman Empire: A Conjuncture in Middle East Environmental History," in *Water on Sand: Environmental Histories of the Middle East and North Africa*, ed. Alan Mikhail. New York: Oxford University Press.

Yaycioğlu, Ali. 2008. *The Provincial Challenge: Regionalism, Crisis and Integration in the Late Ottoman Empire (1792–1812)*. PhD dissertation: Harvard University.

Yerasimos, Stephanos. 2005. "Les Grecs d'Istanbul après de la conquête ottomane: Le repeuplement de la ville et de ses environs (1453–1550)." *Revue du Monde Musulman et de la Méditerranée* (107–10).

Yerasimos, Stephanos. 1992. "L'église Orthodoxe: Pepiniere des états balkaniques," *Revue du Monde Musulman et de la Méditerranée* 66.

Zachariadou, Elizabeth. 1996. *Δέκα Τουρκικά έγγραφα για την Μεγάλη Εκκλησία 1483–1567* [Ten Turkish Documents on the Great Church 1483–1567]. Athens: National Research Center, Institute for Byzantine Studies.

Zachariadou, Elizabeth. 1990–1. "The Neo-Martyr's Message." *Δελτίο Κέντρου Μικρασιατικών Σπουδών* 8.

Zachariadou, Elizabeth. 1966. "Συμβολή στην ιστορία του νοτιοανατολικού Αιγαίου" ["Contribution to the History of the Southeastern Aegean"]. *Σύμμικτα* 1.

Zarinebaf, Fariba. 2005. "Soldiers into Taxfarmers and Reaya into Sharecroppers: The Ottoman Morea in the Early Modern Period," in *A Historical and Economic Geography of Ottoman Greece: The SW Morea in the 18th Century*, Fariba Zarinebaf, John Bennet, and Jack L. Davis. Princeton: American School of Classical Studies.

Zhelyazkova, Antonia. 2002. "Islamization in the Balkans as a Historiographical Problem: The South-East European Perspective," in *The Ottomans and the Balkans*, ed. Fikret Adanir and Suraiya Faroqhi. Leiden: Brill.

Zhelyazkova, Antonia. 1994."The Penetration and Adaptation of Islam in Bosnia from the Fifteenth to the Nineteenth Centuries." *Journal of Islamic Studies* 5(2).

Zilfi, Madeline C. 2000. "Goods in the *Mahalle*: Distributional Encounters in Eighteenth Century Istanbul," in *Consumption Studies and the History of the Ottoman Empire 1550–1922: An Introduction*, ed. D. Quataert. Albany: SUNY Press.

Zilfi, Madeline C. 1988. *The Politics of Piety: The Ottoman Ulema in the Post-Classical Age (1600–1800)*. Minneapolis: Bibliotheca Islamica.

Index

Page numbers in *italics* indicate illustrations, those followed by n indicate notes, and those followed by map indicate a map.

Abravanel, Moses Raphael, 134
Acem, 51
agnosticism, 203
Ahmet III, 85n, 193, 197–205
Ahmet Pasha, Fazıl, 134–5
Aintab, 61
Ali Pasha, Damat (Grand Vezir), 159
alienation of Greeks, 185–7
Amasya, treaty of (1555), 59
Amiroutzes, George, 23, 28
Anatolia, 59, 60, 82, 104–5, 107n, 119
Andros, 36–7, 92
Angelović, Michael, 39
Anscombe, Frederick, 158
Antalya, 41
Anthrakitis, Methodios, 208–9
anti-Greek rhetoric, 26, 27
Apokavkos, Dimitrios, 35, 41
Arab Christians, 93–4
"archons", 62, 114–15
Argyropoulos dynasty, 63
Aristotle, 200
armatole system, 8, 137n
Armenia
  society, 181
  traders, 130
Arsenije III (Patriarch), 160
artistic creation, crisis of, 112–13, 121–2
artistic improvement, 133
Asia Minor, decline of Christians, 104–6
Aşıkpaşazade, 26
askeri, 8, 83–4, 163, 185–6
Athens, as Christian city, 5, 80
ayans, 169–70, 172–3, 183–5, 190n

Babinger, Franz, 55n
Bachstrom, Johann Friedrich, 207

Baer, Marc, 134
Balkans
  cities as stable, 122–5
  conversion to Islam, 71–82
  and Greek lands, 16–19, 21n
  monastic construction, 9–12, 20n, 120–1
  nationalism, 43
  Ottoman, 17map
Barbarossa, Hayreddin, 90–1
Barkan, O.L., 8
Barkey, Karen, 165
Bayezit I, 2, 7, 12, 41, 42
Bayezit II, 29
Belgrade, 157–8, 161
  treaty of (1739), 206
Benakes, Panayiotes, 183
Berat, Albania, 41
beratlı status, 165–6
berats, 12, 29–34, 37, 63–4, 176–7, 178–9, 181
Bessarion, Basilios, 9–10
Bey, Barak (Yenişehir), 3
Bosnia, 78, 158
Braudel, Ferdinand, 73
Brest, Union of (1595-6), 116, 144
Bryer, Anthony, 9, 20n
Bulgaria, 170
  Second Empire, 38
Bulgarian Church, 39
Bulgarians, 38–9
  as *mixovarvaroi*, 45
Bursa, 22, 68
Büyük Kaçğun (Great Flight), 118–19
Byzantine Commonwealth, The, 46
Byzantine Empire, 2, 43–54

Byzantines
  as Christians, 44–5
  elite, 23–4
  identity, 43–54

Çaldiran, battle of (1514), 57, 58
Cami-i Atik, Trabzon, 78
Cantemir, Demetrius, 202
Cappadocia, Anatolia, 74, 172
Cartesianism, 207
Catholic Church, 36–42
  end of the Latin east, 87–94
  versus Orthodox, 140–6
  Reformation, 139–62
celali revolts, 118–19, 122–3, 124
çelebi, 175
Çelebi, Evliya, 80, 81, 124
çelepkeşan system, 16–19, 118
Charles V, 60, 71
Chios, migration from, 130
Christians, 3–6
  Arab Christians, 93–4
  assault on, 40–1
  and commerce, 127–8
  converts, 27–8
  decline of in Asia Minor, 93–4
  in an Islamic empire, 57–86
  resistance to ecclesiastical authority, 177–8
  in the service of the state, 82–4
  as soldiers, 7–9
  soldiers, 82–4
  tax farmers, 126–7
  timar, 7–8
Chronicle of the Morea, The, 48
church building
  urban benefactors for, 11–12
  wealth to build, 10–11
cities, changing, 125–8
cizye (head-tax), 84, 119, 120, 147, 156
Commentarii, 204
commercial privilege, 92–3
communal prayers, 59
communal structures, 125–8, 169–71
confessionalization, age of, 151–3
"Conquering Balkan Orthodox Merchant, The," 164
Constantine XI Paleologos, 23, 24
Constantinople, 22–56
  city of, 24–8
  repopulation of, 24–8
conversion, 40, 41
  Balkans to Islam, 71–82

to Islam, 71–82, 139, 146–62
  of monasteries to mosques, 64–9
çorbacı, 118
Corniactus, Constantine, 99
Costantini, Vera, 106n
Cottunius, Johannes, 203, 204
Council of Florence, 38, 42
countryside, revival of rural life, 6–12
Cretans, commerce, 99–100
Crete, 36, 37, 155–6, 177
  mass conversions, 154–5
Crimean Tartars, 159
crisis of
  artistic creation, 112–13, 121–2
  the elites, 112–14
  the monasteries, 64–9, 112
  patronage, 112–13
Crusius, Martin, 63
Cycladic islands, 90
Cyprus, 91–2
  invasion of, 68

Damascus, 93–4
derbend villages, 6–7, 8, 15, 19n
derbendcis, 8, 84
devaluation of the coinage, 113
devşirme, 27, 54, 55n, 84, 163
  after, 153–6
Dionysios (Patriarch), 64
Dionysiou monastery, Mount Athos, 67
Dousiko monastery, Pindos mountains, 9–10, 12, 69
Dušan, Stefan (Tsar), 39

Ebussuud, 21n, 61, 65, 66–7, 68, 70, 79
ecclesiastical
  boundaries, 36–42
  construction, 69–71
ecnebis, 126, 165, 181
Ecumenical Patriarchate, 29–42
Edirne (Adrianople), 22, 29, 35, 41
education, 208–12
  Greek, 192–3, 195–6, 204
Egypt, conquest of (1517), 60
Eldem, Edhem, 166
elite
  in capital, 135–6
  crisis of, 112–14
  enlightenment, 194–5
  Greek education, 133
  politics, 62–9
enlightenment, popular, 194–5

Index

Esad Efendi, 193, 200, 201–2, 204, 205, 206
estate society, 181
Euboea, 88
Evrenos Bey, 2, 7
experimental science, 195, 207

Famagusta, Cyprus, 91–2
family law, 177
Fethiye mosque, 64
fetvas, 57, 59, 61, 66, 70
Finkel, Caroline, 138n, 162n, 206–7
First School of Ioannina, 209
Florence, Council of, 38, 41
Fotić, Aleksandar, 157–8
Fourth Crusade (1204), 44, 87
Franks, 47–8
  and Orthodox Church, 48
  versus Turks, 87
"Franks Street," 130–1

Galata, 25, 64
  commerce, 95–6
Gallipolli, 40
Gara, Eleni, 5, 74, 123
Gennadios, 29, 35, 41, 55n
George of Sofia, 74
Gerlach, Stephan, 11
Giovanni IV (Duke of Naxos), 90
Gradeva, Rossitsa, 148, 191n
Great Flight (*Büyük Kaçğun*), 118–19
Greek
  education, 192–3, 195–6, 204
  Enlightenment, 164, 192–215
  language, 46–7, 49–50, 81, 105–6, 155, 156
  larger world, 87–107
  merchants, 94–103, 131, 164–6, 187–9
  resentment of Muslims to, 26, 27
  slaves, 25
Greek College of Rome, 143, 195
Greek Fraternity of Venice, 96–9
Greek identity
  Istanbul, 42–54
  separation from Orthodoxy, 204–5
Greek Orthodox Church, 1–2, 36–42, 44–5
  shared religious faith, 100
guilds, 171, 172–4, 180, 182
Gülnüş (Sultan), 199–200, 202
Gyuma, Emmanuel Leontari, 209

Hagia monastery, Andros, 37
Hajdarpasic, Edin, 162n
Halil, Çandarlı (Grand Vezir), 53
haraç, 13, 32–3, 35–6
Hayreddin Pasha, 37, 63, 98
Hellenic imperialism, 103–6
Hellenism, 46–7, 49–50, 53, 79
Hellenization, 103–6, 174–5, 182
  of names, 174–5
Hezarfen Hüseyin Efendi, 202
History of the City of Philosophers, A, 202
History of the Growth and Decay of the Ottoman Empire, The, 202
Holy Apostles, Church of the, Istanbul, 64
Holy League, War of the, 157–61
hospodar, palace of, Bucharest, *108*
households, 135–6
Hungary, Ottoman loss of, 157, 158, 160–1

Ibrahim Pasha, Damat, 198, 199, 206
Ignatius (Archbishop), 38, 42
Imber, Colin, 61, 68
Inalcık, Halil, 32, 55n, 107n, 119, 136n
Ioannina, First School of, 209
Isidorou, Nikolaos, 35, 41
Ismail, Shah, 58–60
Istanbul, 102–3
  commerce, 94–6
  Greek elites, 115–116
  prelate's pectoral, *110*
  see also Constantinople
Ivanova, Svetlana, 171, 184

janissaries, 57, 82–4, 113, 181, 199
Jeremiah (Patriarch), 115–16, 144
Jesuits, 139–62
  missionaries, 140–3, 161n
Jewish community
  loss of privilege, 134
  in Smyrna, 130

kadizadeli, 134–5, 148–9, 200
Kaldellis, Anthony, 44–6, 47, 48–9, 51–2
Kantakouzenos, John, 22, 151
Kantakouzenos, Manoles, 98–9
Kantakouzenos, Michael (şeytanoğlu), 62–3, 114–15, 137n
Kantakouzenos, Thomas, 115, 132
Kantakouzenos dynasty, 7
kanun, 34, 61
Karatza, Ioannikou, 182

Karlowitz, treaty of (1699), 157
Kasim, Haci, 78
Kastoria, 211–12
Katavolinos, Thomas, 35, 41
kefere, 60, 176
Kermeli, Eugenia, 67, 68, 179
Kiel, Machiel, 11, 20n, 82, 85n
Kılıç Ali, 37
Kitromilides, Paschalis, 196, 200–1, 205–6
kızılbaş, 59
Knights of St John, 88, 89–90
Komnenos, David (Emperor), 28, 75–6
Komninos, Nicholas, 204
Konortas, Paraskeuas, 180
Kontaris, Kyrillos, 123
Köprülü dynasty, 133–4, 157
Koresse, Antonios, 63
Koresse family, 98
Korydaleus, Theophilos, 192, 195–6
Kos, 67
Kosovo, 158, 159
Kounoupis, Konstantinos, 63
Kritopoulos, Mitrofanes, 123
Krstić, Tijana, 79
Kunt, Metin, 153
Kurşun mosque, Trikala, 69

Laiou, Sophia, 152
Lane, Winthrop, 129
languages, 202, 203
 Arabic, 60
 bureaucratic, 176
Larissa, 2–3, 6, 74, 127
 as Muslim city, 3–4
Lemnos, 88, 89
Lepanto, battle of (1570), 101
Lesvos, 88
Limnos, 8
Loukaris, Kyrillos (Patriarch), 100, 115–16, 139, 140–1, 176, 192
Lowry, Heath, 8, 27, 60, 62, 74–8, 81, 83
Lucas, Paul, 169
Lwow, 99–100
Lyberatos, Andreas, 118

mahalles, 170–1
Manolakis, 211
Marj Dabiq, battle of (1516), 93
Marmaretos dynasty, 98
martolos, 8, 84
Mavrokordatos, Alexander, 133, 193, 196, 202, 203, 205–6

Mavrokordatos, Nicholas, 195, 199, 200–1, 203, 204–5, 205
Mazower, Mark, 4
medicine, 133–4, 196, 202
medrese complexes, 68, 113, 120, 200, 203, 210
Meeker, Michael, 106, 154
Mehmet, Fatih, 10–11, 52, 53, 54, 75, 104
 treaty with Venice (1454), 36
Mehmet, Vani Efendi, 134–5, 148–9
Mehmet II, 22–9, 57
Mehmet IV, 148–9
Mehmet Paşa Angelović, 24, 27, 28, 39
Mehmet Pasha, Rum, 24, 26
Mehmet Pasha Sokollović (Grand Vizier), 39, 42, 84
merchants and education, 208–12
Mesih Pasha, 24
Meteora monasteries, Mount Athos, 10, 12, 12–13
metropolitan sees, 29, 30map
metropolitans, 41–2, 63, 80, 179–80, 182
 Orthodox, 11–12
migrations, 131, 136, 157–8
millet, 29, 30, 36, 164
mixed marriages, 81
Mocenigo, Zuanne, 100
Moisiodax, Iosipos, 174
Moldavia, 104
monasteries
 agreements, 12–16
 construction in the Balkans, 9–12, 20n, 120–1
 conversion to mosques, 64–9
 crisis of, 64–9, 112
 urban, 14–15
Morea, 157, 158–9, 160, 161
Moreot
 army, 48
 identity, 49
mosques, 59
 conversion from monasteries, 64–9
Mount Athos, 13
Mount Grammos painters, 121, 137n
mountains, 116–22
mültezims, 114, 178–9
Murat II, 4, 13, 41, 42
 centralization, 13–14
Murat III, 37, 65–6, 112–13
Muscovy, 115–16
Muslims
 as artisans, 4

and Greeks, 139–62
non-Muslims inferior, 27
piety, 151–3
resentment to Greeks, 26, 27
see also Islam
Mustafa II, 199
Mustafa Pasha, Fazil, 161
Müteferrika press, 207, 210
Mykonos, 172

nasrani, 60, 176
Nassi, Joseph, 37
Naxos, 37, 178
Nea Mone monastery, Thessaloniki, 14
Necipoğlu, Gülrü, 59, 65, 85n, 112–13
Necipoğlu, Nevra, 14, 53
Neo-Aristotelianism, 192, 193, 195–6, 205, 207
neo-martyrs, 74
  and Ottoman society, 146–51
Neophtyos II (Patriarch), 10
new urbanism, 168–75
Nicolaidis, Efthymios, 197, 205
Nicosia, 91–2
Nikousios, Panayiotis, 131–2, 134, 137n, 140, 143
Notaras, Chrysanthos, 173, 193, 199, 201–2, 206, 208
Notaras, Lucas, 24
Notitiae, 37
Nuh Efendi, 193, 202

Obolensky, Dimitri, 46
Of, 106, 154
Ohrid, 38, 42
  archbishops of, 143–4, 144–6, 182–3
oikoumene, 44–5
On Duties, 203
"On the Road Out of Empire," 165
Orhan (Sultan), 22
Orlov Revolt (1770), 213
Orta Hisar, Trabzon, 76
Ottoman Balkans, 17map
  and Greek lands, 16–19, 21n
Ottoman Enlightenment, 197–9
Ottoman-Habsburg war (1739), 182
Ottomans
  beginning of rule, 1–21
  civil wars, 2
  court, 192–215
  and Greeks, 139–62
  motifs, *108, 109*

  negotiating with the, 12–16
  style, 186–7
Ottoman-Venetian war (1479), 36

Padua, University of, 133, 192, 202
Paleologos, Dimitrios, 10–11, 24
Pammakaristos monastery, Istanbul, 64–6
Panagia, Church of the, St Dimitrios monastery, Thessaly, 69–70
Patriarchate, Ecumenical, 29–42, 175–83
patriarch, 163–91
  as tax farmer, 178–9
Patriarchal History of Istanbul, 64
Patrona Halil rebellion (1730), 206
patronage, 11
  crisis of, 112–13
Pax Ottomanica, 92
Peć, 39, 42, 160, 182–3
Peirce, Leslie, 61
Peloponnese, 47–8
peşkeş, 32–3
Petmezas, Socrates, 52, 124, 166–7, 172
Phanariots, 50, 132–6
  in Ahmet III's court, 205–6
  in Danubian Principalities, 160, 164, 192–3, 196–7
  education, 192–3, 196–7, 202, 203
  as elite, 115, 116, 180, 182, 196–7, 200
  as financiers, 200
  Hellenization, 53, 175, 192–3
  political influence, 181, 182
  philosophy, 195–7, 200, 203
  versus Church, 196–7
Philotheou Parega, 200–1, 203, 204–5
Platimana, Thessaly, 8
Plovdiv, 118, 168–9, 173–4
Poland, 115
Pontos, 105–6, 107n
Porfyrios (Archbishop), 145
printing press, 141, 198, 201, 203, 207, 209–10
  Istanbul, 141, 198, 201, 203, 207
Propaganda Fide, 142–3
provincial society, 183–5

Rafael, 50, 55n
reaya, 80, 84, 163, 165, 176, 185–6
Rhodes, 88, 89–90
Roman empire, 23
Roman identity, 45–8, 50
Romania, 45
Romanians, 160, 161

Rum, 50–2, 55–6n
Russia, war with (1768–74), 212–13
Rüstem Pasha (Grand Vezir), 64

Saadabad, 198, 206
Saadeddin, 27
Saadi Efendi, 202
Safavid dynasty, 58–9, 77
St Benedict's mission, Istanbul, 140
St Dimitrios monastery, Thessaly, 69–70
St George, Church of, Thessaloniki, 65
St John Promodros monastery, Serres, 68
St John's monastery, Patmos, 67
St Nicholas monastery, Ano Vathia, Evoia, 69
St Nicholas monastery, Meteora, 12
St Petka, Church of, Samardzijska, 11
Salakides, George, 127
Samarianis family, 97
Samokov, 172
Samothrace, 89
Samuel (Tsar), 144
Santorini, 178
Sanuto, Marino, 57
sarica, 119
Second Bulgarian Empire, 38
Second Empire, 163–4
sekban, 119
Selim I, 58, 60, 93
Selim II, 66
Serbia, 20n
Serbs, 38–9, 160
şeriat, 23, 26, 61, 62, 69
Serres, 12, 40, 80, 123–4, 173–4
seventeenth-century crisis, 112–38
Severos, Gabriel, 100
Sevlievo, Bulgaria, 73–4
şeytanoğlu (Michael Kantakouzenos), 62–3, 114–15, 137n
Shabbatai Tzevi, 134
sheep market, 116–18
Shi'ism, 60
Siege of Vienna (1683), 157
Sinan Pasha, Koca, 65
sipahis, 7–8, 11, 13, 20n, 82–4, 113–14
skepticism, 203
Skopje, 158
Smederevo, 39
Smyrna, 106, 129–31, 140, 172
Sofia, 11, 148, 168, 171
Spandounes, Theodore, 28
stabilization, 131–6
Stavrides, Theoharis, 9

Stegopole Monastery, Albania, *109*
Stephen the Great, of Moldavia, 104
Stoianovich, Traian, 36, 164
Strupets monastery, Lukovit, Monastery of the Tailor's Guild, 11
Sublime Porte, 52, 56n, 167, 176
Sugar, Peter, 171
Süleyman I, 59, 60–1, 64, 66, 83, 88
Sunni Ottomans, 57
Sunnitization, 151–2
sürgün (forced relocation), 25, 28, 75, 90
Symeon, 29, 35
Synadinos, 80, 124, 125
Syria, 60, 93–4

tahrirs (survey), 13, 72
Tamerlane's defeat of Bayezit, 2
Tarnovo, 38, 42, 55n
Tartarhane, Alexander, 124
tax farming, 26, 27, 114, 125–8, 183
  patriarchs, 178–9
taxes, 6–9, 12–13, 170, 172
  Balkans, 120
  collection by Greeks, 63
  right to collect, 32–4
Terzioğlu, Derin, 151–2
Tezcan, Baki, 126–7, 136n, 153, 162n, 163–4, 165
Thassos, 89
Theofanis, 12
Theofilos, 177
Thessaloniki, 41
  as Christian city, 3–4
  Ottoman conquest of (1387), 13
Thessaly, 1–21, 172
  conquest of, 2–6
  depopulation of, 2–3
Thrace, 59
Thracian islands, 88–9
timar system, 13, 19–20n, 67, 120, 169
Todorov, Nikolai, 94–5
Tonya, Trabzon, 106
Topkapı, Istanbul, 53
Tournefort, 130–1
Trabzon, 23, 28, 74–8, 154–6
  Myrrh flask from, *111*
Trabzonites, 35, 52
travelling painters, 121
Trikala, 3–4, 80
Tsampouras, Theoharis, 135
tuğhra, 12, 21n
"Tulip Age," 198, 206
Turhan, Hatice, 134

Index

Turhan Bey, Ghazi, 2, 6, 20–1n
Turks versus Franks, 87

ulema, 57, 181, 210–11
Union of Brest (1595–6), 116, 144
University of Padua, 133, 192, 202
urban centres, 122–5
urban monasteries, 14–15
Urban VIII (Pope), 143–4, 145
urbanism, new, 168–75
utility of knowledge, 196

vakıf, 6, 66–7, 68
Vani Mehmet Efendi, 134–5, 148–9
varoş, 170–2, 173, 174, 184–5
Venetians
  commerce, 92, 96–9
  as enemy, 158–9
Venice, 36, 63, 96–7
  treaty with Fatih Mehmet (1454), 36
  war with (1463–79), 88
Veroia, 5, 12, 74, 80, 123, 125–6, 126–7
Vidin, 158
Vienna, siege of (1683), 157
virtue, 196, 203
Vlachs, 104

Vlachs, Bosnia, 74
Vlad IV, 104
Vogiatzis, S., 71
Vogorides, Stephanos, 174
Voulgaris, Eugenios, 207
voynuks, 7–8, 11, 83, 84
Vryonis, Spyros, 9, 72, 104–5

Wallachia, 103–4
War of the Holy League, 157–61
war with Russia (1768–74), 212–13
warfare, changes in, 113–14, 118–19
westernization, 186–7
Wortley Montagu, Lady Mary, 168–9, 198

yamaks, 8
Yenişehir (Barak Bey), 3
Yunani, 50, 204–5
Yusuf Bey, 2

Zachariadou, Elizabeth, 11–12, 54, 55n
zaviyes, 79
Zhelyazkova, Antonia, 74
Zile, 176
zimmi, 70, 83, 152, 176–7